MORTEVIVUM

MORTEVIVUM

PHOTOGRAPHY AND THE POLITICS OF THE VISUAL

KIMBERLY JUANITA BROWN

BROWN UNIVERSITY DIGITAL PUBLICATIONS
PROVIDENCE, RHODE ISLAND

THE MIT PRESS
CAMBRIDGE, MASSACHUSETTS
LONDON, ENGLAND

Please scan this QR code to find an open access digital edition of *Mortevivum.*

This publication has been supported by the MIT Press Grant Program for Diverse Voices and the Fund for Diverse Voices.

The MIT Press would like to thank the anonymous peer reviewers who provided comments on drafts of this book. The generous work of academic experts is essential for establishing the authority and quality of our publications. We acknowledge with gratitude the contributions of these otherwise uncredited readers.

This book was set in Halyard by the MIT Press. Printed and bound in the United States of America.

Library of Congress Cataloging-in-Publication Data

Names: Brown, Kimberly Juanita, 1972- author.
Title: Mortevivum : photography and the politics of the visual / Kimberly Juanita Brown.
Description: Cambridge, Massachusetts : The MIT Press, [2024] | Series: On seeing | Includes bibliographical references and index.
Identifiers: LCCN 2023019359 (print) | LCCN 2023019360 (ebook) | ISBN 9780262547642 (paperback) | ISBN 9780262378161 (epub) | ISBN 9780262378178 (pdf)
Subjects: LCSH: Documentary photography--Social aspects. | Documentary photography--Moral and ethical aspects. | Black people--Press coverage. | Racism against Black people--Press coverage. | Violence--Press coverage.
Classification: LCC TR820.5 .B76 2024 (print) | LCC TR820.5 (ebook) | DDC770--dc23/eng/20230712
LC record available at https://lccn.loc.gov/2023019359
LC ebook record available at https://lccn.loc.gov/2023019360

10 9 8 7 6 5 4 3 2 1

For my father, always

We will not die here.

—Michael S. Harper

CONTENTS

SERIES FOREWORD ix

INTRODUCTION: THE MAKING OF PHOTOGRAPHIC BLACKNESS xi

1 **THE EMPIRE** 1

2 **THE VIEWER** 47

3 **THE SENTIMENT** 73

CONCLUSION: WE, STILL 103

ACKNOWLEDGMENTS 117

NOTES 123

INDEX 139

SERIES FOREWORD

Visual culture has always been central to meaning making, and most recently technology has catapulted its global stakes. Today there is greater access and exposure to visual culture than ever before, outpacing our ability to reflect upon its implications. In response to the need for diverse perspectives on the growing impact of visual culture, the MIT Press began work on a new book series in 2018. Conceived over several years of research and intensive discussion with international scholars, the On Seeing series emerged with a commitment to increase visual literacy.

In 2022, the MIT Press and Brown University Digital Publications announced a partnership to launch the series, with inclusivity and access as driving motivations. Books in the On Seeing visual culture series are published in print and in open access, media-rich digital editions to serve the widest possible audience.

Defined by rigorous research, bold positions, and cultural relevance, On Seeing publications shape new conversations about how we see, comprehend, and participate in visual culture, and how we can do so with informed agency. The diverse authors of On Seeing investigate the ways that power relations are inscribed in the visual, and they develop knowledge about how what we see—and what remains hidden from view—is related to justice.

INTRODUCTION: THE MAKING OF PHOTOGRAPHIC BLACKNESS

This is how you make a gelatin silver print: the negative is placed in a photo enlarger, its duplication immersed in chemicals as precise as the movement of time. Silver salts (chlorine, bromide) sustain the emulsion that propels the visualization of the print. It is a living thing. It is a dead offering (or, in the words of Roland Barthes, "it is the living image of a dead thing").[1] And yet, "on top of brown-gray paper," Michael S. Harper writes, "human images rise."[2] Human images in photographic reproductions are sights that compel others to look. Whether this action is to regard with intention or disregard with indifference, looking is a disciplinary and disciplining act[3]—one that nearly two hundred years of photographic history has inculcated into the naturalization of specific investment. And antiblackness blankets this history like a cloak with no beginning and no end, offering only momentary exercises of reprieve. And almost never on purpose.

Analog photography, what Beaumont Newhall referred to as "the mirror with a memory," established itself by the late nineteenth century as a force with which to contend. Between its documentary and artistic pursuits, the genre was also central to the burgeoning eugenics movement in the United States and Great Britain. Along with the spectacular technological achievement that is photography, there is, almost immediately, what John Tagg refers to as its "disciplinary frame."[4] For black subjects, this disciplining, its surveillance and containments, necessitates an ocular vigilance that is difficult to sustain. There are others in the frame, visible or not. These others register in ways that set black subjectivity into disarray. They are the assumed inheritors of a right to their humanity that is not assumed for others.

It is a ghostly apparatus, photographic production, and it always has been. "Photography is a kind of primitive theater," Roland Barthes contends. "A kind of *Tableau Vivant*, a figuration of the motionless and made-up face beneath which we see the dead."[5] When photography and antiblackness are conjoined, black people become the dead that we see. This means that in the generality of a visual imagination that looms large and contains "multitudes," black subjects routinely receive short shrift.[6] In as many ways as black diasporic subjects are presented as bodies of use, photographic accompaniment is regulatory, inflexible, and graphic in its production. To be seen in this environment is to be exposed to the violence of the gaze, particularly when it appears as an objective documentary photograph simply detailing what has already taken place.[7]

These photographs are instructive for what they can tell us about the intersection of race and the visual. In images from the American Civil War, for instance, we see the careful curation of a racial hierarchy that is also gendered male. We see the narrowed roles that African Americans are relegated to occupying and the violent intimacies they must abide to survive. The extended narrative accompanying the photograph

When photography and antiblackness are conjoined, black people become the dead that we see.

confirms the refused access to citizenship that black American soldiers in the Civil War experienced. This erasure looms large in the images and text in Alexander Gardner's 1866 work, *Gardner's Photographic Sketch Book of the Civil War*. About the photograph of an African American soldier photographed serving his military "masters," the text reads: "Although his head resembled an egg, set up at an angle of forty-five degrees, small end on top, yet his moral and intellectual requirements were by no means common. His appreciation of Bible history was shown on many occasions. For instance, he always considered Moses the most remarkable of quartermasters, in that he crossed the Red Sea without pontoons, and conducted the children of Israel forty years through the desert without a wagon trail."[8] The narrative's fixation on John Henry, the only black person represented in the image, is meant to demean in image what is "elevated" in text. An entire photographic universe unfolds along these lines.[9]

Living in the tangible autonomy of existence that is then curtailed by the photographic frame, black subjects breathe life into representation by merely being present in front of *other people's eyes*. "Because, like all other institutions and practices," artist Michèle Pearson Clarke writes, "photography's history reveals a gross complicity with white supremacy, and its emergence during the nineteenth century meant that it was immediately and specifically pressed into colonialist service."[10] Gardner's book is the exploration of photography "pressed into colonialist service" that defines the contours of antiblackness visualized. Clarke continues, "Photography, then, did not so much record the reality of Blackness as signify and construct a way of seeing it."[11] To "signify and construct" is the great power repeatedly deployed then disavowed when photography and antiblackness converge. Performing the structural racism it embodies, the viewer's indifference is ultimately the most telling. Measured quantitatively, a viewing audience predisposed to accept the tenets of white supremacy will have little in the way of expansive engagement when

An entire photographic universe unfolds along these lines.

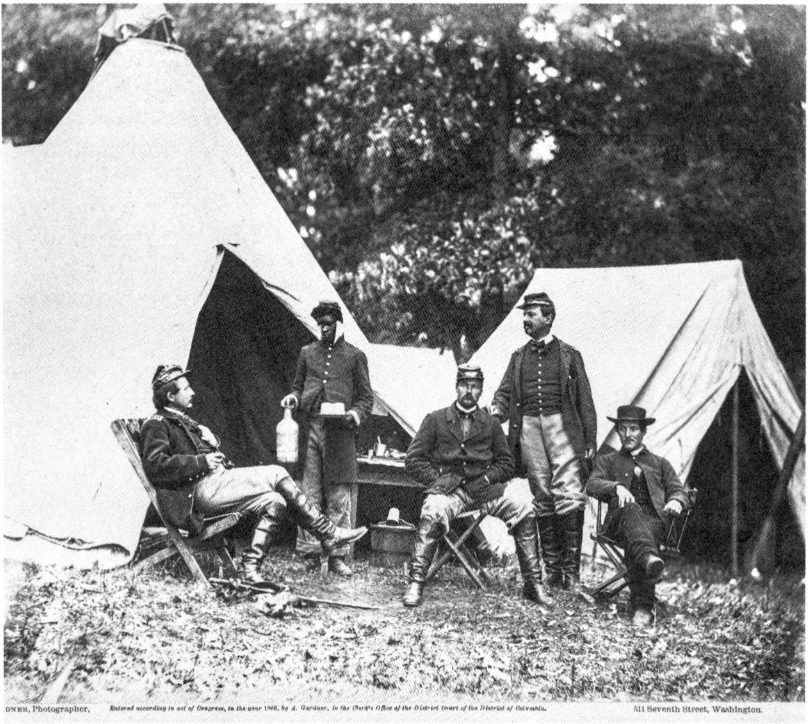

Figure 0.1 Alexander Gardner, *What Do I Want, John Henry?*, Warrenton, Virginia, November 1862. Courtesy of Getty Images.

presented with black subjects in a photographic print. There is a temporal collapse when blackness and photography converge, which threatens to flatten the interaction. This flattening is a direct consequence of the lack of care proscribed to black subjects within documentary photography in the nineteenth and twentieth centuries. Prominent African Americans from Frederick Douglass to W. E. B. Du Bois worked tirelessly in the early decades of photography's emergence to illuminate the inner lives of black Americans through the medium that was referred to as "painting with light."[12]

For Du Bois in particular, his curation of portraits for the 1900 Paris Exposition is one important example. "Black photographers," Deborah Willis writes, "whose work Du Bois drew on for the Paris Exposition, offered a provocative challenge to the blatantly stereotypical images of African Americans as inferior, unattractive, and unintelligent. Their photographs served as evidence that black Americans were as multifaceted as anyone else, and they played a key role in making the black experience visible."[13] Beyond visibility, there was an essential mandate that viewers invest in the aesthetic production of black subjects. In this way, they could be visually retrieved with their humanity fully intact. However, photography's history (and by extension photography studies) is a catalog of othering, surveillance, and the violence of objectification. Bongani Madondo argues that "photography, on its own, is a technological response to the tableaux of its surroundings . . . it is history's roving third eye."[14] *Mortevivum* explores this "third eye" as it exists on the cusp of the twenty-first century, where it seems work is still to be done to render black lives legible outside destruction.

The destruction is the point. Its aims are imagistic and corporeal, representational and juridical. In its aggregate form, antiblackness sutures the line between active and passive racist participation. It requires very little to keep itself going, having relied for so long on the violent foundation it was built upon. "Narrative temporality," Lisa Lowe reminds us, "is itself a powerful vehicle of liberal progress, as evidenced in the emplotment of slave emancipation, in which the slave subject develops in time, constituting a story of an enslaved past that culminates in freedom achieved in the present."[15] The Gardner photograph in figure 0.2 is an example of this narrative temporality, one which would shape viewers' perceptions of black belonging in a national framework after the end of the American Civil War.

Two young black men facilitate a cockfight for the pleasure of the white soldiers and superiors who surround them. They kneel in the center of frame, each one with a bird in hand, and both focused intensely on the task before them. The twelve white men forming a circular boundary constitute the surveillance managers that these men must navigate. A presumptive jury of nonpeers, they are entertained and excited, perplexed, and bored. The ranges of facial and bodily gestures and clothing choices are meant to signal a visual hierarchy that race exacerbates. To the imagined question of what to do about the millions of black subjects on the cusp of freedom from enslavement, this photograph, like the one that precedes it, has an answer: excessive, demoralizing utility and the refusal of anything resembling inclusion. Out of this photographic conundrum we can see how the progression of violent engagements with black flesh evolved. Martin A. Berger writes, "For European-Americans, whiteness was not a standalone construct but one produced by a confluence of other dominant markers of identity. Objects were coded white to the extent that they exhibited (valued) traits associated with their essential nature."[16] Krista Thompson notes that photographs from the Caribbean in the nineteenth century presented black Jamaicans as "picturesque inhabitants who had been 'civilized' and disciplined by colonial rule."[17] Social stasis was thus photographically engineered. From there, it was not difficult to produce the imagistic scaffolding that facilitates photographic black death.

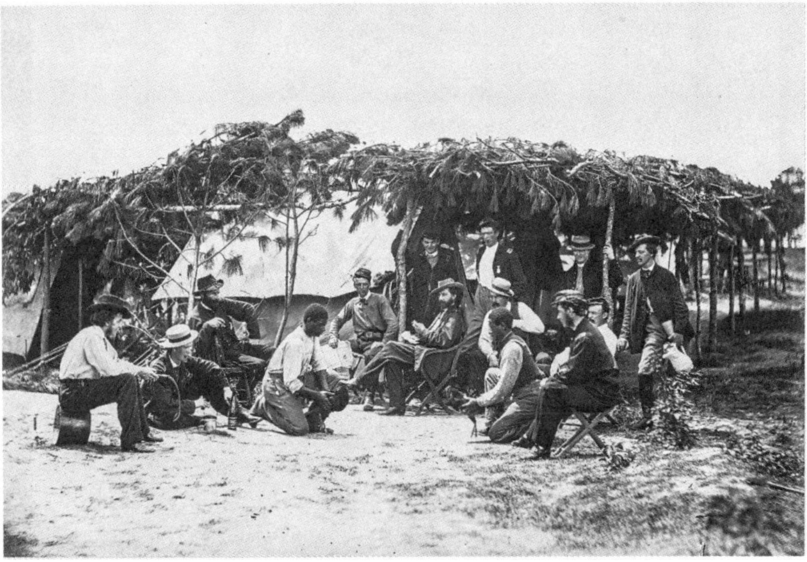

Figure 0.2
Alexander Gardner, *A Fancy Group, in Front of Petersburg*, August 1864. Courtesy of Getty Images.

MORTEVIVUM

Mortevivum is the term I have come up with to understand this particular photographic phenomenon: the hyperavailability of images in the media that traffic in tropes of impending black death. These tropes cohere around an ocular logic steeped in racial violence (and the nostalgia engendered therein), and they make any tragedy, any crisis, an opportunity for viewers to find pleasure in black peoples' pain. The easy accessibility of a range of visual imagery adhering to these tenets constitutes the repetition of a *way of looking* measured by their staying power. Since photography's invention, black life has been presented as fraught, short, agonizingly filled with violence, and indifferent to intervention. Living death in a series of still frames, refusing complex humanity.

Divided into three chapters, *Mortevivum* constructs the late modern advent of photography as uniquely positioned to make profligate the *fungibility*, to use Saidiya Hartman's term, to continually frame the contours of black subjectivity. For the book, I examine four interlocking "locations" of visualizing slaughter: South Africa, Rwanda, Haiti, and the United States. Photography's ability to render blackness as stagnation (via loss, crime, famine, poverty, and death) is visually normalized and held in place by the power of the imagery and our collective inability to see beyond the limitations of our cultural bifurcations. I am interested in how the viewer receives and processes images of the dying and the dead, particularly when those in the photographs are black. What I am calling a *cartography of the ocular* (moving from national location to national location, but always under the cover of blackness) has specific dimensions: a viable and recognizable enemy, the failure of other people's sovereignty, and the global ability to reinforce white supremacist ideals.

Cartographies of the ocular manage to span the reach of antiblackness in the global world. They tell us how blackness is treated as a forfeiture of worth, offering evidence of this forfeiture in an avalanche of graphic imagery. An examination of Pulitzer Prize–winning photographs from the last forty years is instructive. Violent imagery coalesces around black subjects from present-day Zimbabwe to Ethiopia, to California, New Jersey, and Liberia. If we were to draw out a map illustrating instances of antiblackness, it would cover the known world. This book is the way I make sense of the depth and breadth of imagistic othering rendered black.

For mortevivum is, in its very construction, a photographic production. Although it has tendrils of other properties of representation, the term as I am deploying it is about the force and the power of photography in the field of production over which so much has been inferred and assumed. Documentary photography, to be precise, for it is within the space of the document that an adherence to what is constructed as evidence and realism in this genre takes center stage. Black subjects are perceived and remanded to the space of photographic stasis that consumes and corrupts their ability to be autonomous outside of the violence of antiblackness.

What could be more insistently destructive than the swift mobility of print imagery in daily newspapers, digitized and received in various forms of immediate consumption? This project explores photography's import and utility on the cusp of the twenty-first century—at the tail end of analog photography, the beginning of the photographic digitization of imagery and the burgeoning prowess of the World Wide Web. This is a project that looks back to anticipate the forward thrust of a post–September 11 permissive objectification, as after 2001, the dead become a swirling mix of Middle Eastern and South Asian subjects, rendered as deserving of a photographic death and a permanently suspended life.[18]

THE BODY ENTERS THE ARCHIVE

This is how you read a photographic image: I was greeted with marked illustrations of antiblack violence when, after living in Orlando, Florida, for five years, I returned to the city of my birth, New York. I arrived in early June 1994. Moving from one bus/train station to another, I had to readjust to the common presence of newsstands that dotted the city. I would linger as I had previously in front of these ubiquitous kiosks, surveying a range of daily newspaper front covers, deciding which would be worthy of my fifty cents. It took me months to work out why I was noticing something in repetitive patterns that I might have missed had I not spent some years away from the bustle of New York City. Each day as I maneuvered the streets in silence, I was met with jarring photographic renderings of black death. As I instinctively averted my eyes, I remember being unsettled, but I was unsure as to why. I knew enough about the "if it bleeds, it leads" mantra of late twentieth-century journalism, but here was something else. It was devoid of living "human images" and instead trafficked in specific dead bodies—corpses for which there was no need for regard. It was then that it hit me: all the dead bodies shown on the front page of multiple newspapers were black. It was as if there was an implicit agreement that black subjects were fungible in ways others were not. Furthermore, everyone looking at these photographs understood this too.

Indeed, antiblackness so organized the visual disposability of black subjects that the final decade of the twentieth century is filled with examples, large and small, of this repeated expendability found in documentary photography. Of the repetition of images of dead black bodies in daily newspapers during the 1990s, Deborah E. McDowell writes, "These post-mortems circulate specifically within a journalistic economy linked to the dissecting and quantifying obsessions of social science linked especially to its historically racialized obsessions with separating the 'informative' from the 'deviant.'"[19] Blackness intertwined with "objective" data acquisition is an engorged abscess of racialization always on the verge of rupture. When it finally bursts, it renders the wound of white supremacy healed (falsely), and always at the expense of black people. These images have very little to do with the purported evidence of news dissemination. Their informative offerings are always spurious and always open to critique. McDowell continues: "And even if they are seen, these post-mortems do not invite protest. Perhaps they do not strike readers as gruesome because the press has accustomed them to viewing the face of black death. Indeed, in contemporary public media and discourse, death is synonymous with blackness and constitutes the absolute limit of 'difference.'"[20] Blackness and death as "synonyms" is the tally here. How else to understand the century-long deployment of photographs against black humanity, the submersion of subjectivity alongside a rigid visual framework that constricts a fully embodied black presentation?

THE SUBJECT AS OBJECT

Photography has helped facilitate a subject/object fallacy wherein, under the guise of the evidentiary, black subjects are presented as objects of crises waiting for an external (white) articulation. *Legibility* here means being legible to viewers who traffic in the visual demise of those registering as black. The length and depth of this trafficking is a foreshadowing event that produces its own mechanism of engagement. To unpack and unfurl its significance, we must go back to move forward. If global antiblackness is the atmosphere, as Christina Sharpe reminds us, then photography clings invisibly to the skin like mist. This makes the ephemeral/stasis structure of mortevivum an unwieldy navigation.

Visual constituencies make the archive of unbelonging tenable and available. Where harm is done, they ask us to tread lightly while attending to all there is to see. Where value is assumed and expected, there is its constant reinforcement and a willingness to extend ocular grace. Where there is an understanding of collective disposability, dispossession is the navigation and the end point. The black subject's quotidian existence is balanced between photographic dispossession and disregard, informed by a system that claims lives in the light and in the dark. So here we are, at a photographic demarcation point that now includes the continuing costs of white supremacy on black subjects globally.

Along with my reintroduction to newspaper imagery in the mid-1990s, there was a hovering poetic interlude—a space where it seemed black poets felt the need to engage the properties of the photograph that circumscribed black life. These articulations concern the force of photography and its historical longevity, an extension of life buttressed by the value placed on the genre's purported claims. Lucille Clifton's poem "the photograph: a lynching" is presented as a series of questions meant to expose the violence of lynching photography's long history.

is it the cut glass
of their eyes
looking up toward
the new gnarled branch
of the black man
hanging from a tree?

is it the white milk pleated
collar of the woman
smiling toward the camera,
her fingers loose around
a christian cross drooping
against her breast?

is it all of us
captured by history into an
accurate album? will we be
required to view it together
under a gathering sky?[21]

The long and horrific history of lynching photography in the United States is the origin point for a cruel framework set against black subjectivity. As Jacqueline Goldsby reminds us, it was the prurient spectacle offered by lynchings that held the white gaze with the promise of blackness aligned with death. Drawing on Roland Barthes's exploration of the specificity of this thing that "has happened only once," Goldsby writes: "Every lynching that ended in murder was its own 'occasion' of and 'encounter' with reality's final limit—death." And yet, for Goldsby, "once taken, moments captured by still-camera pictures do not exist in the historical present. For lynching to be represented in this medium, then, made the violence easier to disavow because photography transformed it into a spectacle that would prove impossible either to ignore or to see."[22] This crosshatching of regard and disregard creates a spectacle that mediates photography's mundane violences and sets them on fire. The mechanisim, photography, does not burn. It somehow evades that level of destruction in favor of the scars it leaves on some others, not all. This has more to do with cultural shifts in the imaginary that cleave to repetitive narratives.

I emphasize lynching imagery here for a number of reasons. The spectacular production of lynching photographs has a long, horrendous history. These photographs tell us something important about the communal ethos of white supremacist violence and the pleasure derived from its participants. As a terrorizing apparatus that brings pleasure and satisfaction to its participants, the anonymity among visibility is striking. These were not people hiding from photographers. They sought them out. They did not slink away from lynching scenes; they sent postcards, purchased at the lynching events, to friends and relatives across the country. Vicarious murder was the pursuit, and yet one would be hard-pressed to locate the attendees in the historical record. Mortevivum is the deployment of a contemporary application of vicarious murder. And much like a righteous viewer/participant at a public lynching, there are many ways to absolve oneself of the true gravity of the crime.

James Baldwin's 1965 short story "Going to Meet the Man" offers us the parameters of the visual production of the lynching photograph without reproducing the visual image itself. Instead, Baldwin orders the before, during, and after of the event through the prism of white supremacist ideology embodied by the main character, Jesse. Past, present, and foreseeable future coalesce as Jesse negotiates the violence of his desire and the racism that precedes it. "Going to Meet the Man" layers racial hegemony over the physical proximity negotiated by each of the characters in the story. The narrative opens with a scene of stifled/failed intimacy in the space of the marital bed, as Jesse tries but fails to be aroused by his wife, Grace. His impotence hints at his sense of fragile masculinity. He is unable to be with Grace sexually or visualize his wife in this moment as he imagines that every black person he has ever known, abused, violated, or interacted with is there in the bed with them.

As his mind wanders, while Grace drifts off to sleep, his subconscious mind takes over as he recalls aloud the details of the beating given to a young black man at the sheriff's office that day (he is a deputy sheriff). Baldwin writes, "As he talked, he began to hurt all over with that peculiar excitement which refused to be released."[23] At the center of Baldwin's story is the national inheritance of violence and the spectacle of racial terror that functions like a series of moving images made into still frames. Saidiya Hartman writes in *Scenes of Subjection*: "Blacks were envisioned fundamentally as vehicles for white enjoyment, in all of its sundry and unspeakable expressions."[24] Between the marital bed, where Jesse and Grace fail to make love, and the memory of a road trip taken in the cavernous space of the family vehicle, the distance between public and private sites of intimacy are all comingled with black trauma, exploitation, and murder. In this way, Baldwin represents the domestic production of racial terror and patriarchy within its externalized public imagined community—that of the white voyeurs/participants of the mob lynching. Baldwin presents us with an interwoven tapestry of violence and desire that is passed from generation to generation.

In Baldwin's ocular arrangement, lynching photographs embedded in the long arc of US history present the excessive and repetitive display of black visualized death, yet his story focuses instead on the interiority of those who traveled distances near and far to participate in these acts of mob violence and corporeal obliteration. Indeed, these people brought their children to these lynchings, and wore their best clothes. The story seeks to answer the questions, Who were these people? Where did they come from? And why were they so eager to document this violence photographically? Baldwin intimates that in viewing the gruesome murdered bodies of black lynching victims, we are looking at the wrong people.

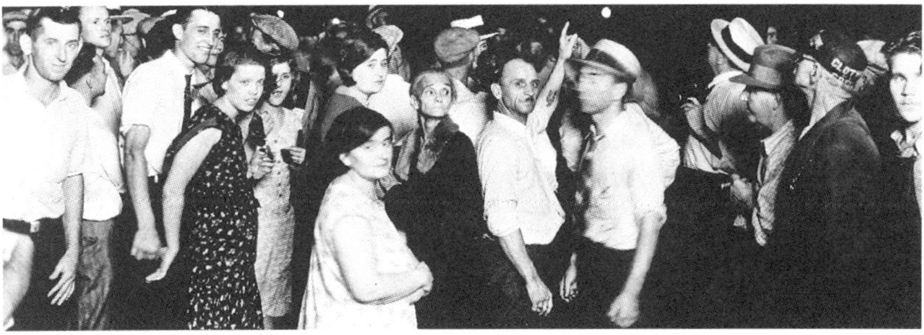

Figure 0.3
Detail. Lynching of Thomas Shipp and Abram Smith, Marion, Indiana, August 7, 1930. Courtesy of Getty Images. This image has been altered from its original form.

"Going to Meet the Man" builds around a memory from Jesse's past when his parents took him to witness his first lynching. As Jesse's family journeys from home into an open field to watch the excruciating hanging and burning of an unnamed black man, we bear witness through Jesse's eyes, fixed on his father (also named Jesse), and then his mother, among the crowd. Baldwin writes, "He watched his mother's face. Her eyes were very bright, her mouth was open: she was more beautiful than he had ever seen her and more strange." Jesse's mother has dressed for the occasion, choosing a ribbon to place in her hair as an adornment. It is essential that she offer the crowd, as well as the soon-to-be lynched man, a vision of white womanhood worth dying for, worth killing for.[25] As the eyes (Jesse's) watch the eyes (his mother's) that are eagerly absorbing the sight of the lynching, desire is formed. "He wanted death to come quickly," Baldwin writes of Jesse while he is submerged within the mob. However, "they wanted to make death wait."[26]

Sandy Alexandre considers the place of landscape in the context of public lynching scenes. She writes of lynching trees: "Their branches and their height: perfect for human display. Their status as natural objects: conveniently implicated in white society's efforts to naturalize what is (in effect) a social crime. Their being symbols of life: ironizing, in plain view, the gruesome scenes of death that take place on their watch."[27] Baldwin claims the landscape as just one more instrument of terror for black subjects. He makes clear that inside or out, in the presumed safety of home or the industry of work, there is no place that white supremacy will leave without terror.

The arc of Baldwin's imaginative trajectory is something akin to the photographic entanglements of race, class, gender, nation, and space. In "Going to Meet the Man," the subtle interplay of staging and seeing reveals an American self-portrait: a violently constructed articulation of white supremacy that presents itself as order, beauty, and virility, a repeating lie that finds the true image of itself in the repetition of that lie. Jesse remembers: "He could not see over the backs of the people in front of him. The sounds of laughing and cursing and wrath—and something else—rolled in waves from the front of the mob to the back. Those in front expressed their delight at what they saw, and this delight rolled backward, wave upon wave, across the clearing, more acrid than the smoke. His father reached down suddenly and sat Jesse on his shoulders."[28] In assuming the viewer's familiarity with lynching photographs, Baldwin is suturing racial violence to the vagaries of leisure and spectacle, the "delight" disallowing the force of white anonymity to dominate what we already know about crowds like the one in the story. Here the lynched man's body serves as an afterimage of the violent photographs that will haunt the southern landscape, then disappear into the temporal archive of history. Baldwin's photographic production, the ebb and the flow of his gestural, expressive, contemplative visual display, is part of his decades-long engagement with the world of the visual.

After the lynching, Jesse and his family walk away, into the attendant violence of their whiteness and the safety it affords them. Meanwhile, "the black body was on the ground, the chain which had held it was being rolled up by one of his father's friends. Whatever the fire had left undone, the hands and the knives and the stones of the people had accomplished. The head was caved in, one eye was torn out, one ear was hanging. But one had to look carefully to realize this, for it was, now, merely, a black charred object on the black, charred ground."[29] To encounter Baldwin's prose is to delve beneath the depths of human frailty and foreclosure, knowing how violently imagistic is what is buried there. It is to consider the primacy of the visual as it orients the lives and labors of the citizens it refuses or holds close. To think of Baldwin, then, as one of the country's foremost theorists of race and the visual is to place him within the canon of interlocutors without whom we would have no contemporary discourse of contemporary visuality. His powers of observation were the enduring result of measured, potent analysis, cultivated over the course of many years, through several literary genres and in photographic presentations.

According to Mark Sealy, "Colonial and racist trophy photographs therefore serve as fragments and frames from within the grand narrative of white supremacist visual ideologies. They allow us to enter the catastrophic frames of violent colonial and racist times, and they become important articulations that signify the dark cultural codes constructed against people of African descent or others classified as inferior."[30] These "important articulations" are a hierarchical road well-traveled and rarely mentioned. Photographs serve as guideposts along this road, able to emulate interest as benign even as the violence of ocular practices is ever-present. Under the ruse of "evidence," blackness survives through the destructive properties of the visual. Misrecognition meets indifference in a surfeit of imagery meant to foreclose the autonomy, will, and humanity of the subject. To be encased in this imagery, held beneath its twisted apparatus of the gaze, is to enter a carnival house of mirrors where the black subject is the only object of engagement. "The circus and the audience," Baldwin writes in *The Evidence of Things Not Seen*, "are absolutely indispensible to the hygiene of the state."[31] The spectacle is the point. Without it, Baldwin suggests, internal chaos will produce the kind of havoc that a deputy sheriff will find impossible to control.

The hypersurveillance black people experience at the hands of the state or as part of some consumerist ethos makes the double consciousness that W. E. B. Du Bois discussed in the early part of the twentieth century photographic in its extension. "The historical formation of surveillance is not outside of the historical formation of slavery," Simone Browne reminds us.[32] Nor is it outside the history of imperial possession. It is, as is now understood, an interlacing of possession and disregard, the permissive inculcation of ocular violence. Someone must be available for this ocular violence, for it has to exist and extend itself forward. Black diasporic subjects are the canvas upon which so much is thrown: racial, national, juridical, and cultural detritus get tossed onto them like projections on a film screen. However, this film has no locatable producer. It runs without a discernible source of power.

Antiblackness so measures the power of looking, seeing, and unseeing that Ralph Ellison structured his novel *Invisible Man* around this peculiar relationship between seeing and invisibility. Toni Morrison perfected the violence/indifference matrix in her novel *The Bluest Eye*. When protagonist Pecola Breedlove hands her money to the white immigrant shopkeeper, the exchange is instructive: "At some fixed point in time and space he senses that he need not waste the effort of a glance," Morrison writes. "He does not see her, because for him there was nothing to see."[33] Antiblackness informs the line of sight and reveals a repetition of responses that suggest viewers "need not waste the effort of a glance"; black people go about their lives with the knowledge of this corporeal vulnerability for which no one, other than themselves, is responsible. Thus, with none of the protections of the state, but with all of its violent inflictions, photography offers one more option to view black people in pain for the viewer's enjoyment.

Some may challenge the idea that there is pleasure in this endeavor; however, one way to refute this is to see how agitated people get when you ask them to stop. Over a dozen years of conversations and presentations, the most consistent question I have received is about the evidentiary. In essence, I am asked about the essential nature of photographic evidence. "Don't we need these photographs to know what is happening?" I am asked. To which my current response is, "What is the evidence we have that white people die?" The response to this question often results in awkward silence. It is precisely this understanding that white supremacy provides but disavows. White lives are valuable—too valuable to be reduced to photographic objects. They will not be visualized as dead bodies strewn across the front pages of newspapers. They will not be displayed anonymously as symbols of crisis and disorder. Their suffering will not be fodder for the failures of the state. It's the privilege of an invisibly operating sempervivum where the perception is that dignified representation is the domain of white subjects, who are precious and therefore deserving of life. This is how the violent pushback against a phrase like *black lives matter* is so energized.

What is embedded in an insistance that the particularities of blackness justify documentation of the infliction of violence that would be appalling to consider for others? Here, that the "all" is not just unrealizable but pointedly antiblack, for other racialized subjects can be sustained within "all," but *only black is black*. Photography gives the illusion of realism, allowing viewers to cement black progress with the visual residue of regression. This ensures that black lives are encapsulated within a two-dimensional space of cultural decline as if it is impossible to imagine what is beyond the photographic frame.

Mortevivum highlights the space between the materiality of the photograph (the living thing) and the visualization of antiblackness (the dead offering). It is here that imminent death is engineered within and beyond the photograph as a projected death drive forced upon black subjects so that others may understand themselves through other peoples' bodies. The black diaspora exists for these viewers as a kind of cudgel against actual death, for in this sense the gravity of death is presented as a quotidian act of nothingness for the darker races. Aime Cesaire writes: "I make no secret of my opinion that at the present time the barbarism of Western Europe has reached an incredibly high level being only surpassed—for surpassed, it is true—by the barbarism of the United States."[34] We know that the "barbarism of the United States" is a nearly boundless series of violations against humanity that the country has yet to acknowledge and reconcile. We also know how racial stratification has buttressed and extended the line of sight for these violations and how easily the country has navigated both its innocence and its defense.[35]

Photograpy's global emergence in the nineteenth century grafted onto the eugenics movement and imperial dispossession writ large. It is how the mandates of capture and progress severely restricted the line of sight for black subjects who had to use the same frame that was intended to contain them. "The camera relieves us of the burden of memory," John Berger laments. "It surveys us like God, and it surveys for us. Yet no other God has been so cynical, for the camera records in order to forget."[36] It is the violence within forgetting that emphasizes black stasis on photographic film. This book endeavers to undermine the harm inherent in a refusal to acknowledge harm. When photography is aligned with blackness, it is suffused with a "serious pathology" that Morrison reminds us is always hovering in the shadows. And because it is hovering, this makes every interaction with the archive fraught with the pursuit of discernable destruction. As Stuart Hall has theorized, "The ideological construction of black people as a 'problem population' and the police practice of containment in the black communities mutually reinforce and supress one another. Nevertheless, ideology is a practice. It has its own specific way of working."[37] In other words, ideology works visually.

Chapter 1 of *Mortevivum*, "The Empire," explores the struggle with unbelonging that black South Africans share with

African Americans in the historical order of racial segregation. Since the election of the National Party in 1948, South Africa has functioned within the racial and juridical rule of a white minority and the resistance of and to a black majority. Photographs manage the daily acts of removal, capture, violence, and denial perpetrated against black South Africans. "For years, apartheid politicians—and these, one should not forget, include apartheid's last president—did not regard the liberation aspirations of blacks with any seriousness," writes Pumla Gobodo-Madikizela.[38] And images in the national media bear this out.

This chapter brings together empires within nations and their relationship to racial subjugation. South Africa and the United States are intertwined in a loop of racial violence meant to remind black subjects of their lower-class status mandated via the state. For South Africa, this is done via the apartheid regime, while the United States has a longer history of de facto and de jure racial classification. It begins during slavery and continues after slavery is abolished with the end of the Civil War in 1865. Apartheid ends officially, with the election of Nelson Mandela in 1994, but the reverberations of the regime are still currently in effect. Images reinforce the way apartheid rendered its black subjects outside citizenship and outside regard. Similarly, Jim Crow segregation in the United States and its attendant imagery extended the visualization of dehumanization from the nineteenth century to the end of the twentieth. From the end of the Civil War through the hideous decades of the American reconstruction era and beyond, white supremacy revealed itself via presentations of dead black bodies that are striking in their ubiquity, revealing a long history of visualizing the vioent deaths of African Americans.

Chapter 2, "The Viewer," concerns the proliferation of death that Rwanda represents during the 1994 genocide, which exists devoid of the photographs that would correspond to the slaughter of one million people in one hundred days. Instead, news media outlets mostly minimized or ignored the violence taking place in the small, central east African nation, preferring, apparently, to allow the war to reach its organic end without intervention. The gruesome images of dead bodies in various stages of decay do emerge. They emerge in the aftermath of the genocide, when most of the victims of the genocide are beyond any humanitarian intervention. These images, then, are not released at the behest of the victims' families, or to highlight the determination of the perpetrators of violence. They are meant to remind viewers that blackness comes with a corresponding violence that no human intervention can abate.

This chapter interrogates the desire on the part of the viewer to participate in a proximity to death, using black people's bodies with the understanding that this vicarious exchange allows the viewer to see everything and nothing at all in the endeavor. Antiblackness disallows points of reflection and consideration of the dead, as Rwanda occupies an unwieldy place in the documented presentation of a nation in crisis. This is where all previous mandates about photographing the dead and dying are violently, relentlessly deepened. And a deafening silence during the war and genocide translates to a visual cacophony afterward, when victims' and survivors' pleas have been ignored.

Chapter 3 of *Mortevivum*, "The Sentiment," concerns Haiti in the public imaginary. The first black republic in the Western hemisphere is also the first nation to violently abolish slavery and create a nation out of its ashes. I argue that Haiti's success as a former colony of France is continually undermined by photographic "evidence" of its sovereign failure. Images try to reinforce the idea that the formerly enslaved cannot overthrow their masters and survive to tell the tale.

When the US military was deployed to Haiti in September 1994, it was to facilitate what was called Operation Uphold Democracy, an effort to overturn the military coup that removed the democratically elected President Jean-Bertrand Aristide. Lasting only a few months, the intervention was documented with hundreds of photographs in daily newspapers and weekly magazines, all seemingly intent on offering the nation up as devoid of leadership, autonomy, and agency. Indeed, the vast majority of images of the dead discussed in this book are from Haiti, where the US military was perpetually present, and so were photojournalists whose documented images reinforce the narrative of Haiti's failed sovereignty.

Mortevivum takes a purposeful textual movement from south to north and back again to illustrate the circumnavigation of antiblackness where it occurs over time. As such, I am moving through several temporal locations in order to grapple with the global nature of antiblackness that pervades photographic archives of the present and past and impedes gestures of resistance for the future. The photograph as a living thing, antiblackness as a dead offering: We live in a repetition of imagery signaling who lives and who dies on a gelatin silver print. On a page in a book. On the cover of a newspaper. And in the memory of millions.

1

THE EMPIRE

the photograph—who you were—
will be waiting when you return.
—Natasha Trethewey

Decades after he is imprisoned for subversion, Nelson Mandela is poised to be the first black president of the Republic of South Africa. The Sunday, May 1, 1994, front page of the *New York Times* features a photograph of Mandela looking serious and solemn, eyes slightly lowered as if deep in thought. Bill Keller's article "The Man for South Africa's Future" traces Mandela's unlikely political trajectory from state prisoner to "president-in-waiting." So much of the essay seems constructed to soften any imagined hard edges the reader supposes Mandela may possess. The soon-to-be president is called "the most practical of men." Keller continues: "He is not unfeeling, but passion—even anger at what he has endured—does not drive him or distract him. He enjoys debate, but he is not a great philosopher or intellectual. He has principles, but he will bend them if they stand in the way of his objective—which, for the last half century, has been ending white domination."[1] With so much hinging on the unification of a postapartheid South Africa, offering Mandela as a "practical" man, one devoid of "philosophical" or "intellectual" diversions, aligns cleanly with a (white) readership necessitating "civilized" reactions to the savagery of white supremacy. Aided by an Associated Press photograph, Mandela's eyes do not meet those of the viewers. There is an undertone of gravity in the image, as if the future president is attempting to take in the totality of meaning that his presidency symbolizes. Because of this, each visual gesture—the slight furrowing of his brow, the way his hands come together, open, yet clasped—is filled with fifty-odd years of symbolic meaning.

In those first few paragraphs of the *New York Times* piece, Keller also describes Mandela's decision, soon after his release, to build a vacation home that is "an exact brick replica of the warden's house" where he lived for months recovering from illness and where he met "secretly" with representatives of the state.[2] This detail is important, for it situates Mandela as less of a threat to the status quo. Indeed, Keller marks the duplication of the warden's bungalow as Mandela himself explains it: pure pragmatism. In the enclosure of a prison domicile, a narrative arc works to sustain an acceptable transition of power. The kind that many white people can find a way to live with as it is grounded in civility's appendage: practicality. "The body is the place of captivity," Dionne Brand writes, and Mandela's imagined and real imprisonment is one he brings with him into postimprisonment, prepresidential shape.[3] It seems vital (and subsequent *New York Times* articles reinforce this) that the preservation of white order remains even when the black majority has political control over the nation. Thus, while Mandela's image offers us a contemplative and thoughtful visual representation, it shows a man holding the totality of a bruised nation in his partially clasped hands—an impossible

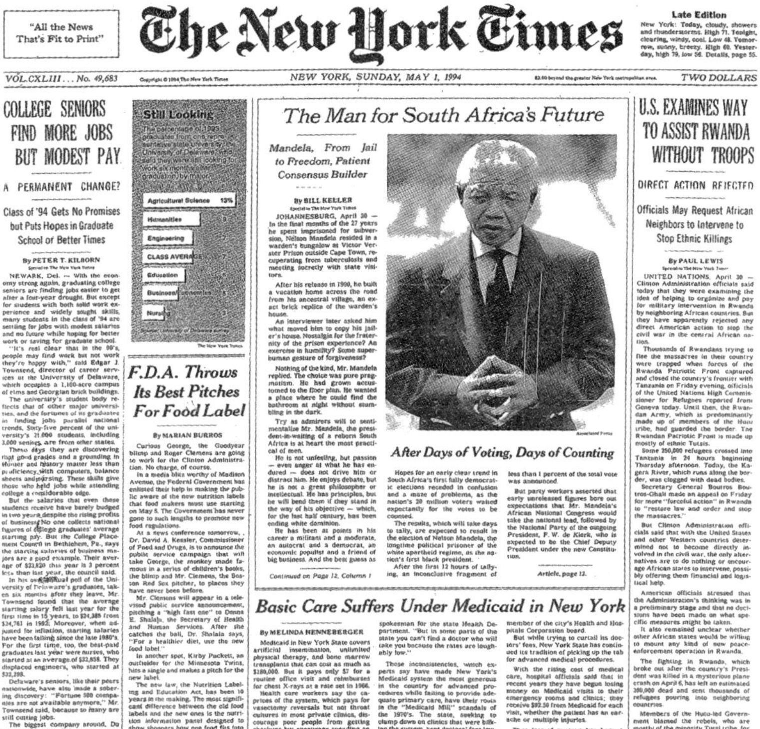

"All the News That's Fit to Print"

The New York Times

Late Edition

New York: Today, cloudy, showers and thunderstorms. High 71. Tonight, clearing, windy, cool. Low 48. Tomorrow, sunny, breezy. High 60. Yesterday, high 79, low 56. Details, page 55.

VOL.CXLIII . . . No. 49,683 — NEW YORK, SUNDAY, MAY 1, 1994 — TWO DOLLARS

COLLEGE SENIORS FIND MORE JOBS BUT MODEST PAY

A PERMANENT CHANGE?

Class of '94 Gets No Promises but Puts Hopes in Graduate School of Better Times

By PETER T. KILBORN

Still Looking

The Man for South Africa's Future

Mandela, From Jail to Freedom, Patient Consensus Builder

By BILL KELLER

After Days of Voting, Days of Counting

U.S. EXAMINES WAY TO ASSIST RWANDA WITHOUT TROOPS

DIRECT ACTION REJECTED

Officials May Request African Neighbors to Intervene to Stop Ethnic Killings

By PAUL LEWIS

F.D.A. Throws Its Best Pitches For Food Label

By MARIAN BURROS

Basic Care Suffers Under Medicaid in New York

By MELINDA HENNEBERGER

Rwandans Fleeing

Air Force Academy Zooms In on Sex Cases

By ERIC SCHMITT

Air Force cadets assembled recently before marching to lunch.

INSIDE

Battle Over Smog Rules

Overhauling Regents' Tests

Tensions in Staten Island

War Stories, From Boys

TODAY'S SECTIONS

Figure 1.1

Cover page of the *New York Times*, May 1, 1994. Courtesy of PARS International.

human endeavor. One nation is dead, and another is born to replace it. But can life emerge out of such a violent death?

Decades mark South Africa's experiment with racial apartheid through photography, an ocular conundrum. From 1948, when the white supremacist National Party was voted into power, until 1994, when apartheid "officially" ended and Nelson Mandela was elected president, photography centralized the way the world learned about the violence that accompanied the apartheid regime. Because 1994 is a significant year in South Africa's racial trajectory, *Mortevivum* opens here in this geographic space of fluctuating sovereignties mired in deep, interlocking histories. "In many ways," Achille Mbembe writes, "our world remains a 'world of races,' whether we admit it or not." Mbembe continues: "Although this fact is often denied, the racial signifier is still in many ways the inescapable language for the stories people tell about themselves, about their relationship with the Other, about memory, and about power."[4] Decades mark this terrain of "inescapable language" with the violence enacted by the apartheid regime and thus pull the viewer into the frame.

Gelatin silver prints created during this time present South Africa as a space of binary opposition: black and white, negative and positive. Something about photography's originating construction (interior versus exterior) reinforces a racialized binary that gets played out symbolically. This chapter will ponder the presence (or lack thereof) of black subjectivity as it exists within the ocular space of mortevivum. Mortevivum is the photographic dividing line of death's proximity to blackness that writers and cultural practitioners must continually negotiate. It is the "voyage through death to life upon these shores" that Robert Hayden's poem "Middle Passage" presents as a thematic organizing principle of slavery's life and slavery's afterlife.[5] Its conceptual refraction, sempervivum, on the other hand, orders the structure of whiteness as the visual corollary of a racial elongation of human life—the ocular production of the *live forever*. If whiteness functions as sempervivum, the logic goes, it can only do so by signaling or referencing its inversion—mortevivum, which has a register of default blackness.[6]

I take seriously Toni Morrison's declaration that "slavery broke the world in half, it broke it in every way." And in taking this seriously, I am invested in thinking about the world-altering mechanisms of transatlantic racial slavery and imperialism that are yoked together in order to upend the order of the world. Morrison continues: "You can't do that for hundreds of years and it not take a toll. They had to dehumanize, not just the slaves but themselves. They have had to reconstruct everything in order to make that system appear true."[7] Colonial archives, oral histories, and legal documents bear out the horrendous nature of Atlantic slavery and imperialism. Furthermore, the place that white supremacy occupies in the world tells us something important about the force and the power of the need to "make that system appear true." By the time photography was invented, racial slavery had become a fixture of the Western world. Photographs reinforce a hierarchical racial fantasy that slavery and imperialism exacerbated.

ETYMOLOGIES

From the Latin *imperium*, meaning "to command," we receive our current deployment of the word *empire*.[8] In the context of South Africa, I am most invested in the definition that follows: "An extensive sphere of activity controlled by one person or group."[9] *To command.* The "extensive sphere of activity" structured around white supremacy made an empire out of whiteness and contained it in the movements and restrictions of groups of people over time. We have seen this before—namely, in the racial stratification of the United States, where for decades after the end of the Civil War (1861–1865), black Americans were regulated under a "sphere of activity controlled" by white supremacy. Their ability to live, to move about, to work, to own property or be autonomously rendered was constrained within white supremacist strictures, similar to its construction in South

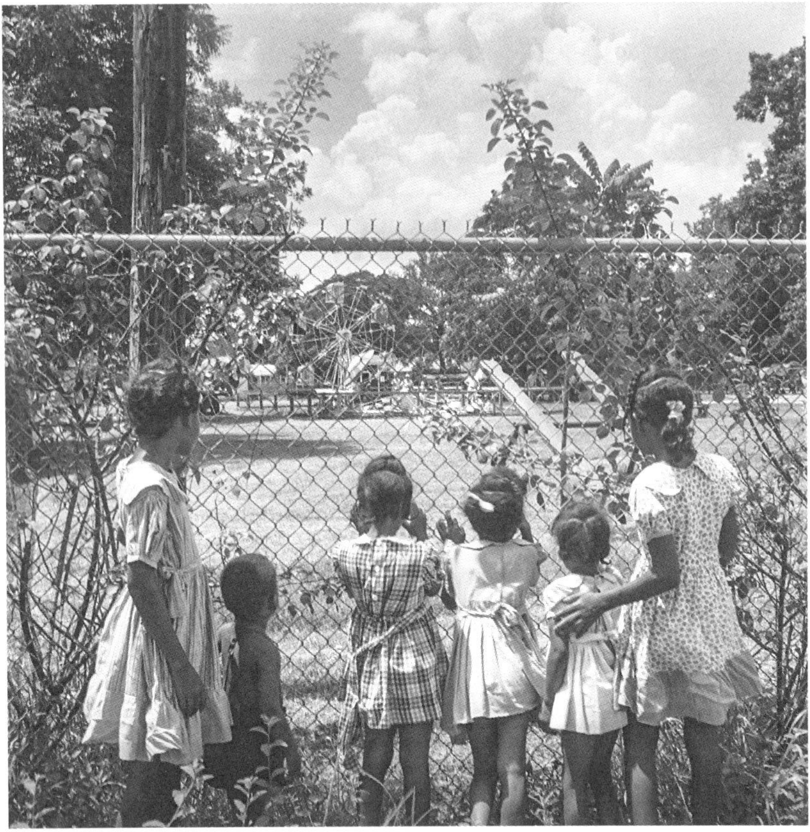

Figure 1.2 Gordon Parks, *Outside Looking In*, Mobile, Alabama, 1956 (printed 2012), High Museum of Art, Atlanta. Courtesy of the Gordon Parks Foundation.

Africa. Here I aim my focus in this bifurcated direction between the United States and South Africa, and at the imagistic scaffolding that impacts imperial regimes structured by race but within national borders.

REPERCUSSIONS

The past has a photographic history as well. In one iteration, found in Peter Magubane's 1976 photograph *Soweto Riots*, we see two women standing near the left of the center of the frame of the photograph. They orient the eye of the viewer. The center contains *nobody*. But there is a body on the ground—someone no longer alive, but occupying space. Wrapped in plaid (Basotho) blankets, and each exposing one hand that emerges through the sleeve of space the blanket provides, the women stand. Someone has died the evening before this early

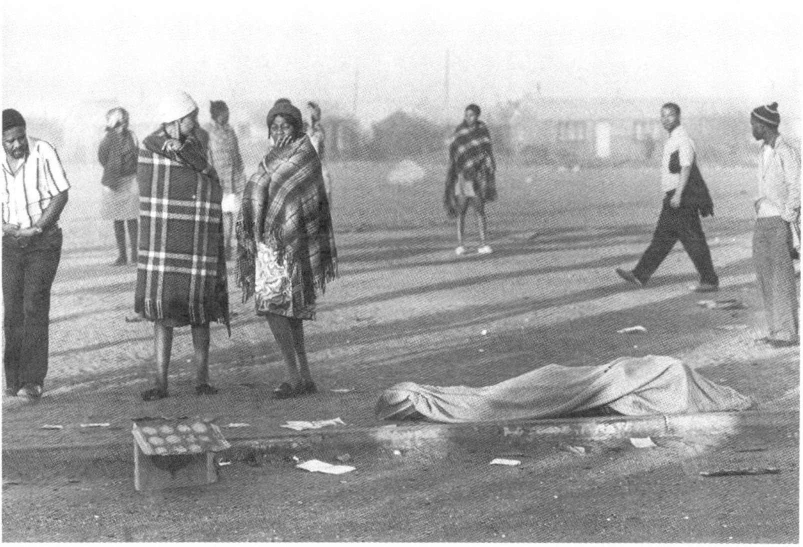

Figure 1.3 Peter Magubane, *Soweto Riots*, 1976. Courtesy of the International Center of Photography (https://www.icp.org).

morning shot was taken. One woman is turned away from the body; one is turned in the direction of the body. She looks down and over. The violence of the evening before is both indexical and evidentiary.[10]

Three men frame the outer edges of the photograph, providing it with corporeal margins—one on the left, and two on the right. One of the men directs his eye to the body on the ground, one gazes back at the photographer, and the last man turns his gaze away from both ocular possibilities. Together, their bodies center the two rows of women (six in all) encased within the boundary of the image. Ten people: nine living, one dead.

In Magubane's photograph, we see an archive at work, and it is an image that reframes the intent of an empire within a nation. It is a scene of temporal fluidity, an intertextual vision of the layering of black unbelonging. In the photo, a group of black South Africans are assembled around a dead body after the Soweto protests begin taking place. Each of the people present attends to or avoids the sight of the body. The body itself is a problem—its placement in the image's foreground, its status among the dead, and its presence in close proximity to those gathered about it. As the photo intimates, the space between blackness and death is so close that it is often impossible for Western practices of the ocular to tell the difference.

A visible tether joins the men and women in the image to the person who has just recently passed from life to death. This is what renders the photographic scene with its taut emotive extension. Not one person in the image will voluntarily cross the threshold of this death, a subjectivity that Giorgio Agamben might call killable but not mournable.[11] Stopping inches away from the body, they address it as its own cruel visual display. They both recognize and resist the demarcation of what Saidiya Hartman would call their photographic *fungibility*, and the imprint of too many inculcations of temporal duress.[12] The image is useful to ponder the present absence of blackness photographically, and within the ocular space of what I call a *cartography of the ocular*. This cartography has layered antiblack dimensions: the seeming absence of empire, the collapsing of historical exclusions, and the repetition of racial subjections. This joins black Americans and black South Africans under a similar rubric of photographic removal, where a racial hierarchy presents itself invisibly while enforcing itself so violently.

Once black bodies are removed from lynching photographs, the question remains: Who were these people and why were they so eager to be photographed? For Ken Gonzalez-Day, "The history of lynching demonstrates that without a legal code of law, justice is little more than fleeting passion—mob rule."[13] And this is most often how lynchings are written about,

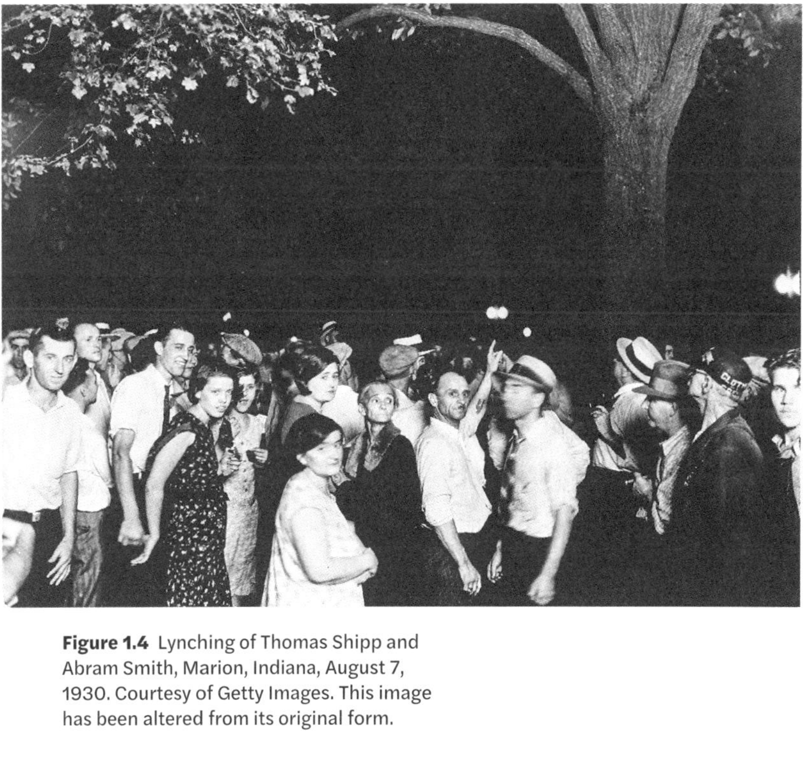

Figure 1.4 Lynching of Thomas Shipp and Abram Smith, Marion, Indiana, August 7, 1930. Courtesy of Getty Images. This image has been altered from its original form.

as demonstrations of vigilante justice, a way for community members to right wrongs that have been done in the glaring light of day. This is all tangled up with race, class, gender, and geography in the United States. And it has a back history as old as the nation itself. Tina Campt writes, "The materiality of the photo secures neither its indexical accuracy nor transparency; it leads us to question it instead."[14] In this case, these questions go beyond the details of the photograph and through the cultural arena of which they are a part. What does Indiana in the 1930s have to tell us about how racial mores evolved in the decades that preceded it?

PHOTOGRAPHIC HISTORIES OF VIOLENCE

Five black men fill the photographic space with the visible labor their bodies represent. One stands, and three are bent over as they negotiate the Virginia earth and the burial task they must perform. In the forefront of the image, the viewer's eye is drawn to the seated black man and the skeletal remains of American Civil War soldiers alongside him. He gazes back at the camera, his head tilted slightly to the left, close to the first of five skulls that look like macabre extensions of his own body. The five skulls anchor the five living figures in the image and provide a figurative line of defense against possible threat. The Civil War was imagined as a white man's war; visually devoid of black soldiers and their corporeal sacrifice, the imagery that remains is instead a visual register of white sacrifice. White soldiers dying for the sins of the country and the sins of black people—that is, the sin that is slavery. The photographic archive of the war is one of astounding substance and meaning, but also astounding absence and refusal. There, in the precise envisioning of the archive, we see few images of African Americans outside their prescribed roles of subservience; they are presented mostly as servants, refugees, contraband, gravediggers. We can imagine that the graves dug signify these men's own buried or submerged citizenship that does not allow black Americans to firmly situate themselves within the geographic space of the

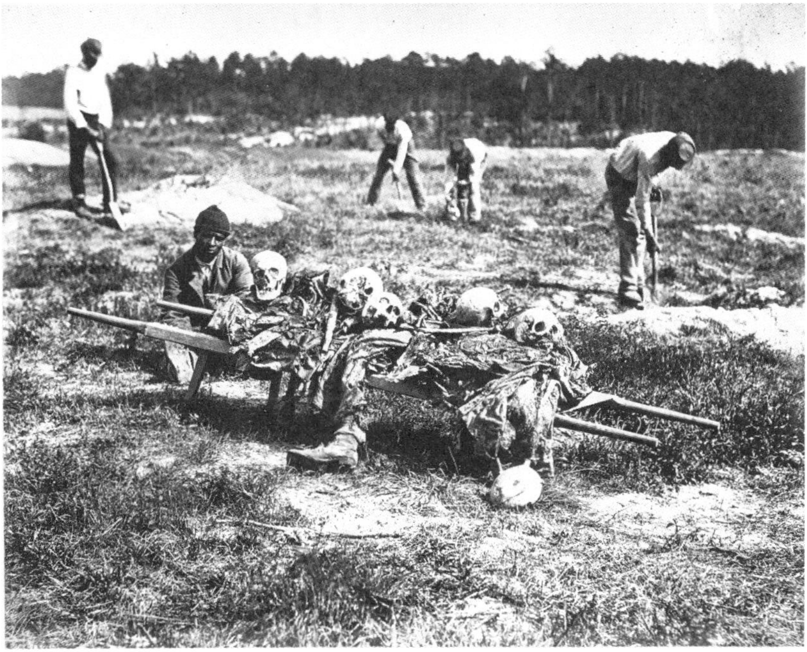

Figure 1.5 John Reekie, *A Burial Party, Cold Harbor, Virginia*, 1865. Courtesy of Getty Images.

nation. Instead, they are seen to be ever awaiting a future reconciliation that is never to arrive—but is always on its way.

These men form the boundary of a burial party for white soldiers as their bodies intimate a proximity to death that they negotiate alone. In this way, the fraught negotiation of national and familial cohesion is organized around a narrative reconciliation making them brothers or soldiers of the war, but only if they are white. Black Americans, as this image intimates, exist on the periphery of the national family, and documentary photographs illustrate this repeatedly. Further, these images tether blackness to death as legible, as destined and in proximate certainty.

Something of the memory of the American Civil War haunts the present, aided by documentary photographs. Beyond the six hundred thousand dead and the catastrophe of its ruined landscape, something else is present, palpable and visible. It is a hovering sense of national mourning that has not sustained African Americans within the national imaginary. "A scaffolding of bone we tread upon, forgetting," according to poet Natasha Trethewey.[15] A past and a future tense of racial hegemony. It begins in the photographic archive of dead Civil War soldiers, iconic images of stone-still battlefields littered with bodies that occupy the visual field, facilitating a process of mourning that reinforces citizenship and national belonging, yet black soldiers exist outside of this framework.

A perusal of the Prints and Photographs Division at the Library of Congress shows the available archive has its limitations. Before a search for African American soldiers in the Civil War can begin, the researcher is informed that "images of African American soldiers are not well-represented" in the archive. Instead, "most photographs show African Americans as civilians attached to the military, and as 'contraband' and refugees."[16] These images signal the visualization of a repeated metaphor of black subjectivity occupying an impossible duality of property and person, of contraband and comrade, and of refugee and citizen.

The paucity of images of African Americans in the photographic archive of the Civil War (composed of nearly one million images) replicates an erasure of visible blackness when that blackness is a part of the discourse of the event. In the aftermath of the Civil War and its ghostly remembrances, in the sliver of space between slavery's demise and the spectacular production of lynching photography, the recovery mission of the nation doubled black death against a refusal of citizenship, necessitating the production of photographic memory on the part of African Americans to make space for the imagistic absence of black subjects and black subjectivity.

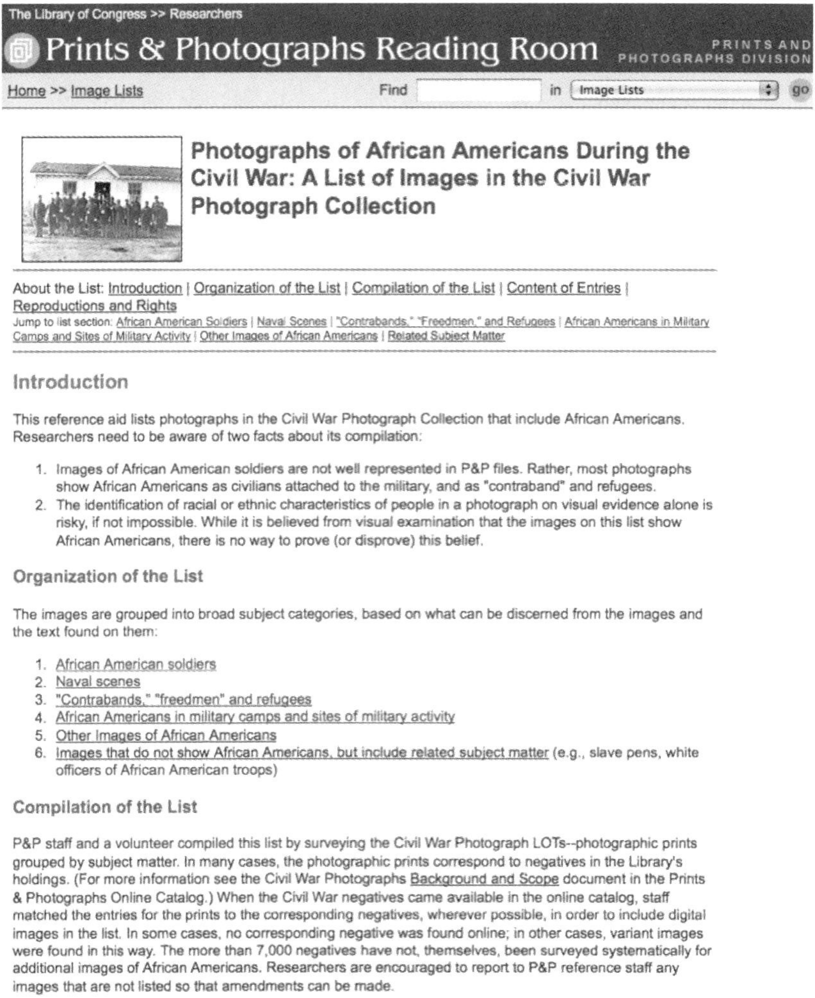
The Library of Congress >> Researchers

Prints & Photographs Reading Room

PRINTS AND PHOTOGRAPHS DIVISION

Home >> Image Lists Find in Image Lists go

Photographs of African Americans During the Civil War: A List of Images in the Civil War Photograph Collection

About the List: Introduction | Organization of the List | Compilation of the List | Content of Entries | Reproductions and Rights

Jump to list section: African American Soldiers | Naval Scenes | "Contrabands," "Freedmen," and Refugees | African Americans in Military Camps and Sites of Military Activity | Other Images of African Americans | Related Subject Matter

Introduction

This reference aid lists photographs in the Civil War Photograph Collection that include African Americans. Researchers need to be aware of two facts about its compilation:

1. Images of African American soldiers are not well represented in P&P files. Rather, most photographs show African Americans as civilians attached to the military, and as "contraband" and refugees.
2. The identification of racial or ethnic characteristics of people in a photograph on visual evidence alone is risky, if not impossible. While it is believed from visual examination that the images on this list show African Americans, there is no way to prove (or disprove) this belief.

Organization of the List

The images are grouped into broad subject categories, based on what can be discerned from the images and the text found on them:

1. African American soldiers
2. Naval scenes
3. "Contrabands," "freedmen" and refugees
4. African Americans in military camps and sites of military activity
5. Other Images of African Americans
6. Images that do not show African Americans, but include related subject matter (e.g., slave pens, white officers of African American troops)

Compilation of the List

P&P staff and a volunteer compiled this list by surveying the Civil War Photograph LOTs--photographic prints grouped by subject matter. In many cases, the photographic prints correspond to negatives in the Library's holdings. (For more information see the Civil War Photographs Background and Scope document in the Prints & Photographs Online Catalog.) When the Civil War negatives came available in the online catalog, staff matched the entries for the prints to the corresponding negatives, wherever possible, in order to include digital images in the list. In some cases, no corresponding negative was found online; in other cases, variant images were found in this way. The more than 7,000 negatives have not, themselves, been surveyed systematically for additional images of African Americans. Researchers are encouraged to report to P&P reference staff any images that are not listed so that amendments can be made.

Figure 1.6 Library of Congress, Prints and Photographs Division (http://www.loc.gov/pictures/).

Of the famous Gardner photographs of deceased white Civil War soldiers blanketing battlefields across the country, Susan Sontag writes, "With our dead, there has always been a powerful interdiction against showing the naked face." For Sontag, this is what gives the images their exceptional force, as "Union and Confederate soldiers lie on their backs, with the faces of some clearly visible."[17] It is a consolidation of racial alignment that allows this to be visualized and held in memory. White soldiers, even the traitorous Confederates, are seen as the epitome of sacrifice—to die for the preservation of an idea, white supremacy—while black soldiers register as the contraband white lives are sacrificed *for*.

Encased in a refusal to incorporate black people into the national imaginary, contemporary literature about the Civil War is more than just a reclaiming of the available archive: it is a reconfiguration of what it means to read against the grain of what is already there. I want to think about the photographic space opened by the onset of the Civil War as one that framed black subjectivity in increasingly narrowing parameters, even as a separate African American archive existed. I also want to think about the space of contemporary photography as expansive enough to imagine black futurity against the containing register of race and nation.

Decades after the Civil War ends, stereographs of black laborers culling cotton appeared in the United States. These images then, visually out of time, are also solidified through a photographic stasis that attempts to hold black Americans in a state of enslavement that seemingly never ends. The never-ending extension of slavery's presence is the disciplinary framework of racialized violence we have come to know. How then to discuss the pleasures of looking when those doing the looking are white, while the wounded, exploited, and dead are black? Black writers, artists, and activists have not had the luxury of passive attention. Not when "photographs of dead black bodies surrounded by happy white onlookers" are a central feature of lynching images in the United States.[18]

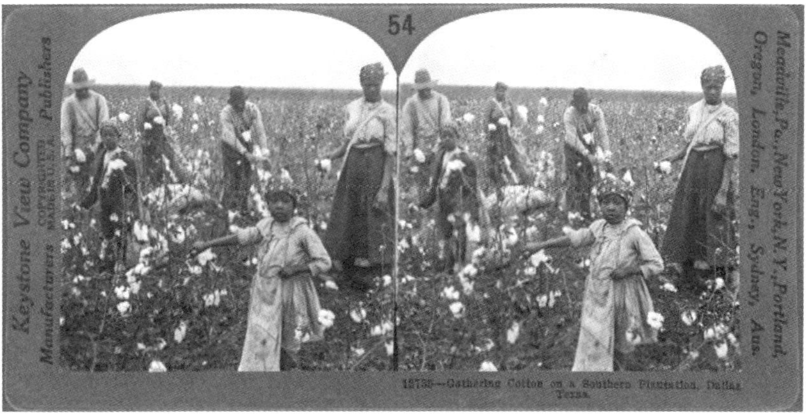

Figure 1.7 *Gathering Cotton on a Southern Plantation*, Dallas, Texas, 1900. Courtesy of the New York Public Library.

The doubling mechanism of mortevivum is the schematic cartography of unbelonging that hinges on the absence of black bodies in the photographic archive of the American Civil War, and the hyperpresence of black bodies in images of the dead at the end of the twentieth century. Whiteness constructs the documentary photographic space within its own binary logic, marking the photograph in and through the bodies that it contains. If whiteness is sempervivum (the live forever) of the American Civil War in this documentary logic, then blackness functions as a default mortevivum (the death living).

In a comparative study of the United States and South Africa, Tiffany Willoughby-Herard writes, "The pursuit of whiteness leaves people less human, less capable of accountability for their own debasement, and yet thoroughly meritorious in their own view because by standard markers of socioeconomic status, they are successful." Willoughby-Herard insists that "we begin to talk about whiteness as pathology, whiteness as diminished selfhood, whiteness as soul injury, and whiteness as death."[19] *Whiteness as death.* What spectacular production of death has whiteness, in its imperialist production, wrought?

How might we consider how photography functions as an aid as well as a traitor to the mission of the propaganda of white supremacy? *Soweto Riots* utilizes shadows to illuminate *that which cannot be gleaned without effort*: the space of desire in the temporal iteration of blackness in its proximity to death. As I discuss in chapter 3 of *Mortevivum*, shadows and photographic practices align to promote an aesthetic of haunting that refers itself forward in time. If the empire is a shadow, its cloaking mechanism is also its ubiquity. Photographic terms oscillate between light and shadow, mutations of exposure and imagistic clarity. To this, South African apartheid adds its own enclosure—an archival world producing shadows for light and light for shadow.

Because racial empires are constructed around the idea of implemented order (i.e., white sovereignty) and the containment of a duplicating threat (black sovereignty), they exist to stifle the movement and will of those considered undesirable, recalcitrant, unassimilable. Photography is a necessary appendage of empire, and its racial dimensions are part of what allows it to have such a potent legacy. Archives of the colonial experiment in South Africa detail an aggressive campaign of disruption and bodily violence that has yet to be reckoned with in the public imagination. That specific set of decades—1948 to 1994—is its own imperial curation, and photographs dominate. So many images from the period have been reproduced so often as to be infamous in their ubiquity, like the United States in the nineteenth century and the 1950s and 1960s.

THE RIFF

Decades of removal, segregation, and racial violence converge in this image. It travels across temporalities. From the front page of the *New York Times* in 1963, it moved to every major city in the United States and multiple international news outlets, including *Life Magazine*. If it were described to you, its contours and graphic overtones relayed in words, you would recognize it sight unseen. The term *iconic* fails at the task of registering the total photographic symbolism of the civil rights movement era contained in the image. In Birmingham, Alabama, there is a monument based on Bill Hudson's famous photograph of fifteen-year-old Walter Gadsden. It is a photograph of convergence. I think of Gadsden as one of the few members of black photographic production who is disallowed the basic tenets of privacy and whose relationship to this image remains a static force, holding him in time, over time, as an object of suffering.

Four years after this photograph was taken, another emerged with similar visual constituencies. This one was taken at football game in Johannesburg, South Africa, and in it, another young man resists an imminent attack by a German shepherd. Both photographs traffic in what Martin A. Berger calls "sufficient signs of black inactivity and all white activity to read a reassuring narrative of race," and as such, the images traverse national boundaries to reassert racial supremacy.[20] Is it possible that Hudson's photograph of Gadsden inspired the latter one by Magubane? Could it be that the infusion of German shepherds in South Africa directly results from

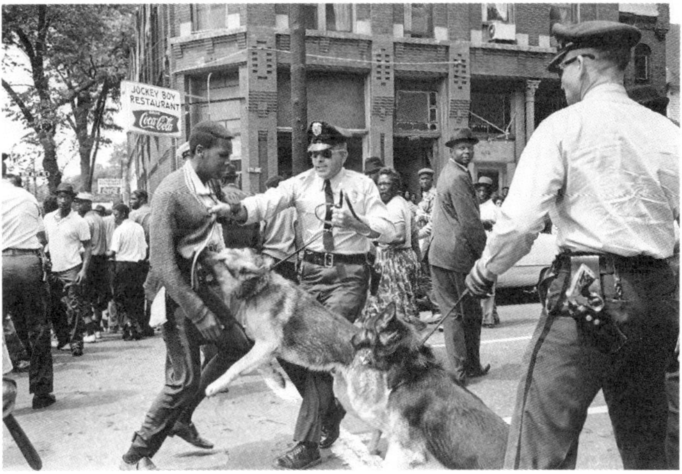

Figure 1.8 Bill Hudson, *Police Dog Attack*, Birmingham, Alabama, 1963.

photographs like Hudson's from the United States? Magubane says in part about the photograph: "A policeman with a dog is a fearful thing. One of those dogs will rip you open. They never used dogs before but now they are common."[21] And so the question is, When exactly did it become common to use German shepherds in the facilitation of controlling black crowds in apartheid-era South Africa? What is the genealogy of this photographic phenomenon?

In Bénédicte Boisseron's *Afro-Dog: Blackness and the Animal Question*, Boisseron demarcates the fraught space between "canine aggression and black civil disobedience" that lingers as an aftereffect of slavery in the Americas and apartheid in South Africa. She writes, "What brings the dog, the slave, and the civil rights protester together under the same 'ferocious' stigma is their common claim to freedom, perceived ultimately as a feral claim." Photographically, the presence of the German shepherd is often read as the chaotic disorder of black resistance. Boisseron continues: "The human and the dog compound each other's constructed viciousness in a mutual 'becoming against,' the consequence of which is that the image of the vicious dog pursuing the slave has become a part of a collective consciousness that compulsively recreates—and each time reignites—the association of the vicious dog with truant blacks."[22] In a kind of visual fetish, viewers sublimate the desire for racial order onto the dog that ferociously represents the state, teeth locked onto flesh for the purpose of white supremacy.

Within and beyond a photographic history of exceptional aggression, black subjects negotiate space on gelatin silver prints alongside imminent or actual canine attacks. "It is just possible," John Berger writes in *About Looking*, "that photography is the prophecy of a human memory yet to be socially and politically achieved. Such a memory would encompass any image of the past, however tragic, however guilty, within its own continuity."[23] This continuity is a neither/nor, both/and construction, moving geographically, historically,

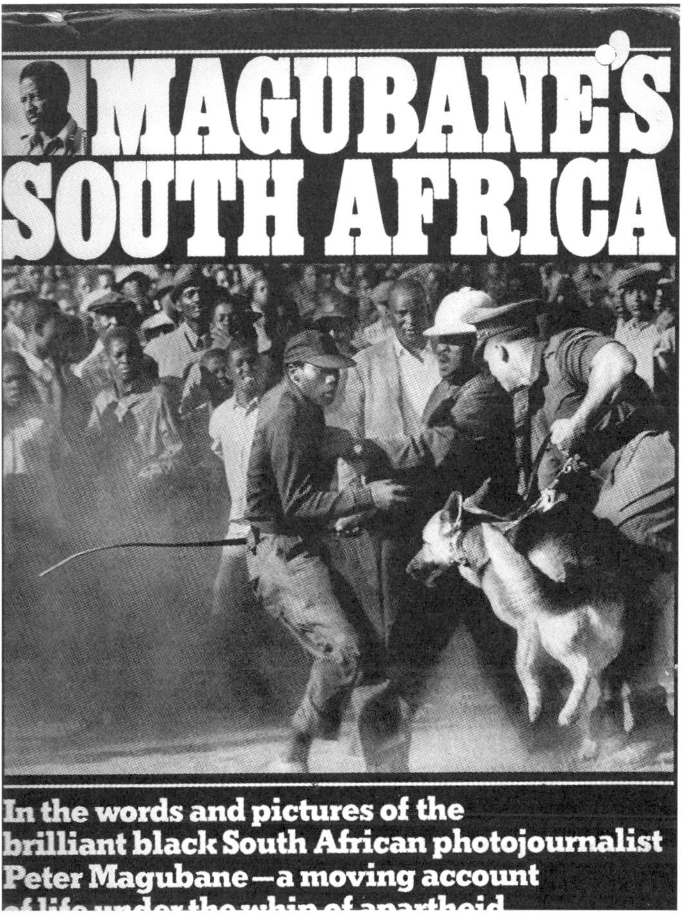

Figure 1.9 Peter Magubane, *Magubane's South Africa.*

culturally, and linguistically across time. What if we attended to this construction for its antiblack contours to see what is already there?

TO SEE WHAT IS ALREADY THERE

The 2012 exhibition at the International Center of Photography (ICP), *Rise and Fall of Apartheid*, depended heavily on the spectacular reproduction of black suffering.[24] This it largely delivered, despite, I believe, its intent. Along with graphic images of black South Africans fighting against the regime of the racist state, there were interspersed images connotating the violence that, both unyielding and horrifying in its display, appears as a fixed event in the history of apartheid. Yet hung prominently in the ICP's café area was a large white sheet with the words "They Will Never Kill Us All." A future perfect statement ("they will never kill us all") that is also a statistical threat to white supremacy ("never kill us"). But it is much more than this. While presenting the state's ultimate goal ("kill"), the sheet is a response to what is a numerical impossibility ("kill us all"). As viewers circle their way around the exhibit on the first floor, the sign in the café is at the natural end of their journey. As they take in the totality of the exhibition and sit in the café enjoying a light snack or a coffee drink, the image appears to reinforce the perpetual nature of embattled states that attend black subjectivities. Presented with the casual effort one puts into placing a landscape painting on a hotel room wall, there is something compelling here but otherwise unremarkable, for the viewer to consider but not necessarily engage with. The landscape is a place the viewer never has to visit, unfixed and remote. It is an island where otherness lives. What could fix the gaze in this direction for more than the moment it takes one to read the line of text? That is a question for the archive, its silences and sounds, and the indifference that animates the viewer's relationship to black subjects.

And so maybe a theory of photographic distrust is borne here—out of three centuries of the visual culture of racial hegemony. A space of black exceptionality combines Orlando

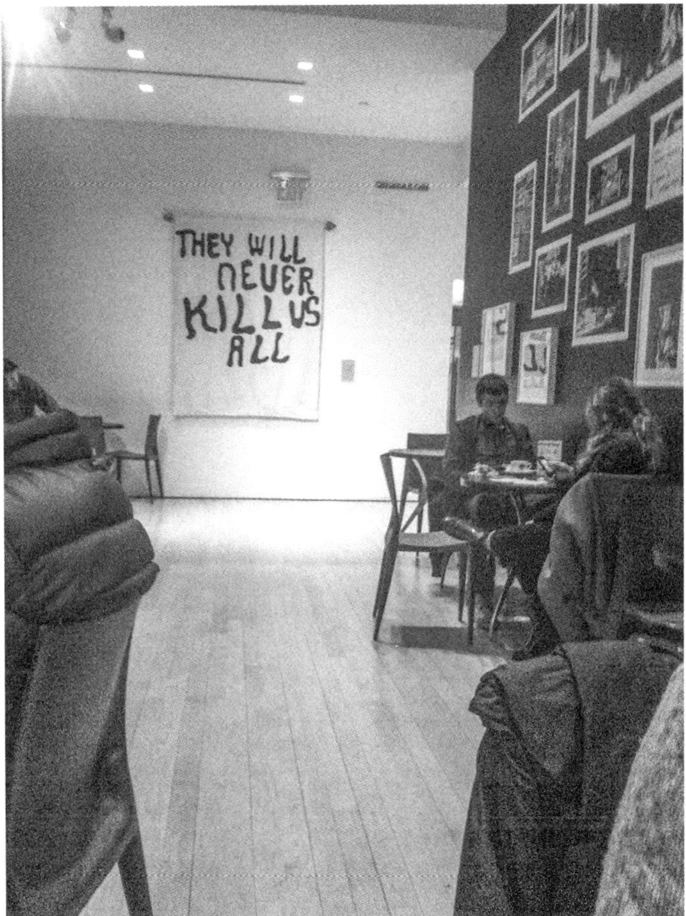

Figure 1.10 A sign displayed in the café at the International Center of Photography during the 2012 *Rise and Fall of Apartheid* exhibition.

Patterson's articulation of "natal alienation" with Charles Mills and Saidiya Hartman's delineation of the borders of black citizenship. In the symbolic register of the photographic imaginary, the empire still holds sway. Frantz Fanon writes: "This explosive population growth, those hysterical masses, those blank faces, those shapeless, obese bodies . . . these children who seem not to belong to anyone . . . all this forms part of the colonial vocabulary."[25] It also forms part of an imperial ocular expectation, trained and molded into melancholic terms. "The repetition of tragic southern African themes," writes Paul Gilroy, is "deployed to contest and then seize the position of the victim."[26] What Saidiya Hartman refers to as the "slipperiness of empathy" within the structural resonance of American slavery has Gilroy's version of *postcolonial melancholia* at its core.[27] "In that slippage," Christina Sharpe maintains, "is also the multiple ways that oppressive social systems—apartheid, ethnocentrism, and slavery—drive people in all places in the power structure 'mad.'"[28] In this "madness," there are the unstated performative deployments of projected rage, poised and perfected for nearly two hundred photographic years.

The visuality of this deployment is an ocularity that has its lens turned toward the proliferation of specific pained and nonliving bodies and the racial aftermath of indifference. In these moments of carnivorous voyeurism, we allow the image to culturally inform the very thing we see, regardless of the medium through which we see it. Photographs say, "I duplicate and extend your line of sight; you do the rest." And we agree. "What the camera does," John Berger argues, "and what the eye itself can never do, is fix the appearance of that event. It removes its appearance from the flow of appearances, and it preserves it, not perhaps forever but for as long as the film exists."[29] If we were to negotiate the terms of *not perhaps forever*, there would be a distinct racial dialogue that routinely places blackness outside the periphery of the temporal.

Archives of indifference permeate the photographic framework of black South Africa as subjectivity modulates racial visibility and civic transparency. *Soweto Riots* is a photograph of temporal conflation and elongation. An image of the witness, the voyeur, and the victim. A photograph of blurring visual constituencies: the figure, the subject, and the pawn. In the temporal demarcation of 1976, when this photograph was taken, we can also imagine the repetition of 1960 and 1994. "We thus live in an era," Ariella Azoulay contends, "in which it's difficult to conceive of one single human activity that does not use photography or at least provide an opportunity for it to be deployed in the past, present, or future."[30] The subjects in the photograph comport the management of the visual dissonance of a dead body in this image and enact past, present, and future in one frame. The past includes the American Civil War and the 1960 Sharpeville massacre; the present the US civil rights movement and the Soweto uprising; and the future anticipates the final death blow to the system of apartheid in South Africa in 1994.

There is a disturbing history of photographic violence attending black subjects, throughout the African diaspora and within the African continent. In the United States, these images conjure up a cartography of unbelonging, placing black bodies at the center of a sentient divide. From the space of the gaze, the viewer participates in what W. J. T. Mitchell calls the "ocular violence of racism," by "observing" the photographic display of disjuncture.[31] The viewer is present, therefore, not only to indict a voyeuristic participation in the violence and bloodshed of othered bodies, but also to engage the element of desire in the continual proliferation of a certain kind of black representation—a visual wailing cast in light and dark.

Magubane's photograph also parses out articulations of gender that are not always present in the available archive. The veneer of safety within a category of unbelonging cannot sustain itself here. This absence of acknowledged inflictions of violence blankets the imagery involving black women. This photograph, framed by the two women standing closest to the body on the ground, marks this precise proximity (and its gendered pronouncement) as central to the composition of the image, as the two women are central to the framework of violence and removal, situated within this space of national violence.

Magubane's image details the outward imperative of graphic death that, by this date in 1976, had become part and parcel of the haunting of colonial and postcolonial photographic practices. This is bodily injury under the accepted racial demarcation of expendable otherness. And the photographer framing the sight does so after state-imposed imprisonment, violations of his citizenship, and financial sanctions. "I had spent a total of 586 days in solitary, six months in ordinary jail, and five years as a ghost," he writes in *Magubane's South Africa*. "I had never been convicted of any crime."[32] Locating his professional isolation, juridical removal, and imprisonment within the elongated structure of subjective temporal shifts, Magubane marks time through the containing register of a silenced visual archive—his own.

THEIR DEAD AMONG US

Death hovers and drifts over the photographic invisibility of black soldiers during the Civil War. Death frames the hideous decades of the reconstruction era and the spectacle of lynching that dominates the US imaginary thereafter. Photography posits black people in the United States as a default symbolic register. It explains a contemporary fascination with the digital proliferation of the imagery of black death. It details the particular national refusal to enclose African Americans within the safety of citizenship. It is the thing, according to Natasha Trethewey, "which must be accounted for."[33] It is the voyage nations obfuscate in order to continually *refuse to regard*. In the aftermath of the American Civil War, during the rise of American lynchings, Jacqueline Goldsby writes, "Lynching photographs figure the dead as signs of pure abjection, who radiate no thought, no speech, no action, no will; who, through their appearance in the picture's field of vision, become invisible."[34] It is what philosopher Charles Mills refers to as "a dark ontology," the process of seeing black subjectivity outside of the realm of fungibility, and it is something the nation is still grappling with.[35]

Buried in the earth in both marked and unmarked graves are the bodies of the 180,000 black Civil War soldiers who enlisted in the Union army during the war. Natasha Trethewey's 2006 book of poetry *Native Guard* tells the story of one such African American soldier fighting for the Union. The Native Guard infantry regiment was based in Port Hudson, Louisiana, where formerly enslaved people and free men enlisted with the Union. The poem begins in 1862 (the year the regiment is reconfigured from the Confederacy to the Union) and ends the year the Civil War ends in 1865. The poem is an ode to the all-black regiment and its members' pursuit of freedom and racial purpose. In the final stanza, the speaker reflects on the "things that must be accounted for," a list of incomprehensible violence enacted upon those other victims of the American Civil War, African Americans:

1865

These are things which must be accounted for:
slaughter under the white flag of surrender—
black massacre at Fort Pillow; our new name,
the Corps d'Afrique—words that take the *native*
from our claim; mossbacks and freedmen—exiles
in their own homeland; the diseased, the maimed,
every lost limb, and what remains: phantom
ache, memory haunting an empty sleeve;
the hog-eaten at Gettysburg, unmarked
in their graves; all the dead letters, unanswered;
untold stories of those that time will render
mute. Beneath the battlefields, green again,
the dead molder—a scaffolding of bone
we tread upon, forgetting. Truth be told.[36]

Part of the useful availability of black bodies during the Civil War corresponds to their visual absence after the war ends. In producing Civil War monuments of the citizen-soldier, Kirk

Savage asserts that the search was for an "American type." And unsurprisingly, "what it meant for a face to be 'American' was not easy to define, but whiteness was a prerequisite—so obvious to most that it needed no comment." As a consequence, "the figure of the black soldier, inextricably linked to the memory of slavery, became unrepresentable."[37] Trethewey's poem "Native Guard" attends to the dead in a way that makes black presence available to the archive and representable. The poem functions as a found photograph layered with meaning and as a present commentary on the purposes of oral and written testimony. The speaker, using a pilfered notebook (taken from a Confederate homestead), marks down all that he sees like an image-maker assigned to collect documentary evidence. In the exhaustive extension of the black soldier's body during the war, there is no unification, not even in death. The speaker produces this unification out of sheer force of will and history.

According to Karla F. C. Holloway, contemporary African American funereal practices developed from the segregated and exclusionary procedures of handling the dead during the latter half of the nineteenth and early part of the twentieth century, and also from when black bodies during the Civil War were left "unclaimed," stateless corpses belonging to no nation. In addition, she writes, "Black culture's stories of death and dying were inextricably linked to the ways in which the nation experienced, perceived, and represented African America."[38] Mortevivum is the imagistic corollary to the production of insular white collectivity. The "our" that "our dead" intimates, and its concomitant exclusionary register, "their dead." In this refusal to absorb black Americans into the constituency of the nation, they personify the very idea of removal as an impossible endeavor, nevertheless repeatedly attempted. Claudia Rankine's *Citizen: An American Lyric* grapples with the juxtaposition of word against image as Rankine, a poet, grapples with the borders of the racialized body in the linguistic world. She writes: "Words work as release—well-oiled doors opening and closing between intention, gesture. A pulse in the neck, the shiftiness of the hands, an unconscious blink, the conversations you have with your eyes translate everything and nothing. What will be needed, what goes unfelt, unsaid—what has been duplicated, redacted here, redacted there, altered to hide or disguise—words encoding the bodies they cover. And despite everything the body remains."[39]

The body and its remains blanket the Magubane photograph with diagonal constituencies as black subjectivity takes on the veil of witnessing, crowding out the divisibility of each of the figures in the photograph while also closing in on the borders of the photo and creating a more insular space. Through this mechanism, black South Africans are asked to prove a legibility of citizenship even as physical and metaphorical removal takes place. Within state-sanctioned violence and subjection, there is the desire for participatory engagement. "Here we see the first syntheses between massacre and bureaucracy," writes Achille Mbembe in his essay "Necropolitics"—"that incarnation of Western rationality."[40] Magubane plays on the texture of this demarcation "between massacre and bureaucracy" playing itself out in the townships outside Johannesburg in the 1960s and 1970s. Life and death, movement and stillness, proximity and distance, shadows falling on earth—everything converges in this image. Clashes, actually, as it appears the photographed subjects mark this visual dissonance with the distance of their bodies away and apart from that of the decedent, but close enough to register the collective interiority of this loss.

The signification of transnational blackness in documentary form (prior to September 11, 2001) was one that invited a vision of corporeal obliteration, fetishized it photographically, and released the imagery as an ocular engagement recognizably compelling to a mass audience already racially immured. The viewer's (Western, first-world, and white) projected investment extends the proliferation of the maimed (or contained) black-world subject, offering the viewer the ability to slaughter with the eye those who have been slaughtered out of time. This is what it means to live forever in the psychic photographic space of black peoples' demise.

Thus, the South African scene from 1976 has the familiar afterlife of tyranny: the Sharpeville massacre in South Africa occurred in March 1960, soon after indigenous Africans resisted the mandates that stripped their state citizenship. This photograph, taken in 1976 during the onslaught of the Soweto uprising, refers back to 1960 and the unprovoked massacre that followed a series of rigid separatist policies now filed under the lexicon of a racist regime. By the time South Africa's national experiment with apartheid came to an end in 1994, there was a temporal layering of contingent imagery that replicated this scene. The message is subtle, but clear: some people are supposed to die and do so repeatedly for the benefit (and citizenship) of others.

The Sharpeville massacre takes its name from the South African township bearing the burden of history on its shoulders. On what should have been a less than eventful day with a planned protest against the extension of the pass laws (requiring black men and women to carry a reference book with personal details contained within it), police opened fire on the group, killing sixty-nine and injuring hundreds more. If we think about the intersection of race, violence, and photography codifying black subjectivities within and beyond the corporeal framework, the role of the witness is of particular importance. The viewer (of, for instance, newspaper imagery) as an after-witness yields to the on-site purveyor of the violence taking place—the people photographed alongside the maimed and the injured, their bodies providing the extended envisioning of projected desire. I want to think about the containment of space within these photographs as a solidification of racialized violence, violence that is part of the imagistic archive producing and extending the cartography of indifference. A violence that is as prevalent photographically as it is resistant to its own unpacking. This often marks temporal conflation as it is rendered here as pre-, post-, and neocolonial, inventing a lineage of similar imagery across disparate locations, framed to invoke the slippery nature of other people's sovereignty. "In the colonial world," Frantz Fanon laments, "the emotional sensitivity of the native is kept on the surface of his skin like an open sore."[41] This "open sore" is visually rendered as reproduced documented assaults against black flesh, and it is this sore that photography can reopen and infect. "Can you be black and look at this?," the question that Elizabeth Alexander asks as she examines the ubiquitous violence of the Rodney King video, is present here as well.[42] *To be black and to look at this* is to engage in the photographic dimensions of empire, to view the empire through the binary logic of sempervivum: white life and liberty rendered through black death and the constant invocation of unfreedom, of unbelonging. "Photography functions on a horizontal plane," Ariella Azoulay writes. "It is present everywhere—actually or potentially."[43]

Lynching photography in the United States presents the witnessing of black death as an insular racial experience: white ease, pleasure, pride, and interest against black caution, anger, anxiety, and dread. At the same historical moment (the 1960s) that multiple African nations were gaining independence, South Africa's experiment with apartheid was immortalized photographically through images much like Magubane's. What is particular about this image is its early morning reckoning, its divided and multiple constituencies, its projection beyond time and through the impact of decades of displacement, marginalization, forced removal, murder, and indifference.

In layering the Civil War soldier and his duties with the black soldiers' awareness of the permutations of the war event, Trethewey joins them together in a proximity to the dead. This proximity, often reproduced photographically, connects black labor to the dirges, the ditches, and the dangers of war participation, while also articulating their closer proximity to death by "those who still would have us slaves." And so the enemy is everywhere—literally, for black soldiers, just as it is clear that danger and violence is everywhere for black people. White soldiers, who can cloak the visual markers of the Union or the Confederacy, are able, after the end of the war, to negotiate a difficult but possible reconciliation, which renders them as deserving of national respect and admiration. The speaker's journal is another "page of history," a palimpsest that troubles the negotiation of the past in the present:

April 1863
When men die, we eat their share of hardtack
trying not to recall their hollow sockets,
the worm-stitch of their cheeks.
Today we buried
the last of our dead from Pascagoula,
and those who died retreating to our ship—
white sailors in blue firing upon us
as if we were the enemy. I'd thought
the fighting over, then watched a man fall
beside me, knees-first as in prayer, then
another, his arms outstretched as if borne
upon the cross. Smoke that rose from each gun
seemed a soul departing. The Colonel said:
an unfortunate incident; said:
their names shall deck the page of history.[44]

"Native Guard" attends to the dead in a way that makes black presence available to the archive—a found photograph filled with meaning. "Some men shall deck the page of history / as it is written on stone. Some will not." The speaker, using a pilfered notebook (taken from a Confederate homestead) marks down all that he sees like an image-maker assigned to collect documentary evidence.

June 1863
Some names shall deck the page of history
as it is written on stone. Some will not.
Yesterday, word came of colored troops, dead

on the battlefield at Port Hudson; how
General Banks was heard to say *I have*
no dead there, and left them, unclaimed. Last night,
I dreamt their eyes still open—dim, clouded
as the eyes of fish washed ashore, yet fixed—
staring back at me. Still, more come today
eager to enlist. Their bodies—haggard
faces, gaunt limbs—bring news of the mainland.
Starved, they suffer like our prisoners. Dying,
they plead for what we do not have to give.
Death makes equals of us all: a fair master.[45]

Replicating the violence of the gaze, the "fixed" eyes "staring back," the speaker is haunted by dreams of open eyes that have the capacity to see beyond death to the refusal of the consideration given soldiers who are white. Moreover, death's equality even extends to the color of the skin. With white bodies turning black after death, Drew Gilpin Faust writes, "Soldiers looked with horror upon bodies that seemed to change color as they rotted, commenting frequently upon a transformation that must have borne considerable significance in a society and a war in which race and skin color were of definitive importance."[46] Here, the earth holds information: bodies, lives, and the fictions of racial supremacy. We just have to look.

FOREVER, CONTAINED

Opening in 2001, South Africa's Apartheid Museum is the first of its kind, a *live forever* of a different sort. Located in Johannesburg, the museum's ambitious design is meant to signal the better future of a postapartheid world. Inside the structure, visitors are meant to experience the racial stratification of the regime as soon as they enter the museum. Admission cards produce a binary of "white" and "nonwhite" identity in order to critique apartheid's classification system. "Your ticket to the museum has randomly classified you as either 'white' or 'nonwhite,'" the ticket holder is informed. They are then instructed to "use the

Here, the earth holds information: bodies, lives, and the fictions of racial supremacy. We just have to look.

entrance to the museum" in accordance with the ticket classification. This binary logic separates the entrances, and so visitors immediately perform privilege or racial subjugation based on the statistical whimsy of an entrance card. The second person allows for a familiar intimacy to float just above the surface and hover close at hand. With an uncanny ability to reinforce the very hierarchy it purports to deconstruct, white visitors, in a ubiquitous consolidation, may have their whiteness reified by an experiment in memory making that rhetorically orders what was initially a juridical practice. In 2001, seven years after the end of the apartheid regime, a museum opened to relegate the system to the past. It is still participating in this endeavor.

The temporal framework of apartheid gives the second half of the twentieth century a precise visual location through which to process the photography of antiblackness projected against a world stage. For nearly fifty years, documentary photographs punctuated media coverage of the violence apartheid engendered; from forced removals in places like Sophiatown (Kofifi) to the stripping away of citizenship rights for black South Africans, Afrikaans being chosen as the official language in schools, the renaming of geographies from indigenous African names to Dutch/European names, and ceaseless murders, beatings, and arrests. It is a precise marking that troubles the discourses embedded within—namely, histories of empire, African studies, visual culture studies, black studies, and gender studies. It is to trouble what Tina Campt calls the "lower frequencies of transfiguration enacted at the level of the quotidian, in the everyday traffic of black folks with objects that are both mundane and special: photographs."[47]

Documentary photographs manage the fissures of citizenship that clamor for visibility in the modern era. Carrying the memory of black South African death imagistically, coverage of apartheid's slow but eventual demise enfolds the dead in a blanket of racial tension that unravels without care. The viewer is central to this unfolding, as an assumed investment structures the order of how much viewers are willing to absorb.

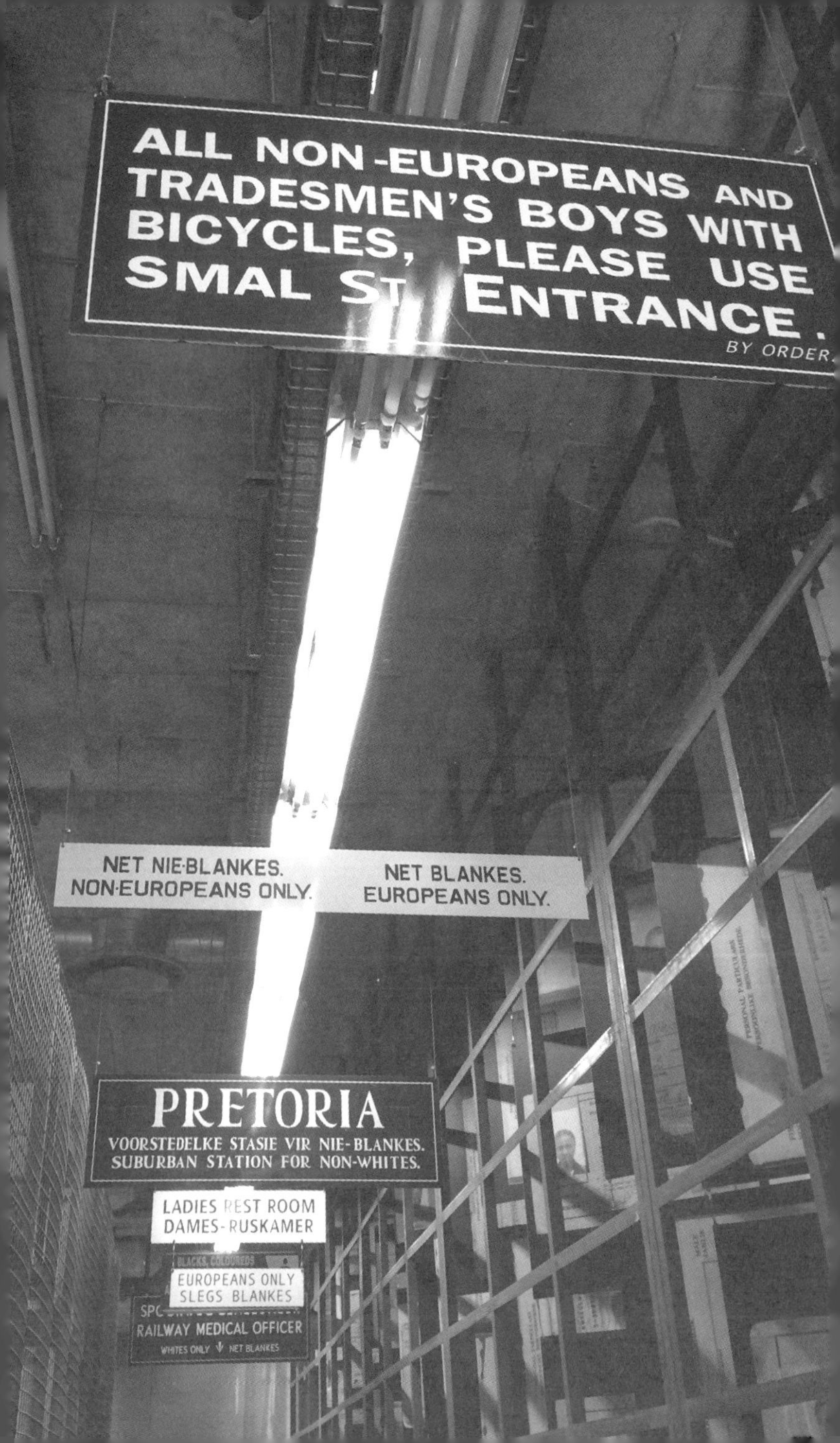
ALL NON-EUROPEANS AND TRADESMEN'S BOYS WITH BICYCLES, PLEASE USE SMAL ST. ENTRANCE.
BY ORDER.
NET NIE-BLANKES.
NON-EUROPEANS ONLY.
NET BLANKES.
EUROPEANS ONLY.
PRETORIA
VOORSTEDELKE STASIE VIR NIE-BLANKES.
SUBURBAN STATION FOR NON-WHITES.
LADIES REST ROOM
DAMES-RUSKAMER
EUROPEANS ONLY
SLEGS BLANKES
RAILWAY MEDICAL OFFICER
WHITES ONLY NET BLANKES

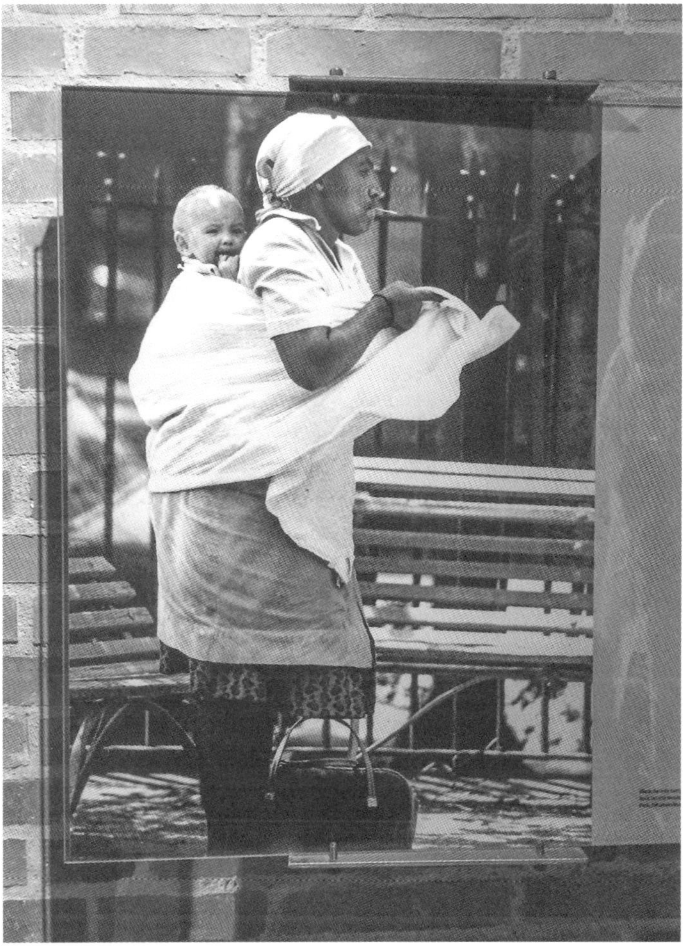

Figure 1.11 Apartheid Museum, Johannesburg, South Africa. Photograph by the author.

Figure 1.12 Apartheid Museum, Johannesburg, South Africa. Photograph by the author.

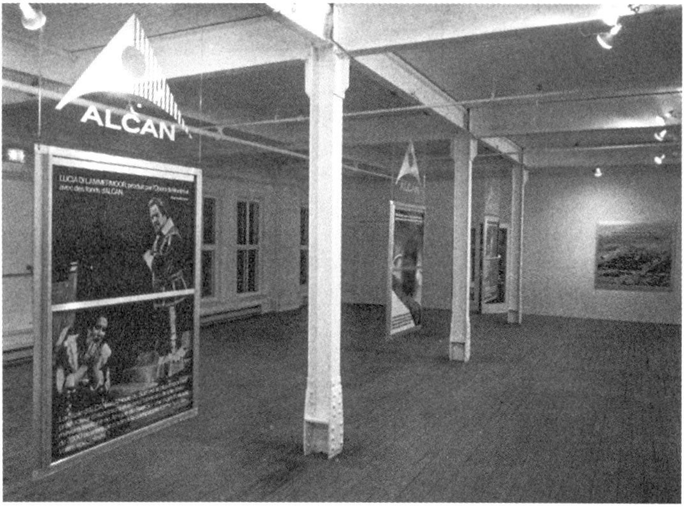

Figure 1.13 Hans Haacke, *Voici Alcan*, exhibition at Galerie France Morin, Montreal, 1983. Courtesy of MIT Libraries.

Somewhere between collusion and implied consent, a viewership adapts to the implicit needs of antiblackness. Compartmentalized photographs appearing in the media negotiate a binary between *legitimate death* and *illegitimate life*. The former allows the visual space for predetermined incommensurability; the latter is an example of surfeit populations eligible for culling.

Photographs crowd the interior of the Apartheid Museum with spatial intimacy, then spread outward like propaganda. The physical enclosure of the museum connotes the binary production of a worldview structured as black and white (even as the racial category of "colored" also exists). Even the nuances mark a precise territory. How, then, are viewers to navigate a haunted space of racialized trauma while attending to the difficult work of apartheid's antiblack violence? What ways of measuring cognitive recognition are available to the viewer? And how has the history of photography in South

Africa produced an archive of imperial practice barely fifty years into its modern existence? Part of this project concerns the iterations of belonging that reinforce the space whiteness occupies as it constructs modernity as a pale mission of purposeful invasion. Empires engage photography for its disciplinary mechanisms, what Susan Sontag calls "collective instruction."[48]

In the popular imaginary concerning this temporal overlay, photographic images solidify the stark binary logic placing black South Africans outside the orientation of self-possession, of sovereignty. In 1983 the Galerie France Morin in Montreal featured an art piece by Hans Haacke with a postmortem photograph of black South African political activist Steve Biko. Biko's dead body is the center image in a triptych, and is bracketed by images of living, vibrant stage performers from the Montreal Opera. They are as alive in the photographs as Biko is dead on a coroner's table. "Even though *Voici Alcan* was made for an exhibition in Quebec," Haacke states in an interview, "the Tate Gallery audience in London could relate to it, particularly because, due to the historical and close trade relations between the U.K. and South Africa, apartheid is a hot topic in London."[49] Audiences in London could also relate to the image because the dead body of Steve Biko is presented as the central image, reinforcing a hierarchy of life and death that is racially bound. Although certainly a protest image, *Voici Alcan* also visually reproduces the violence it seeks to indict. In order to highlight the constancy of black death against its binary variable of white life, documentary images (even when in art productions) offer black suffering as a way to understand the aftermath of empire.

THE AFTERMATH OF EMPIRE

James Q. Whitman's *Hitler's American Model: The United States and the Making of Nazi Race Law* draws out the historical connection between racist Nazi policies and racial segregation in the United States: "In the early twentieth century the United

States was not just a country with racism. It was *the* leading racist jurisdiction—so much so that even Nazi Germany looked to America for inspiration." Whitman continues:

> In the early twentieth century the United States, with its deeply rooted white supremacy and its vibrant and innovative legal culture, was the country at the forefront of the creation of racist law. That is how the Nazis saw matters, and they were not the only ones. The same was true in Brazil, just as it was true in Australia and South Africa, just as it was true of the German colonial administrators who went hunting for a model for the making of anti-miscegenation law. And while the Nazis liked to mention South Africa as a fellow traveler, in practice they found very little South African law to cite in the early 1930s. Their overwhelming interest was in the "classic example," the United States of America.[50]

Although there is a vibrant national policy of self-congratulation as it concerns America's racist past (and how the country managed to "overcome" it), many of the images from the US civil rights movement are simply repetitions of corporeal violence against African Americans. They illustrate the peculiar lens through which viewers were galvanized to bring about change while also cementing the idea of perpetual black suffering. Leigh Raiford uses the term *critical black memory* to encapsulate the surfeit of imagery that must be held in tandem with black narratives. "Black memory," she writes, "also describes and carries within it the failures of the past: the failure to produce the desired political transformations, the failure to create or sustain a culture of mourning or to successfully work through that mourning. . . . Black memory has also been a burden, turning experiences into icons, forcing racial and gender conformity and eliciting prescribed responses to racial events."[51] Some of those responses can be found in the viewer's expectations that conform to perceptions of the lack of agency on the part of black subjects.

Thinking through an imperialist lens as it relates to antiblackness requires a spatial analysis that takes the global seriously. Lisa Lowe's *The Intimacies of Four Continents* tracks goods, people, and racial concepts as they move across geographies and inform the way modernity comes into being. If you are paying attention to the archive, she writes, "one notes explicit descriptions and enumerations, as well as the rhetorical peculiarities of the documents, the places where particular figures, tropes, or circumlocutions are repeated to cover gaps or tensions."[52] One also notes that these "gaps" and "tensions" play themselves out photographically soon after the invention of the medium, which corresponds to the mandates of the end of the industrial age, or the "age of mechanical reproduction" that Walter Benjamin examined nearly one year after the invention of photography.

The viewer has much to manage: where to center the eye, hold the gaze . . . what to keep, disregard, and deeply notice. In a photograph published in the *New York Times* in April 1994 (figure 1.14), Zulu protesters march in support of "their King's demand for a sovereign state." The image shows a group of people moving forward, front-flanked by two police officers. Bodies fill the frame of the photograph, giving the viewer the sense of a claustrophobic crowding that moves beyond the frame itself. It is possible to read this image as the culminating metaphor for the propulsion of black South African agency, but I suspect this was not the reason the image was chosen. With no singular figure for the viewer to hold in visual harmony unobscured (unlike the May 1, 1994, front-page image of Nelson Mandela, the default center moves ever so slightly to the right. There, one of the two officers, head turned to the left, occupies visual space. If the forward progression (political, juridical) of a new South Africa is to be documented in the media, outlets like the *New York Times* will only do so if the subtle (or graphic) metaphor of white guidance against black sovereignty can be rendered visually. Nevertheless, by 1994, South Africa existed within the structures of the photographic imaginary as the symbolic register of this work of both extermination and settlement. In the latter half of the year, the

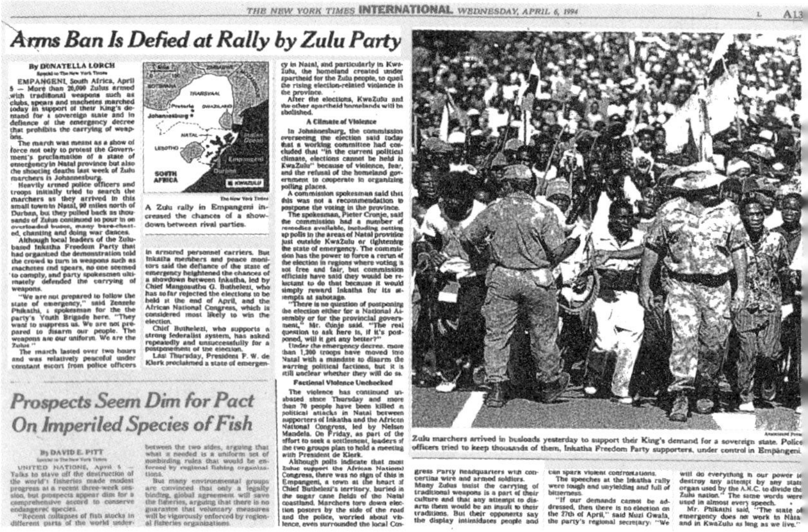

THE NEW YORK TIMES INTERNATIONAL WEDNESDAY, APRIL 6, 1994 A13

Arms Ban Is Defied at Rally by Zulu Party

By DONATELLA LORCH

Special to The New York Times

EMPANGENI, South Africa, April 5 — More than 20,000 Zulus armed with traditional weapons such as clubs, spears and machetes marched today in support of their King's demand for a sovereign state and in defiance of the emergency decree that prohibits the carrying of weapons.

The march was meant as a show of force not only to protest the Government's proclamation of a state of emergency in Natal province but also the shooting deaths last week of Zulu marchers in Johannesburg.

Heavily armed police officers and troops initially tried to search the marchers as they arrived in this small town in Natal, 90 miles north of Durban, but they pulled back as thousands of Zulus continued to pour in on overloaded buses, many bare-chested, chanting and doing war dances.

Although local leaders of the Zulu-based Inkatha Freedom Party that had organized the demonstration told the crowd to turn in weapons such as machetes and spears, no one seemed to comply, and party spokesmen ultimately defended the carrying of weapons.

"We are not prepared to follow the state of emergency," said Zenzele Phikathi, a spokesman for the the party's Youth Brigade here. "They want to suppress us. We are not prepared to disarm our people. The weapons are our uniform. We are the Zulus."

The march lasted over two hours and was relatively peaceful under constant escort from police officers in armored personnel carriers. But Inkatha members and peace monitors said the defiance of the state of emergency heightened the chances of a showdown between Inkatha, led by Chief Mangosuthu G. Buthelezi, who has so far rejected the elections to be held at the end of April, and the African National Congress, which is considered most likely to win the election.

Chief Buthelezi, who supports a strong federalist system, has asked repeatedly and unsuccessfully for a postponement of the election.

Last Thursday, President F. W. de Klerk proclaimed a state of emergency in Natal, and particularly in KwaZulu, the homeland created under apartheid for the Zulu people, to quell the rising election-related violence in the province.

After the elections, KwaZulu and the other apartheid homelands will be abolished.

A Climate of Violence

In Johannesburg, the commission overseeing the election said today that a working committee had concluded that "in the current political climate, elections cannot be held in KwaZulu" because of violence, fear, and the refusal of the homeland government to cooperate in organizing polling places.

A commission spokesman said that this was not a recommendation to postpone the voting in the province.

The spokesman, Pieter Cronje, said the commission had a number of remedies available, including setting up polls in the areas of Natal province just outside KwaZulu or tightening the state of emergency. The commission has the power to force a rerun of the election in regions where voting is not free and fair, but commission officials have said they would be reluctant to do that because it would simply reward Inkatha for its attempts at sabotage.

"There is no question of postponing the election either for a National Assembly or for the provincial government," Mr. Cronje said. "The real question to ask here is, if it's postponed, will it get any better?"

Under the emergency decree, more than 1,200 troops have moved into Natal with a mandate to disarm the warring political factions, but it is still unclear whether they will do so.

Factional Violence Unchecked

The violence has continued unabated since Thursday and more than 70 people have been killed in political attacks in Natal between supporters of Inkatha and the African National Congress, led by Nelson Mandela. On Friday, as part of the effort to seek a settlement, leaders of the two groups plan to hold a meeting with President de Klerk.

Although polls indicate that most Zulus support the African National Congress, there was no sign of this in Empangeni, a town at the heart of Chief Buthelezi's territory, buried in the sugar cane fields of the Natal coastland. Marchers tore down election posters by the side of the road and the police, worried about violence, even surrounded the local Congress Party headquarters with concertina wire and armed soldiers.

Many Zulus insist the carrying of traditional weapons is a part of their culture and that any attempt to disarm them would be an insult to their traditions. But their opponents say the display intimidates people and can spark violent confrontations.

The speeches at the Inkatha rally were tough and unyielding and full of bitterness.

"If our demands cannot be addressed, then there is no election on the 27th of April," said Nuzi Gwala, the party's regional secretary. "We will do everything in our power to destroy any attempt by any state organ used by the A.N.C. to divide the Zulu nation." The same words were used in almost every speech.

Mr. Phikathi said, "The state of emergency does not work in Natal and in KwaZulu as long as we live."

The New York Times

A Zulu rally in Empangeni increased the chances of a showdown between rival parties.

Associated Press

Zulu marchers arrived in busloads yesterday to support their King's demand for a sovereign state. Police officers tried to keep thousands of them, Inkatha Freedom Party supporters, under control in Empangeni.

Prospects Seem Dim for Pact On Imperiled Species of Fish

By DAVID E. PITT

Special to The New York Times

UNITED NATIONS, April 5 — Talks to stave off the destruction of the world's fisheries made modest progress at a recent three-week session, but prospects appear dim for a comprehensive accord to conserve endangered species.

"Recent collapses of fish stocks in different parts of the world under-

between the two sides, arguing that what is needed is a uniform set of nonbinding rules that would be enforced by regional fishing organizations.

But many environmental groups are convinced that only a legally binding, global agreement will save the fisheries, arguing that there is no guarantee that voluntary measures will be vigorously enforced by regional fisheries organizations.

Figure 1.14 Interior page of the *New York Times*, April 6, 1994. Courtesy of PARS International.

"new" nation being reformulated considered what it might mean for a white minority to be on the margins of the visible sphere of political power. Conversations about the reconfiguration of the national flag, the falling of monuments, and the renaming of streets and bridges filled the op-ed pages of newspapers like the *New York Times*. Photographs were disinvested of previous racial tensions and words replaced imagery. But even this has a past and a present tense.

FUTURE TENSE

Documentary photographs occupy symbolic and literal space in the Apartheid Museum. It is a space that negotiates the concept of empire through a hierarchy of the visual that reinforces the protective comfort of white supremacy. Like many other spaces of representation involving black subjects, this one emphasizes white comfort while demonstrating the far-reaching capacities of black pain. If the empire is an eye, then it is one part sight and one part blindness, for it moves between these two spheres of visibility. Data collecting, surveillance, and the production of propaganda materials frame imperial directives. For a large swath of photographic history, imperial constructions dictate the manner and mode of exchange. "All photographs are, to some extent, souvenirs," Zahid Chaudhary writes, "insofar as they give shape and signification in the midst of the uncertainty of the present at the moment the aperture is set to work, and the resulting photograph invokes the distance from the past, which is now handed down as a framed scene in the midst of the disappearing present's uncertainty."[53] Apartheid, as a particularly photographic regime, swiftly recycles imperial imagery in place in other national contexts so that the fullest measure of hierarchical structure is sustained.

The shadow of the empire is indigenous to the photograph, and so is its undoing. Life, death, and everything in between exist here. The solemn May 1, 1994, photograph of Mandela has a counterpart in the image of the newly elected president displayed on the newspaper's front cover on May 3. Francis Cline's piece "A Joy Born in Pain Dances in the Street" features a smiling Mandela, mid-dance, claiming victory in the historic presidential election. This time his image is to the right of the middle of the front page, as a photograph of buoyant celebrants react to the final vote tally for the next leader of South Africa. The top image takes some time to parse out—multiple people and their exuberant expressions/bodily gestures converge in the photograph to illustrate what is referenced by Mandela's centralized image. There is movement in both images, and one can read in this movement the forward progress resisted by a recalcitrant white supremacist regime, or the end result of continued black agitation. Either way, the photographs are informative in their ability to offer ways through and around apartheid without disturbing the haunting presence of white supremacy. The question then remains, What is to come after apartheid? Perhaps the answer lies in what has already been allowed to exist.

Documentary photographs grapple with the effect/affect dualism that navigates the parameters of visible and intangible subjectivities. Some of the choices made by editors and newspaper staff are practical and accidental. Some are not. But documentary photographs allow a space to explore the often binary opposition of black and white (of photographs and people). Often, particularly within the space of a daily international newspaper, words are set against imagery, and black subjectivities are strewn about, devoid of the attention to detail that would reinforce their humanity. “A general imperial right to seize and take was practiced as given and unlimited,” Ariella Azoulay writes. “The use of the camera was built on this *right to take*—to take *photographs* in worlds that were ‘opened up’ for them by imperial agents who socialized them to see this right as inalienable, given to them for the sake of humanity, and could be exercised regardless of the will of those depicted as paradigmatic victims of imperial violence.”[54] The photographic conundrum of apartheid, with its signposts and signals, is symbolically disappeared through the hard-won “success” of Mandela’s election and the “joy dances in the street” visually held together on the front page of the *New York Times*. This is the through line: There is no need to look back. Only forward. And only forward can all of the violence, dispossession, and bloodshed be resolved. Much like South Africa’s Truth and Reconciliation Commission, the motto of which was Healing Our Past, this is a reverse trajectory, suturing the past with the present but focused intently on the future. Mandela’s inauguration speech announced in part: “The time for the healing of the wounds has come. The moment to bridge the chasms that divide us has come. The time to build is upon us.”[55] And indeed, this is what the photographs imply. From healing wounds to bridging chasms, the visual rhetoric presented in popular media mutes the force of the apartheid regime in order to refuse the need to examine the past.

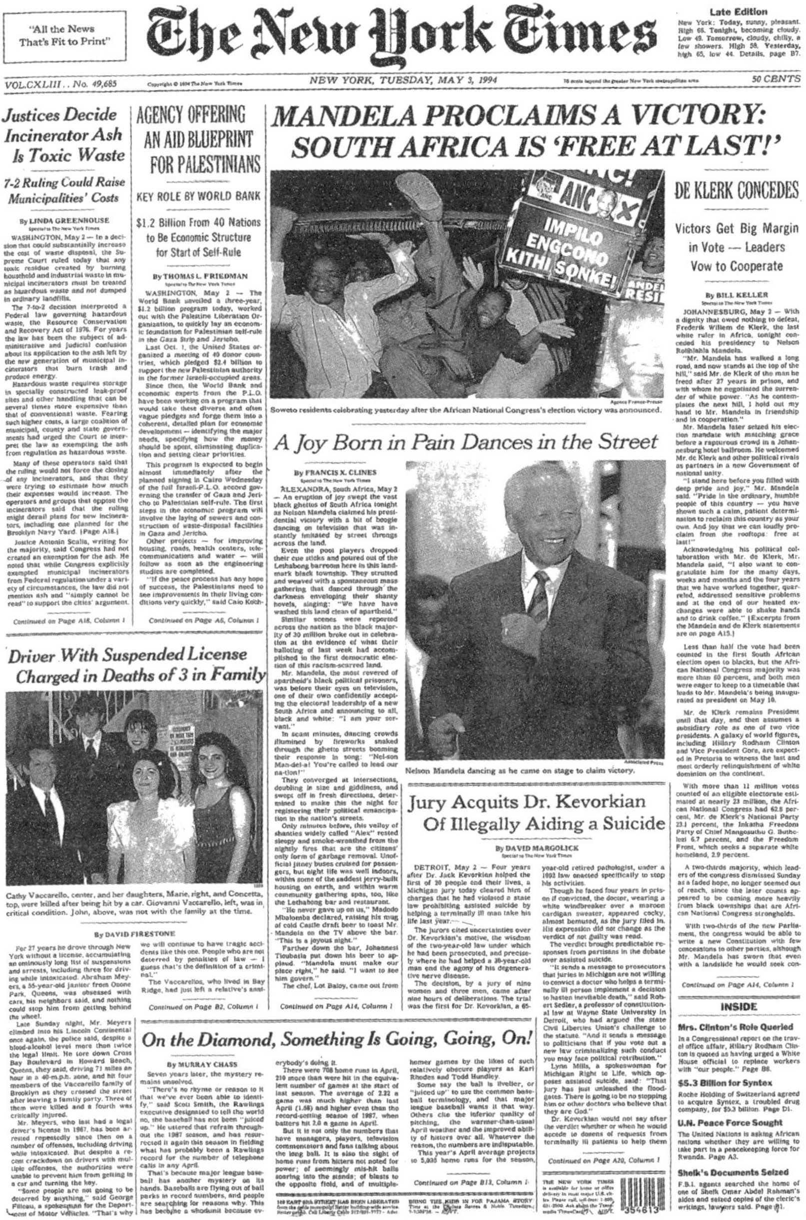

"All the News That's Fit to Print"

The New York Times

Late Edition

New York: Today, sunny, pleasant. High 66. Tonight, becoming cloudy. Low 49. Tomorrow, cloudy, chilly, a few showers. High 58. Yesterday, high 65, low 44. Details, page B7.

VOL.CXLIII . . No. 49,685 — Copyright © 1994 The New York Times — NEW YORK, TUESDAY, MAY 3, 1994 — 75 cents beyond the greater New York metropolitan area. — 50 CENTS

MANDELA PROCLAIMS A VICTORY: SOUTH AFRICA IS 'FREE AT LAST!'

Justices Decide Incinerator Ash Is Toxic Waste

7-2 Ruling Could Raise Municipalities' Costs

By LINDA GREENHOUSE
Special to The New York Times

WASHINGTON, May 2 — In a decision that could substantially increase the cost of waste disposal, the Supreme Court ruled today that any toxic residue created by burning household and industrial waste in municipal incinerators must be treated as hazardous waste and not dumped in ordinary landfills.

The 7-to-2 decision interpreted a Federal law governing hazardous waste, the Resource Conservation and Recovery Act of 1976. For years the law has been the subject of administrative and judicial confusion about its application to the ash left by the new generation of municipal incinerators that burn trash and produce energy.

Hazardous waste requires storage in specially constructed leak-proof sites and other handling that can be several times more expensive than that of conventional waste. Fearing such higher costs, a large coalition of municipal, county and state governments had urged the Court to interpret the law as exempting the ash from regulation as hazardous waste.

Many of these operators said that the ruling would not force the closing of any incinerators, and that they were trying to estimate how much their expenses would increase. The operators and groups that oppose the incinerators said that the ruling might derail plans for new incinerators, including one planned for the Brooklyn Navy Yard. [Page A18.]

Justice Antonin Scalia, writing for the majority, said Congress had not created an exemption for the ash. He noted that while Congress explicitly exempted municipal incinerators from Federal regulation under a variety of circumstances, the law did not mention ash and "simply cannot be read" to support the cities' argument.

Continued on Page A18, Column 1

AGENCY OFFERING AN AID BLUEPRINT FOR PALESTINIANS

KEY ROLE BY WORLD BANK

$1.2 Billion From 40 Nations to Be Economic Structure for Start of Self-Rule

By THOMAS L. FRIEDMAN
Special to The New York Times

WASHINGTON, May 2 — The World Bank unveiled a three-year, $1.2 billion program today, worked out with the Palestine Liberation Organization, to quickly lay an economic foundation for Palestinian self-rule in the Gaza Strip and Jericho.

Last Oct. 1, the United States organized a meeting of 40 donor countries, which pledged $2.4 billion to support the new Palestinian authority in the former Israeli-occupied areas.

Since then, the World Bank and economic experts from the P.L.O. have been working on a program that would take these diverse and often vague pledges and forge them into a coherent, detailed plan for economic development — identifying the major needs, specifying how the money should be spent, eliminating duplication and setting clear priorities.

This program is expected to begin almost immediately after the planned signing in Cairo Wednesday of the full Israeli-P.L.O. accord governing the transfer of Gaza and Jericho to Palestinian self-rule. The first steps in the economic program will involve the laying of sewers and construction of waste-disposal facilities in Gaza and Jericho.

Other projects — for improving housing, roads, health centers, telecommunications and water — will follow as soon as the engineering studies are completed.

"If the peace process has any hope of success, the Palestinians need to see improvements in their living conditions very quickly," said Caio Koch-

Continued on Page A6, Column 1

Agence France-Presse

Soweto residents celebrating yesterday after the African National Congress's election victory was announced.

DE KLERK CONCEDES

Victors Get Big Margin in Vote — Leaders Vow to Cooperate

By BILL KELLER
Special to The New York Times

JOHANNESBURG, May 2 — With a dignity that owed nothing to defeat, Frederik Willem de Klerk, the last white ruler in Africa, tonight conceded his presidency to Nelson Rolihlahla Mandela.

"Mr. Mandela has walked a long road, and now stands at the top of the hill," said Mr. de Klerk of the man he freed after 27 years in prison, and with whom he negotiated the surrender of white power. "As he contemplates the next hill, I hold out my hand to Mr. Mandela in friendship and in cooperation."

Mr. Mandela later seized his election mandate with matching grace before a rapturous crowd in a Johannesburg hotel ballroom. He welcomed Mr. de Klerk and other political rivals as partners in a new Government of national unity.

"I stand here before you filled with deep pride and joy," Mr. Mandela said. "Pride in the ordinary, humble people of this country — you have shown such a calm, patient determination to reclaim this country as your own. And joy that we can loudly proclaim from the rooftops: free at last!"

Acknowledging his political collaboration with Mr. de Klerk, Mr. Mandela said, "I also want to congratulate him for the many days, weeks and months and the four years that we have worked together, quarreled, addressed sensitive problems and at the end of our heated exchanges were able to shake hands and to drink coffee." [Excerpts from the Mandela and de Klerk statements are on page A15.]

Less than half the vote had been counted in the first South African election open to blacks, but the African National Congress majority was more than 60 percent, and both men were eager to keep to a timetable that leads to Mr. Mandela's being inaugurated as president on May 10.

Mr. de Klerk remains President until that day, and then assumes a subsidiary role as one of two vice presidents. A galaxy of world figures, including Hillary Rodham Clinton and Vice President Gore, are expected in Pretoria to witness the last and most orderly relinquishment of white dominion on the continent.

With more than 11 million votes counted of an eligible electorate estimated at nearly 23 million, the African National Congress had 62.8 percent, Mr. de Klerk's National Party 23.1 percent, the Inkatha Freedom Party of Chief Mangosuthu G. Buthelezi 6.7 percent, and the Freedom Front, which seeks a separate white homeland, 2.9 percent.

A two-thirds majority, which leaders of the congress dismissed Sunday as a faded hope, no longer seemed out of reach, since the later counts appeared to be coming more heavily from black townships that are African National Congress strongholds.

With two-thirds of the new Parliament, the congress would be able to write a new Constitution with few concessions to other parties, although Mr. Mandela has sworn that even with a landslide he would seek con-

Continued on Page A14, Column 1

A Joy Born in Pain Dances in the Street

By FRANCIS X. CLINES
Special to The New York Times

ALEXANDRA, South Africa, May 2 — An eruption of joy swept the vast black ghettos of South Africa tonight as Nelson Mandela claimed his presidential victory with a bit of boogie dancing on television that was instantly imitated by street throngs across the land.

Even the pool players dropped their cue sticks and poured out of the Lethabong barroom here in this landmark black township. They strutted and weaved with a spontaneous mass gathering that danced through the darkness enveloping their shanty hovels, singing: "We have have washed this land clean of apartheid."

Similar scenes were reported across the nation as the black majority of 30 million broke out in celebration at the evidence of what their balloting of last week had accomplished in the first democratic election of this racism-scarred land.

Mr. Mandela, the most revered of apartheid's black political prisoners, was before their eyes on television, one of their own confidently accepting the electoral leadership of a new South Africa and announcing to all, black and white: "I am your servant."

In scant minutes, dancing crowds illumined by fireworks snaked through the ghetto streets booming their response in song: "Nel-son Man-del-a! You're called to lead our na-tion!"

They converged at intersections, doubling in size and giddiness, and swept off in fresh directions, determined to make this the night for registering their political emancipation in the nation's streets.

Only minutes before, this valley of shanties widely called "Alex" rested sleepy and smoke-wreathed from the nightly fires that are the citizens' only form of garbage removal. Unofficial jitney buses cruised for passengers, but night life was well indoors, within some of the saddest jerry-built housing on earth, and within warm community gathering spas, too, like the Lethabong bar and restaurant.

"He never gave up on us," Madodo Mbalomba declared, raising his mug of cold Castle draft beer to toast Mr. Mandela on the TV above the bar. "This is a joyous night."

Farther down the bar, Johannesi Tloubatla put down his beer to applaud. "Mandela must make our place right," he said. "I want to see him govern."

The chef, Lot Baloy, came out from

Continued on Page A14, Column 1

Associated Press

Nelson Mandela dancing as he came on stage to claim victory.

Driver With Suspended License Charged in Deaths of 3 in Family

Cathy Vaccarello, center, and her daughters, Marie, right, and Concetta, top, were killed after being hit by a car. Giovanni Vaccarello, left, was in critical condition. John, above, was not with the family at the time.

By DAVID FIRESTONE

For 27 years he drove through New York without a license, accumulating an ominously long list of suspensions and arrests, including three for driving while intoxicated. Abraham Meyers, a 55-year-old janitor from Ozone Park, Queens, was obsessed with cars, his neighbors said, and nothing could stop him from getting behind the wheel.

Late Sunday night, Mr. Meyers climbed into his Lincoln Continental once again, the police said, despite a blood-alcohol level more than twice the legal limit. He tore down Cross Bay Boulevard in Howard Beach, Queens, they said, driving 71 miles an hour in a 40-m.p.h. zone, and hit four members of the Vaccarello family of Brooklyn as they crossed the street after leaving a family party. Three of them were killed and a fourth was critically injured.

Mr. Meyers, who last had a legal driver's license in 1967, has been arrested repeatedly since then on a number of offenses, including driving while intoxicated. But despite a recent crackdown on drivers with multiple offenses, the authorities were unable to prevent him from getting in a car and turning the key.

"Some people are not going to be deterred by anything," said George Filieau, a spokesman for the Department of Motor Vehicles. "That's why we will continue to have tragic accidents like this one. People who are not deterred by penalties of law — I guess that's the definition of a criminal."

The Vaccarellos, who lived in Bay Ridge, had just left a relative's anni-

Continued on Page B2, Column 1

Jury Acquits Dr. Kevorkian Of Illegally Aiding a Suicide

By DAVID MARGOLICK
Special to The New York Times

DETROIT, May 2 — Four years after Dr. Jack Kevorkian helped the first of 20 people end their lives, a Michigan jury today cleared him of charges that he had violated a state law prohibiting assisted suicide by helping a terminally ill man take his life last year.

The jurors cited uncertainties over Dr. Kevorkian's motive, the wisdom of the two-year-old law under which he had been prosecuted, and precisely where he had helped a 30-year-old man end the agony of his degenerative nerve disease.

The decision, by a jury of nine women and three men, came after nine hours of deliberations. The trial was the first for Dr. Kevorkian, a 65-year-old retired pathologist, under a 1992 law enacted specifically to stop his activities.

Though he faced four years in prison if convicted, the doctor, wearing a white windbreaker over a maroon cardigan sweater, appeared cocky, almost bemused, as the jury filed in. His expression did not change as the verdict of not guilty was read.

The verdict brought predictable responses from partisans in the debate over assisted suicide.

"It sends a message to prosecutors that juries in Michigan are not willing to convict a doctor who helps a terminally ill person implement a decision to hasten inevitable death," said Robert Sedler, a professor of constitutional law at Wayne State University in Detroit, who had argued the state Civil Liberties Union's challenge to the statute. "And it sends a message to politicians that if you vote out a new law criminalizing such conduct you may face political retribution."

Lynn Mills, a spokeswoman for Michigan Right to Life, which opposes assisted suicide, said: "That jury has just unleashed the floodgates. There is going to be no stopping him or other doctors who believe that they are God."

Dr. Kevorkian would not say after the verdict whether or when he would accede to dozens of requests from terminally ill patients to help them

Continued on Page A20, Column 1

On the Diamond, Something Is Going, Going, On!

By MURRAY CHASS

Seven years later, the mystery remains unsolved.

"There's no rhyme or reason to it that we've ever been able to identify," said Scott Smith, the Rawlings executive designated to tell the world no, the baseball has not been "juiced up." He uttered that refrain throughout the 1987 season, and has resurrected it again this season in fielding what has probably been a Rawlings record for the number of telephone calls in any April.

That's because major league baseball has another mystery on its hands. Baseballs are flying out of ball parks in record numbers, and people are searching for reasons why. This has become a whodunit because everybody's doing it.

There were 708 home runs in April, 210 more than were hit in the equivalent number of games at the start of last season. The average of 2.22 a game was much higher than last April (1.58) and higher even than the record-setting season of 1987, when batters hit 2.0 a game in April.

But it is not only the numbers that have managers, players, television commentators and fans talking about the long ball. It is also the sight of home runs from hitters not noted for power; of seemingly mis-hit balls soaring into the stands; of blasts to the opposite field, and of multiple-homer games by the likes of such relatively obscure players as Karl Rhodes and Todd Hundley.

Some say the ball is livelier, or "juiced up" to use the common baseball terminology, and that major league baseball wants it that way. Others cite the inferior quality of pitching, the warmer-than-usual April weather and the improved ability of hitters over all. Whatever the reason, the numbers are indisputable.

This year's April average projects to 5,035 home runs for the season,

Continued on Page B13, Column 1

INSIDE

Mrs. Clinton's Role Queried

In a Congressional report on the travel office affair, Hillary Rodham Clinton is quoted as having urged a White House official to replace workers with "our people." Page B8.

$5.3 Billion for Syntex

Roche Holding of Switzerland agreed to acquire Syntex, a troubled drug company, for $5.3 billion. Page D1.

U.N. Peace Force Sought

The United Nations is asking African nations whether they are willing to take part in a peacekeeping force for Rwanda. Page A3.

Sheik's Documents Seized

F.B.I. agents searched the home of one of Sheik Omar Abdel Rahman's aides and seized copies of the cleric's writings, lawyers said. Page B1.

Figure 1.15 Front page of the *New York Times*, May 3, 1994. Courtesy of PARS International.

The empire is an archive of photographs rendered in the service of a separatist state. The United States' Jim Crow era of racial segregation doubled as the imagistic referent of a scopic regime, and one meant to surveil and impose its mandates on black subjects violently. It was also meant to solidify the hierarchy of white over black in the psyche of southern citizens navigating a post–Civil War America. That South Africa's apartheid regime took hold in the 1950s just as the United States was witnessing the demise of racial segregation in the South is not accidental. If we consider the work of observation, duplication, and data collecting done by white South Africans in the decades after de jure segregation began in the US South, we know that photography and its ability to quickly render the impossible binary of racial demarcation via a visual apparatus was central to this experiment.

Two women stand near the left of the center of the frame of the photograph. And they orient the eye of the viewer. The center contains *no body*. But there is a body on the ground. Someone no longer alive, but occupying space. One body, its photographic archive, and the transnational empire left lingering in its wake. This is a photograph of shadows on ground, of the singular mandates and imperatives that find their way into an image whether the viewer sees a body, a subject, a figure, an empire, or the faint outline of the imprint of loss.

The empire is a shadow, marked by figures both there (visible) and not there (invisible). Black suffering, rendered photographically, keeps the shadow in play and the center of subjectivity off to the side where it can be both seen and disregarded. If antiblackness is the weather, as Christina Sharpe writes, if it "necessitates changeability and improvisation," then photography is how the "weather" registers visually to others.[56] And photography is the mode and the medium of that register. Weather must be survivable. Bearable. Possible to evade when necessary. In short, weather must be able to *be* weathered, and there is little of the history of photography that offers this to the viewer. Not because these images are not present, not available, but because they are not allowed to usurp the force of white supremacy in the desire of viewers to disregard black agency upon seeing black subjects in the frame. And that has everything to do with the ubiquitous force of antiblackness in the very air we breathe.

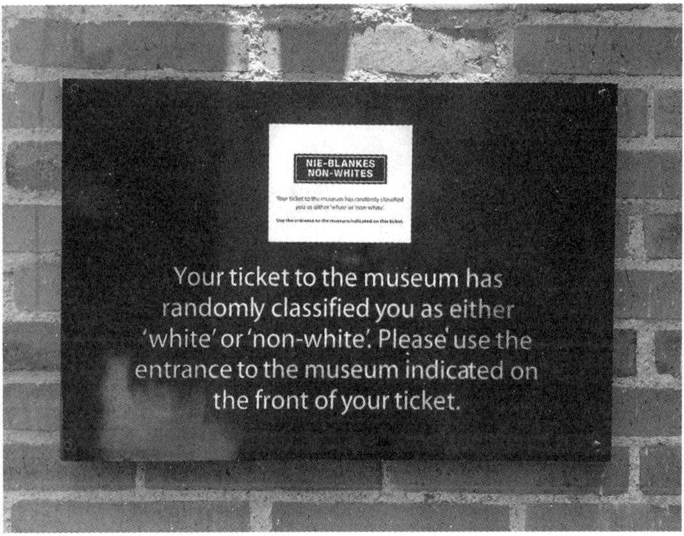

Figure 1.16 Apartheid Museum entrance sign. Photograph by the author.

2

THE VIEWER

Defend the dead
—M. NourBese Philip

Moments of absence punctuate the photographic landscape of the Rwandan genocide, as if nothing newsworthy is taking place. Dailies like the *New York Times* provide sporadic reports like flashing lights warning others of danger. Othering is a large part of the point. The trace of empire, interethnic conflicts, and global abandonment are offered up through the apparatus of the visual. Rwanda is the point of no return. The deep end of an imagistic ocean that meets no horizon.

There are one million stories for every photograph we have not seen. Narratives told and retold by those witnesses; the victims and perpetrators, their family members and friends. In the documentary archive of photographic images, though, corpses. Bones. Partial skeletons and human remains. Viewers sift through what is left of the dead and parse out what is important about the act. Survivors fall outside of the purview of the imaginable.

Survivors. Plural noun. Those who are left behind. Alfredo Jaar's book *Let There Be Light: The Rwanda Project 1994–1998* features as its cover image two children, arms locked in a comforting embrace, their backs turned away from us. There is, in the photograph, the remnant of a secret between them, one which is unavailable to the viewer, and to the naked eye. They are, in the words of Ben Okri, "the best things . . . growing in secret."[1] And yet this secret, both between them and within them, is there: available, but also obscured. The photograph offers a sliver of information: a slight vein extends from one hand to the forearm, and an eyelash points the viewer in the direction of one child's gaze—downcast, but only slightly. We are refused full entry into the frame of the photograph, which somehow feels correct. What is it that we believe it is our right to see here? Moreover, what will we do with the body

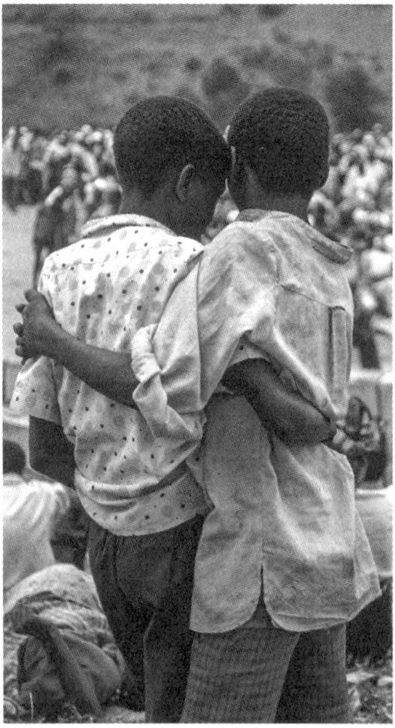

Figure 2.1 Alfredo Jaar, *Embrace 4*. © Alfredo Jaar. Courtesy of Galerie Lelong & Co. and the artist.

once we possess it in this way? In the aftermath of the Rwandan genocide, what is the role of the witness, and what is the viewer's responsibility? For those of us engaged as it is, in the demanding work of remembering the dead, how do we imagine the visualization of healing that is still taking place?

Of his elegant artistic work, Jaar has said, "There must be another way to talk about violence without recurring to violence"—and this is where I want to begin this chapter, by considering the possibilities engendered by refusing to capitulate to spectacles of violence that have held black people in a state of rigid dehumanization. Jaar seems intent on retaining some level of anonymity for his subjects.[2] They are nearly silhouettes against the framework of imagistic offering. In other photographs from the same series, they hold each other more closely—so tightly that no light gets through as they lean into each other, keeping the rest of the world at bay. The visual harmony intimated by these photographs obscures the gathering,

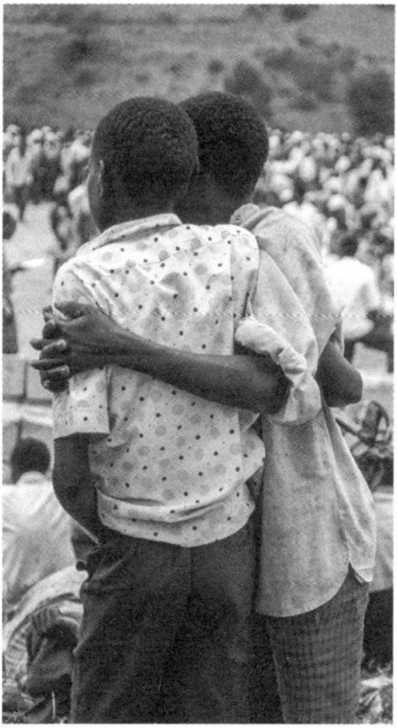

Figure 2.2 Alfredo Jaar, *Embrace 3.* © Alfredo Jaar. Courtesy Galerie Lelong & Co. and the artist.

There are one million stories for every photograph we have not seen.

which is rendered out of focus and beyond the viewer's line of sight. "The photograph is laborious," Roland Barthes reminds us, "only when it fakes."[3] Jaar uses *Let There Be Light* instead to indict the global community's failure to respond to the genocide in real time, before nearly a million people lost their lives. That is the thing to see that is not visible, but the image is heavy with that absence.

According to Jae Emerling, "Jaar explains the pace of the work as an attempt to alter the viewers' habits who move from work to work, image to image far too quickly. The slowness of the text is deliberately frustrating and viewers grow impatient," but, Emerling argues, "it is an aesthetic experience Jaar constructs, one that is about temporality, memory, attentiveness, an ethical encounter with apprehension."[4] Jaar's pacing constitutes a practice of approach for the viewer in which they can bring their patience, their attentiveness, and their apprehension with them to the series.

Thus far I have attempted to find a way to attend to the black enclosures that photography engenders, the sliver of space through which there is a rendering of humanity that necessitates vigilant looking on the viewer's part. I'm interested in the limits of empathy, particularly when black subjects are presented as tangential to the centrality of their photographic presence. Examining photographic archives from 1994 has repeatedly brought me back to artistic productions that attempt to retrieve black subjectivity from the eyes of others. In my perusal of the *New York Times*, Rwanda looms large as absent presence. As the vast majority of images from this region are aftermath photos, it is difficult to make survivors legible to the viewer, nor does the newspaper try.

How might we reconcile the current documentary project with the presence of *blackness as fungibility* that normalizes visual imagery? I am interested in the space of possibility that mourning facilitates, though black people are often left on the periphery of this possibility. What is it about blackness in the public imaginary that has repeatedly aligned it with suffering?

How have artists attempted to illuminate the matter of black precarity? Does it register?

Jaar seems most attuned to the permutations of subjectivity when violence is also central to the production of the image. *Let There Be Light* is punctuated by the absence of news media coverage of the Rwandan genocide by international news organizations, making hypervisible the racial indifference on display. The world watched or it didn't, but there would be no (US, Belgian, French, or British) intervention in Rwanda.[5] There would be only photographs of cadavers, the thumbprint of empire, and a marked disinterest in survivors who are black.

THE EYE IN I

Rwanda occupies a space not of temporal collapse but of temporal stasis, where the genocide both precedes history and then defines it. In a claustrophobic apparatus of ocular containment, the photographic archive yields no center, no symbolic image to set and mark meaning. In a spectacular outgrowth of the coalescence of antiblackness in the global imagination, Rwanda stands in for the failed black state. Tasked with ensuring the safety and the forward progression of its own sovereignty, it could not. All else is data, that acquisition of the legible regard that dictates nominal investment. "If Rwanda was the genocide that happened," Mahmood Mamdani writes, "then South Africa was the genocide that didn't."[6] It is as if the gathered tensions of the two nations is funneled into Rwanda's civil war and genocide. "The genocide that happened" did so in the light of day, and with the auditory assist of radio programs that fomented the acceleration of the violence.[7]

As the country embodying the relationship between genocide, hypervisibility, and global indifference, Rwanda occupies an unwieldy place in the imperial imaginary. From its position as a protectorate under the German empire in the late nineteenth century to the battle over its natural resources with Belgium, the tiny nation in central Africa became illustrative of the failure of black self-governance when civil war erupted in

April 1994 and nearly a million Rwandans (mostly Tutsis) were slaughtered over one hundred days. Coverage of the genocide asks the viewer to negotiate a terrain of not seeing, instead inviting the practiced relationship with antiblackness to be their guide. Regardless of the efforts to refute this, engaging Rwanda as *the* ultimate site of death (but with none of the gravity reserved for Holocaust death camp sites) is how viewers perform visual indifference. History makes it easy if your investment is encapsulated in the facade of popular media as a space of information. The details of ongoing events are produced, but not much else, and this in and of itself is a large part of the problem.

FIRST NAME UNKNOWN

One photograph illustrates this. James Natchwey's image *Rwanda* is a profile of Nyabimana, whom the AP reports as having a "first name unknown." A twenty-six-year-old man presents the right side of his face for inspection; there are four long machete scars visible. The cuts start at his scalp, and the deepest one extends from the side of his (open) mouth. Part of his right ear has been clipped off. Natchwey isolates a moment of exposure, the war, its scars, and the individual lives most affected. Nyambimana has his left hand on his neck, a gesture at once comforting and illustrative of the "evidentiary" quest of documentary photography. He is the evidence of harm that has been done. He is the witness—the survivor.

In the photograph, though, he is something else. A victim with an absent perpetrator. A last name with an "unknown" first. This fragmented and incomplete relationship to Rwandan history is a lack of attention to detail that symbolically structures the genocide so that it exists within and beyond time. Through a contemporary navigation around the cultural memory of the genocide, viewers can skim around and through the imperial archive of subjection that arrives here at a single image of one person and the visualized effects of trauma on the body. The photograph won Natchwey the 1995 World

Press Photo of the Year prize, and its perpetual duplication deepened the viewer's relationship with the space of temporal collapse that deserves further investigation. "As a symbolic operation," Achille Mbembe writes, "representation does not necessarily lead to the possibility of mutual recognition. First, in the consciousness of the representing subject, the represented subject always runs the risk of being transformed into an object or a plaything. By allowing himself the capacity to be represented, he denies himself the capacity to create himself, both for himself and for the world, a self-image."[8] Because of a perceived and enforced absence of sovereignty, the "capacity to be represented" in the few avenues for representation available might appear better than nothing at all. This could only be true if the disciplined expectation of visual presence rendered black were not already such an embedded practice.

In her study of the Vietnam war in photographic memory, Thy Phu considers the swath of imagery making its way through North American media sites that foster the "blinders imposed by abiding assumptions about objectivity as a measure of journalistic truth."[9] Further, when images produced and disseminated fail to adhere to the narrow confines of racial representation, it will not gain traction. Instead, invested viewers will have to do a great deal of work in order to see alternate images representing the same event.

Searching for Pulitzer Prize–winning photographs from the past thirty years is like examining a wound that refuses to heal. Dozens of marked and marginalized people occupy visual space expressly for them to be othered further. In 1995, the Pulitzer went to a group of images from Rwanda taken by Associated Press photographers. Among the many corpses displayed with distanced vigilance by these photographers was another that managed to negotiate intimacy with death as a condition of (im)possibility for black subjectivity. A dead Rwandan child foregrounds the image—maybe nine or ten years in age—at a refugee camp outside Goma in the Democratic Republic of the Congo. The image's background is the refugee camp, as we are privy to scores of refugees, their belongings in bags, suitcases, and other makeshift fabric carriers strong enough to hold a few items. Eight of the refugees are returning the gaze. Every one of those gazes is devastating in its disapproval, its silent judgement.[10] Aside from the ease with which dead black children are photographed and disregarded, there is the disregard of the living—just a few feet back in the image—that is most prominent. The idea, I believe, is that the worst of the devastation of war is over, and now the slow march toward recovery can begin. This is a mandate, not a question, and it has at its center the inability to fathom a world of recovery that is tethered to colonial atonement. Instead, an insular black perpetrator/victim binary emerges and sustains itself through a repeated inculcation of the dead who are also living expressly for the immediacy of corporeal destruction.

HOW WE SEE WHAT WE SEE

Beneath the facade of public information and access, dead black bodies appear. They appear as fodder, as illustration, and as a visual means to an end. They rarely appear to impart knowledge respectfully. Because "antiblackness is the weather," black subjects are exposed to the elements with no reprieve. In a consolidating archive of dead bodies as news leads, black death, at the end of the twentieth century, is the default register. From a post–World War II news media perspective, there is an evolutionary arc, which is graphically positioned at or near the moment of violent death (these are not photographs of people peacefully appearing to be asleep). These acts of aggressive photographic capture correspond with a quantitative metric that leans heavily against black lives mattering outside the data of blackness doubling down on death. Much of this is about the mechanism of engagement—how we see what we see—and the administrative choice makers who ultimately decide *who* is consumed in the visual arena. These choice makers—newspaper and magazine editors, curators, and the like—are primarily white and male, having had the remarkable privilege of orienting the eyes of others toward the repetition of a theme: the problem of black bodies in time—as living, autonomous beings who have agency, purpose, desires, and futures. The photographic production we have been offered as viewers says otherwise. Black destruction, obliteration, capture, and imminent death is the line on the horizon that seems to keep white supremacy from seeing its reflection in the water. White supremacy necessitates a visual component, and if it will not look within, then it must look without. It must fix its gaze in the direction of an apt racial object, expansive enough to elicit interest, disgust, desire, or indifference. Rwanda offers all of these possibilities in a contained months-long time bubble that gave the world an example of failed governance on a devastatingly murderous scale.

But first, there is the absence of imagery. Reports from the region begin with incomplete information—a plane crash. "Hundreds feared dead" in the chaotic aftermath of the plane crash, and a scattering of more uncorroborated information. No photographs. There are more reports, then, sporadic and unsubstantiated. This much is known: On April 6, 1994, President Habyarimana and President Ntaryamira were killed along with ten other passengers and crew members when their aircraft was shot down as it prepared to land in Kigali. Both Habyarimana and Ntaryamira were Hutu. Then the reports came streaming in of the killings taking place all over the country, by citizens against other citizens. No photographs. More reports by UN peacekeepers, clergy, witnesses on the ground. Rwanda becomes a nation of indiscriminate death. There is no before or after to contend with, just the unrelenting power of *now*. As Susan Sontag reminds us, "To catch a death actually happening and embalm it for all time is something only cameras can do." Having an absence of gruesome moment-of-death photos did not ensure that Rwanda would evade photographic capture. It just took more time.

NOW

From 1894 to 1918, present-day Rwanda was part of German East Africa along with Burundi. After World War I and under the Treaty of Versailles, Rwanda came under the administrative control of Belgium. Decades of theft, undermining, and ethnic control by Belgium positioned the ethnic minority Tutsis as the preferred group in the hierarchy of power in Rwanda. "The racialization of the Tutsi/Hutu was not simply an intellectual construct," Mamdani writes. "More to the point, racialization was also an institutional construct. Racial ideology was embedded in institutions, which in turn undergirded racial privilege and reproduced racial ideology."[11] With tensions between the Hutus and Tutsis fraught, Belgium exacerbated those tensions by declaring that the Tutsis were innately better than Hutus and therefore entitled to have power and resources kept from Hutus. Mamdani continues: "The idea that the Tutsi were superior because they came from elsewhere and that the difference between them and the local population was a racial difference, was an idea of colonial origin . . . shared by rival colonists, Belgians, Germans, English, all of whom were convinced that wherever in Africa there was evidence of organized state life, there the ruling groups must have come from elsewhere."[12] By the time the murders began in April, reports treated the country as a double enclosure of self-destruction, as if there were no external European interference shaping political life and death in Rwanda. Photography's absent presence, then, was an elongation of imperial infraction that framed responses to the genocide in real time.

According to Edgar Roskis, in his essay "A Genocide without Images: White Film Noirs," it was not April, May, or June that gave the larger public a full sense of what was happening during the genocide, but later, "between 14 and 20 July," when "picture-chasers from all over the globe, from the most timid to the boldest, the most sensitive to the most cynical, poured into the area."[13] The area they poured into was Goma, in present-day Democratic Republic of the Congo, and they did so when most of the killing in Rwanda had already occurred. The dead and dying were everywhere, and now photographs were everywhere as well. Contextualizing what had taken place in the one hundred days since the April 6, 1994, political assassination of Habyarimana and Ntaryamira, what looms is the deadly assist of news media reports that graphically produced a visual narrative of sovereign chaos rendered through aftermath photographs.

In these aftermath photos, viewers can see how these deaths are framed through the lens of the genocide. Within this, we have the global enforcement of antiblackness that buttresses the space between indifference and fungibility. *How do we see what we see?* Well, this primarily concerns whose job it is to bring this information to a larger public and why they do so in very restricted racial avenues of engagement. Said plainly, the people in control of a larger apparatus of news media dissemination do not look like the people who are positioned as dead on the page or the photograph or the video feed.[14]

In her study of documentary photographs under the Pinochet dictatorship in Chile, Ángeles Donoso Macaya analyzes the multivalent apparatus of representation that was more fluid and capacious than the narrow field of vision I examine in this book. For Donoso Macaya, then, "the practices that different critical texts commented on did not establish a mechanical or illustrative association between photography and reality but the concept of photography as a document and trace became a significant theoretical notion to consider them."[15] Further, as Donoso Macaya suggests, "photographs that circulate in the public sphere, such as news photographs, produce their audiences or spectators."[16] The intersection of photography and antiblackness corrupts the malleability necessary to give black subjects the ability to access three-dimensional existence. This is especially the case when there is any devastation taking place—because news media outlets move with the speed of a crisis event, to place dead black bodies in the center of a frame already constructed with them in mind. "What concerns me here," Saidiya Hartman contends, "is the spectacular nature of black suffering and, conversely, the dissimulation of suffering through spectacle."[17] In a pattern of behavior that has become its own imagistic raison d'etre, the right to expose, highlight, enforce, violate, and demean is preserved as the right to inform, with no negative implications articulated. "Photography is commonly regarded as an instrument for knowing things," Sontag tells us, for "cameras did not simply make it possible to apprehend more by seeing . . . they change seeing itself by fostering the idea of seeing for seeing's sake."[18] In a black diasporic conundrum of the ocular, black subjects must navigate representation through the destructive apparatus of too many images where they are imagined and captured without full agency. We have seen and continue to see these images circulating in public. And our current ability to record some of these scenes of violent subjection on camera phones has opened up new venues for visualizing black death. These are snuff films, for viewers are watching the final moments of someone's life. Taken as evidence or proof of murder, their existence on social media or the evening news is one more avenue where black life is curtailed within the public arena, as white viewers have a high tolerance for black death that they do not seem to possess when graphic images of white death are presented to them.

AFTERMATHS AS AESTHETIC PRODUCTION

Donatella Lorch reports on the Rwandan refugees who "crossed the border into Tanzania by the thousands" to flee the civil war taking place back home. The date of the report on the refugees is May 2, 1994, nearly a month after the slaughter began. Between April and July, reports trickled through, and a fuller exploration of the war and the genocide emerged (slowly). Mamdani writes: "Two trends gathered over time. One accelerated the element of spontaneity, the other reinforced organization. The spread of massacres gave free reign to forces of banditry and pillage.

As banditry and pillage grew, so did random killings. Yet, while there were reports of the poor attacking the well-off, the killings remained directed in the main at those identified as the political enemy, not the class enemy."[19]

Decisions made in the flash of a newsroom meeting clash with the relative swiftness that people in power in these mostly white spaces allocate to black people generally, and black people in crisis specifically. Of this, black subjects will be the exception to every known rule about the ethics of media reporting and respect for the dead. Children will be shown, the names of the dead will not be verified, the newly dead and open-faced corpses will appear with abandon and disregard, and the desires of family members will be ignored. These decisions will place black people outside the circle of consideration and inside a tomb of disregard. This will be done without fanfare or footnote by those who look exactly like those who have been making those decisions for the past one hundred years. The same people who routinely pause when presented with a graphic image of white death. As if this is an oxymoron from which there is no return.

SEMPERVIVUM

I started this project by thinking through the multiple definitions of the term *sempervivum* in the available linguistic archive. I wanted something deployable when considering white supremacy's capacity to set death against others and away from itself. Lynching photography has this capacity—to cement the idea of black death against the perpetuity of white life. It consolidates anonymous whiteness in crowds of onlookers whose regard is a mixture of joy, gravity, righteousness, and wonder. According to Autumn Marie Womack, "By the turn of the twentieth century as the number of lynchings peaked, the public's interminable appetite for spectacular displays of black suffering was sated by an onslaught of lynching photographs." Elizabeth R. Baer uses the term *genocidal gaze* in her study of Germany's colonizing of present-day Namibia. She writes, "When the imperial gaze, prompted by racist hierarchy or by religious or ideological beliefs that engender a confidence in one's superiority, evolves into a consideration of the gazed upon as inconvenient, as no longer deserving to live, the gaze can become deadly." Hiding behind the premise of objective truth, documentary photographs traffic in the photographic destiny of others, who exist in a neoliberal concept of cause and imagistic effect.

Absence marks the force of the genocide through sparse or crowded but intensely gruesome images. So much happens in real time that is unseen by the global community. Witnesses, though, have no such protection. The viewer, in the aftermath of the violence, can do further violence as they peer through the center of each photographic frame and perform a training directive, one allowed by the exigencies of the photograph. Legible mostly as gruesome aftermath corpses, living survivors were disappeared within media coverage that was a situational failure. Privileging dead bodies over living survivors, newspapers and magazines marked the country as a "heart of darkness" from which there was no return.

FUTURE PERFECT

Survivor. Noun. "One who outlives another." Victim and perpetrator appear side by side in a photograph. They make demands of the viewer. Participatory engagement orients the eye to the center of the frame, where the appearance of a resolution is taking place. The work demanded of the viewer is an assumption wrapped in an invitation: the work of representation requires a semblance of formal allegiance. An adherence to structural codes already in existence. A convergence of sightlines. An embodied ritual of recognition.

Appearing in the *New York Times Magazine* in 2014, Pieter Hugo's series "Portraits of Reconciliation" presents Rwandans placed side by side—one victim and one perpetrator—visually performing some form of national redress.[20] Timed to commemorate the twentieth anniversary of the Rwandan genocide, the photographs offer imagery as an instrument of repair, and this is designed to visually reflect a desire for reconciliation.[21] Hugo's images present an uncomfortable corporeal proximity (one person to another) as part of a "reconciliation" that has yet to occur. As Ulrich Baer writes, "Positioning the viewer in reference to an event that resists full absorption into narrative memory changes a crucial methodological question about the status of all photographs of trauma. A constitutive question of both traditional and more recent art-historical inquiries concerns the extent to which the reading of an image might be inflected by (prior) knowledge of its historical contexts."[22] Every one of these coupling photographs is an experiment in ocular allegiance. In the context of the Rwandan genocide, they offer an "after" that mutes the potency of "before." They suggest closure where open wounds are just beginning to heal. They produce a fragile and often illusory visual reconciliation where only a previous gesture appears. Site-specific repair unfolds where those harmed are presented to the viewer with digitally constructed specificity.

The narrative accompanying each photograph in the magazine further alienates the subject from the viewer by offering a shortened account of the genocide by a survivor while also providing equal space on the page to the perpetrator. "Thus," writes Michel-Rolph Trouillot, "the presences and absences embodied in sources (artifacts and bodies that turn an event into fact) or archives (facts collected, thematized, and processed as documents and monuments) are neither neutral or natural. They are created."[23] In the created archive of the genocide, in its collapsed and split trajectories, the demography of those affected by the violent events is rendered as a totality, an encompassing of the months-long siege that resulted in so many dead, so many wounded.

It is word against image as the written statements from both subjects appear beneath each one of Hugo's photographs. They vie for space on the page of the magazine. In each instance, a "survivor" coexists with a "perpetrator," sculpting a binary division that the viewer/reader must negotiate. In the condensed statements from the subjects, we have a kind of dual task. The work of these "portraits" and their corresponding statements is the work of the aftermath of empire, even when it doesn't appear to be the case. Christina Sharpe writes, "Living in the wake means living in and with terror in that in much of what passes for public discourse about terror we, Black people, become the carriers of terror, terror's embodiment, and not the primary objects of terror's multiple enactments; the ground of terror's possibility globally."[24] Drawing a photographic binary between "the one who did it" and "the one who outlives another" is of course one way to visually simplify the deep trauma experienced by Rwandans. It also speaks to the general inability that viewers have with being asked to grapple with multidimensional aspects of black humanity. With subjects who return the gaze, tentatively, forcefully, but who also remain somewhat inaccessible, the work of the viewer is the work of this extended archive.

We know as viewers that this victim and this perpetrator are still alive. We know they are not dead. However, the deaths that hover around them—family members, friends, neighbors, coconspirators, and state officials—are more difficult to glean. This is how genocide can appear when those impacted by the violence are black and assumed to be closely linked to death. Linked in ways that make blackness and death inextricable, and undeniable.

Documentary images thus reinforce the concept—blackness and death—as the natural result of a failure of global sovereignty. The framing is visually instructive, particularly when considering the long photographic history of family portraits and the antiblack legacy they heighten. The proliferation of "family photographs" comprised of people unknown to the photographer (and mostly unnamed) is yet another instance of this exclusionary practice. This too is a kind of family photograph, one that instructs the viewer how to collapse visual constituencies into a cohesive whole. "Blackness has been central to, rather than excluded from, liberal humanism,"

Zakiyyah Iman Jackson writes in *Becoming Human: Matter and Meaning in an Antiblack World*. "The black body is an essential index for the calculation of degree of humanity and the measure of human progress."[25] I am therefore explicitly cognizant of both the engendering and ungendering of photographic practices and am interested in parsing out the particularities of these demarcations.

THE PROBLEM OF "EVIDENCE"

By the violent logic of the scopic regime, documentary photography often aids and abets the fraught terrain of the visual. The repeated demands for "evidence" that a thing happened/harm was done is suffused into disparate archives, where, despite the very evidence sought, harm is either minimized or denied. Of the group of photographs (seventeen in total) winning several AP photographers the prize for Feature Photography in 1995, there are none that offer a version of humanity that retains the same for the subjects. Instead, in a dehumanizing motif of the ocular, what is being offered and preserved is the black subject as object. Bakirathi Mani writes, "I am convinced more than ever that the accumulation of visual objects, photographic and otherwise, cannot contravene the logic of racialization by the neo-liberal state."[26] Further, in the case of Rwanda and news media outlets, the accumulation of dead and decaying bodies coupled with the absence of living subjects led to mortevivum's enveloped insistence. For the viewer, this means their role, circumscribed and curtailed, is reduced to scanning with futility, for there is everything and nothing at all to see. If, as Dionne Brand asserts, "cartography is description, not journey," what of the global traffic in site-specific demarcations of the other?[27] How does photography provide a visual assist, and what are some of the ways of not seeing or refusing to see? Ariella Azoulay writes: "Imagine photographers not taking new photographs of imperial disaster, not submitting news to media corporations predicated on this assumption, not showing up at photo opportunities of statesmen visiting conflict zones for which they should have been accountable, not giving their permission to use their photographs unless photographed persons have negotiated their meaning and their rights to these photographs?"[28] To this I add, imagine a visual universe where to see black subjects was not to envision impending destruction or perpetual destruction. "For the dominant media by no means drowns us in a torrent of images," Jacques Ranciere suggests, "testifying to massacres, massive population transfers and the other horrors that go to make up our planet's present. Quite the reverse," he states, "they reduced their number, taking good care to select and order them."[29] For the most part, this is true. For black subjects, there is this slippage between a lack of care and excessive use. There is no reduction in the proliferation of images, almost as if there is a collective understanding concerning the place of blackness in the world of images.

Embedded in the rush to capture images of violence, devastation, and death, photographic subjects go partially or fully unnamed, as if the objective of the image is to mute any consideration of the subject in the image. In an agreed-upon exchange of disregard, viewers are allowed to let their gaze slide over a group of corpses registering as black and attribute swift death and perpetual destruction on sight. And in this visual grift, the purpose is often to self-soothe with the notion that nothing stands in the way of dispossession for others. Not war, not peace, not the liberal state, nor a moral imperative managed from without. "Thus whatever becomes fact does so with its own inborn absences," Michel-Rolph Trouillot reminds us.[30] The fact of the genocide must compete with its profound absences, and this is where it is possible to do the work that must be done.

An eerie combination of scores of bodies coupled with a lack of media reporting on the genocide warp the memory of the event and its continued ramifications. There are no standout images from the Pulitzer Prize–winning group of Associated Press photographs. Most are horrifically graphic—unspeakably so—but even in the ones that avoid a kind of granular violence, there is the absence of any kind of human focal point that adheres to any kind of logic that preserves the humanity of the subject of the photo. There are *people* in the photographs, it must be said, but they are incidental to the image.

To be incidental to the image in this context is to be somehow beside the gravity of the point. And how can one be beside the gravity of the point when one *is* the point: the human cost of this conflict, this war, and this genocide? Antiblackness is the matter through which all matter is made. Zakiyyah Iman Jackson writes, "I contend while antiblackness is terrifyingly persistent and ongoing as a system, antiblack racism and its (somatic) effects nevertheless unfold processually, bearing the capacity to take form as 'event' and within the ontological expanse of 'emergence' rather than reflect a passive 'legacy' emanating from a reified foundation or immutable structure."[31] The media coverage of the genocide collapsed Rwanda into a murderous event and a series of casualties, but antiblackness in the media is a part of a long history that is "terrifyingly persistent" and photographically held in place.[32]

Jaar demarcates the slow movement of media outlets concerning the genocide and its global coverage. His documentation of the cover stories in *Time* and *Newsweek* speaks to a much longer history of visual indifference catalogued over time. Jaar pairs information about the genocide with the cover images of weekly news magazines to highlight what is missing, minimized, made inessential, and disappeared. "May 22," the left side of the image reads. "The Rwandan Patriotic Front gains full control of Kigali and the airport." The final line points to the growing number of the dead by that date: "300,000 deaths." The following page shows that the cover image of *Newsweek* from May 23 is a grainy photograph of a World War II soldier crawling through the water toward the shore at Omaha Beach, Normandy.[33]

The famous Robert Capa image from 1944 visually sets the tone of investment for the viewer, requiring little more from them than an already-present understanding of the measure of the gravity of war based on race and nation. Like the United States, but on a bigger scale, European nations return to the second world war and its allied success over the Third Reich as proof of some innate national goodness they share. And here, as Paul Gilroy suggests, "that memory of the country at war against foes who are simply, tidily, and uncomplicatedly evil has recently acquired the status of an ethnic myth."[34] Gilroy continues, "It explains not only how the nation remade itself through war and victory but can also be understood as a rejection or deferral of its present problems."[35] The United States is nothing if not a nation "remade . . . through war and victory." From the Civil War to World War II and the Gulf War, the United States imagines its reflection in a mirror that reflects back only what it wants to see. So on the cusp of the fiftieth anniversary of the storming of Normandy, *Newsweek* revisits this moment (with weeks to spare; the event began on June 6, 1944) and makes the choice to continue ignoring the genocide that has claimed three hundred thousand lives. And it does so, again, as if nothing newsworthy is taking place. According to Gilroy, this stance, "and the accompanying inward turn, functions as a 'defensive gesture,'" reifying the inherent value of the memory of World War II against a lack of interest in the victims of the current war taking place in Rwanda.

THE AFTERTHOUGHT

Because most of the photographs coming out of Rwanda through news media outlets are aftermath photos, they lack the urgency of what Barbie Zelizer calls "about to die" images. For Zelizer, the impact of impending death is what gives these images their potency as people know precisely what is at stake with the photographs. Therefore, according to Zelizer, "though people tend to recall more about the news when visuals depict what is happening and exhibit certain empathetic bodily responses to what they see in images, viewers have definite assumptions about what should and should not be shown, and many regularly try to constrain images by notions of decency, taste, appropriateness, and tone."[36] She goes on to claim that "very few photographs in the news actually depict death."[37] This is in fact true, but only if you exclude the default position occupied by black subjects photographically. I contend that black death is such a naturalized photographic documentary position that most white viewers do not notice how ubiquitous it is. Part of the reason they do not notice is that the repetition of people who register as white do not register as dead in the news media. Death is for others, and though the "others" can shift and change over time, default imagistic death is the space black subjects occupy. The viewer's relationship to the subject is one that Lisa Cartwright and Marita Sturken discuss in their book *Practices of Looking: An Introduction to Visual Culture*.[38] "Practices of looking are intimately tied to ideology," they write. "The most important aspect of ideologies is that they appear to be natural or given, rather than part of a system of belief that a culture produces in order to function in a particular way."[39]

Published in 2010, the same year of the earthquake in Haiti, Zelizer's book *About to Die: How News Images Move the Public* is an exploration of public sentiment born from the photographs that depict people who are in danger of imminent death. In fact, Zelizer's book is filled with imagistic examples of this relationship between the viewer and the viewed from very famous photographs, like Richard Drew's *Falling Man* image from the World Trade Center towers on September 11, 2001, to anonymous images taken by witnesses during war. International in scope, Zelizer's project aims to highlight those moments of proximity that the viewer shares with those who are photographed. And while there are black subjects in her archive, they by no means dominate the production of human subjects Zelizer is interested in discussing. In fact, black subjects in Rwanda's genocide upend the argument that Zelizer makes repeatedly in her book. "Impending death," she writes, "can be remotely possible, vaguely possible, distinctly possible, or even probable, but it is never certain, and information conveying certainty is not made available by the news organization."[40] I contend that it is precisely the promise of certainty that gives black subjects the mark of mortevivum, where death is read as imminent *and* certain, the racial demarcation of antiblackness rendered photographically.

Indeed, there is only the how and why to contemplate in Rwanda as the space between absence and graphically produced death is a matter of months. There is, then, not the immediacy of a response that requires swift action. But here, in the space between photography's ability to capture and antiblackness' surveillance within a space of disregard, black subjects are both "about to die" and always somehow beyond the reach of death. They are also contained within a forward movement of death in the print as the repetition of training provides the viewer with the pointed fungibility already heavily rehearsed. This is the vexed space between the evidentiary and the visceral offering of death the photograph possesses.

Shortly after Russia invaded Ukraine in February 2022, African students fleeing Kharkiv, Lviv, and Kyiv were stopped from boarding trains to Poland by Ukrainian security forces and border guards and told that "Blacks were not allowed."[41] The outbreak of war and the vulnerable status of Africans studying in Ukraine were met with racial refusal as there was no stated reason from Ukrainian officials for why black residents were refused refuge from the cities where bombings had begun. Somewhere in the psyche of these officials who were there to provide protection and safety to those fleeing the city, they could not find a way to include African students in the category of the protected. And when later asked about this heavily visible discrepancy, there was no defense provided for the action.

The United States' official response to Russia's war of aggression is instructive as well. Although the two countries were previously intertwined and Russia has worked tirelessly to violently return Ukraine to the country despite resistance from Ukraine. In dealings with the Eastern European nation, there is a sense of an understanding of the country's autonomy, untethered from any previous conflicts with Russia. Images also bear out the international understanding that Ukrainians, embattled and invaded, are fighting for what is rightfully theirs, with the assistance of multiple governments and heads of state. Meanwhile, infantilizing and declaring swift retribution for national self-defense seem to be the gift that black sovereign nations receive in times of need. Or complete silence and neglect.

THE EYE IN TEMPORAL COLLAPSE

Walter Gadsden's immortalization at the age of fifteen on a gelatin silver print is not something he can remove himself from, nor is it the path to black freedom offered up by those in pursuit of something akin to human rights. Instead, his image symbolizes the many ways photographs are placed in the arena of representation in order to constrict the very idea of representation separate and apart from violation. Hugo's photographs, too, statically regard the route to regard as one tempered by the vicissitudes of antiblackness as it is only antiblackness that would attempt to collapse time and murderous violence with the simplification of a series of images meant to reconcile the space between memory and forgetting.

Moments of quiet encase the missing photographs of the Rwandan genocide as if they are enveloped in the lush landscape of the nation, unseen by most. While survivors travel as refugees, traumatized and wounded, newscasters will lean into an externally imposed narrative of destined death, almost as if they have been instructed to do so. In the interim, the narrative constructed around the genocide will imagine it as ordained by a self-destructive god, hell-bent on disappearing a large segment of the nation into the abyss of absent archives.

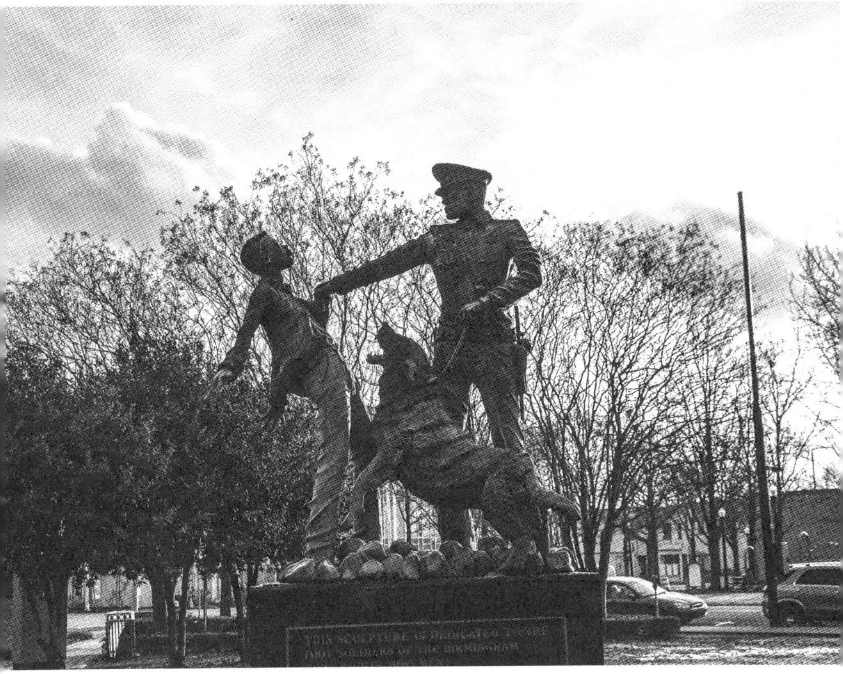

Figure 2.3 Gadsden monument, Birmingham, Alabama. Photograph by the author.

3

THE SENTIMENT

And then there was no more Empire all of a sudden.
Its victories were air, its dominions dirt . . .
—Derek Walcott

Days into the US intervention in Haiti in September 1994, the *New York Times* featured a photo of a coconut vendor lying dead on a Port-au-Prince street, face beaten and body bruised. The headline, "Haitian Police Crush Rally as American Troops Watch," was possibly a critique of US foreign policy at this volatile moment in Haiti's political history, but it's difficult to tell.[1] The image appears to function as both illustration and indictment, making visual the mortal trajectory of both the vendor and the photograph, reinforcing the *that has been* that Roland Barthes reminds us exists in each photographic image.[2] In the image of the deceased vendor, we have no view of American soldiers, no photo of any of the 3,300 troops deployed to the region under orders to observe but not interfere. It is fitting,

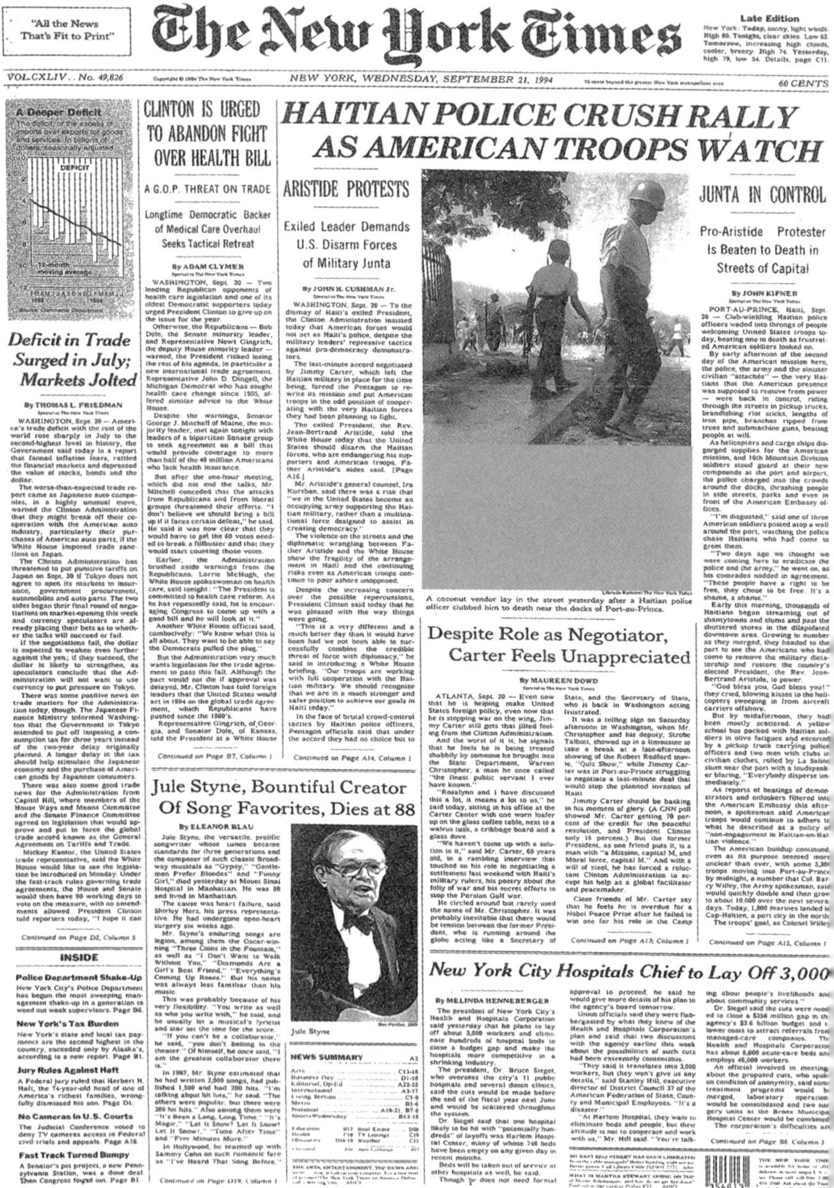

"All the News That's Fit to Print"

The New York Times

Late Edition

New York: Today, sunny, light winds. High 80. Tonight, clear skies. Low 62. Tomorrow, increasing high clouds, cooler, breezy. High 74. Yesterday, high 79, low 54. Details, page C11.

VOL.CXLIV . . No. 49,826 — Copyright © 1994 The New York Times — NEW YORK, WEDNESDAY, SEPTEMBER 21, 1994 — 75 cents beyond the greater New York metropolitan area — 60 CENTS

HAITIAN POLICE CRUSH RALLY AS AMERICAN TROOPS WATCH

ARISTIDE PROTESTS

Exiled Leader Demands U.S. Disarm Forces of Military Junta

By JOHN H. CUSHMAN Jr.

WASHINGTON, Sept. 20 — To the dismay of Haiti's exiled President, the Clinton Administration insisted today that American forces would not act as Haiti's police, despite the military leaders' repressive tactics against pro-democracy demonstrators.

The last-minute accord negotiated by Jimmy Carter, which left the Haitian military in place for the time being, forced the Pentagon to rewrite its mission and put American troops in the odd position of cooperating with the very Haitian forces they had been planning to fight.

The exiled President, the Rev. Jean-Bertrand Aristide, told the White House today that the United States should disarm the Haitian forces, who are endangering his supporters and American troops, Father Aristide's aides said. [Page A16.]

Mr. Aristide's general counsel, Ira Kurzban, said there was a risk that "we in the United States become an occupying army supporting the Haitian military, rather than a multinational force designed to assist in creating democracy."

The violence on the streets and the diplomatic wrangling between Father Aristide and the White House show the fragility of the arrangement in Haiti and the continuing risks even as American troops continue to pour ashore unopposed.

Despite the increasing concern over the possible repercussions, President Clinton said today that he was pleased with the way things were going.

"This is a very different and a much better day than it would have been had we not been able to successfully combine the credible threat of force with diplomacy," he said in introducing a White House briefing. "Our troops are working with full cooperation with the Haitian military. We should recognize that we are in a much stronger and safer position to achieve our goals in Haiti today."

In the face of brutal crowd-control tactics by Haitian police officers, Pentagon officials said that under the accord they had no choice but to

Continued on Page A14, Column 1

A coconut vendor lay in the street yesterday after a Haitian police officer clubbed him to death near the docks of Port-au-Prince.

JUNTA IN CONTROL

Pro-Aristide Protester Is Beaten to Death in Streets of Capital

By JOHN KIFNER

PORT-AU-PRINCE, Haiti, Sept. 20 — Club-wielding Haitian police officers waded into throngs of people welcoming United States troops today, beating one to death as frustrated American soldiers looked on.

By early afternoon of the second day of the American mission here, the police, the army and the sinister civilian "attachés" — the very Haitians that the American presence was supposed to remove from power — were back in control, riding through the streets in pickup trucks, brandishing riot sticks, lengths of iron pipe, branches ripped from trees and submachine guns, beating people at will.

As helicopters and cargo ships disgorged supplies for the American mission, and 10th Mountain Division soldiers stood guard at their new compounds at the port and airport, the police charged into the crowds around the docks, thrashing people in side streets, parks and even in front of the American Embassy offices.

"I'm disgusted," said one of three American soldiers posted atop a wall around the port, watching the police chase Haitians who had come to greet them.

"Two days ago we thought we were coming here to eradicate the police and the army," he went on, as his comrades nodded in agreement. "These people have a right to be free, they chose to be free. It's a shame, a shame."

Early this morning, thousands of Haitians began streaming out of shantytowns and slums and past the shuttered stores in the dilapidated downtown area. Growing in number as they merged, they headed to the port to see the Americans who had come to remove the military dictatorship and restore the country's elected President, the Rev. Jean-Bertrand Aristide, to power.

"God bless you, God bless you!" they cried, blowing kisses to the helicopters sweeping in from aircraft carriers offshore.

But by midafternoon, they had been mostly scattered. A yellow school bus packed with Haitian soldiers in olive fatigues and escorted by a pickup truck carrying police officers and two men with clubs in civilian clothes, roiled by La Saline slum near the port with a loudspeaker blaring, "Everybody disperse immediately."

As reports of beatings of demonstrators and onlookers filtered into the American Embassy this afternoon, a spokesman said American troops would continue to adhere to what he described as a policy of "non-engagement in Haitian-on-Haitian violence."

The American buildup continued, even as its purpose seemed more unclear than ever, with some 3,300 troops moving into Port-au-Prince by midnight, a number that Col. Barry Willey, the Army spokesman, said would quickly double and then grow to about 10,000 over the next several days. Today, 1,800 marines landed in Cap-Haïtien, a port city in the north. The troops' goal, as Colonel Willey

Continued on Page A15, Column 1

CLINTON IS URGED TO ABANDON FIGHT OVER HEALTH BILL

A G.O.P. THREAT ON TRADE

Longtime Democratic Backer of Medical Care Overhaul Seeks Tactical Retreat

By ADAM CLYMER

WASHINGTON, Sept. 20 — Two leading Republican opponents of health care legislation and one of its oldest Democratic supporters today urged President Clinton to give up on the issue for the year.

Otherwise, the Republicans — Bob Dole, the Senate minority leader, and Representative Newt Gingrich, the deputy House minority leader — warned, the President risked losing the rest of his agenda, in particular a new international trade agreement. Representative John D. Dingell, the Michigan Democrat who has sought health care change since 1955, offered similar advice to the White House.

Despite the warnings, Senator George J. Mitchell of Maine, the majority leader, met again tonight with leaders of a bipartisan Senate group to seek agreement on a bill that would provide coverage to more than half of the 40 million Americans who lack health insurance.

But after the one-hour meeting, which did not end the talks, Mr. Mitchell conceded that the attacks from Republicans and from liberal groups threatened their efforts. "I don't believe we should bring a bill up if it faces certain defeat," he said. He said it was now clear that they would have to get the 60 votes needed to break a filibuster and that they would start counting those votes.

Earlier, the Administration brushed aside warnings from the Republicans. Lorrie McHugh, the White House spokeswoman on health care, said tonight: "The President is committed to health care reform. As he has repeatedly said, he is encouraging Congress to come up with a good bill and he will look at it."

Another White House official said, combatively: "We know what this is all about. They want to be able to say the Democrats pulled the plug."

But the Administration very much wants legislation for the trade agreement to pass this fall. Although the pact would not die if approval was delayed, Mr. Clinton has told foreign leaders that the United States would act in 1994 on the global trade agreement, which Republicans have pushed since the 1980's.

Representative Gingrich, of Georgia, and Senator Dole, of Kansas, told the President at a White House

Continued on Page B7, Column 1

A Deeper Deficit

The deficit, or the excess of imports over exports, for goods and services. In billions of dollars, seasonally adjusted.

DEFICIT

12-month moving average

Source: Commerce Department

Deficit in Trade Surged in July; Markets Jolted

By THOMAS L. FRIEDMAN

WASHINGTON, Sept. 20 — America's trade deficit with the rest of the world rose sharply in July to the second-highest level in history, the Government said today in a report that fanned inflation fears, rattled the financial markets and depressed the value of stocks, bonds and the dollar.

The worse-than-expected trade report came as Japanese auto companies, in a highly unusual move, warned the Clinton Administration that they might break off their cooperation with the American auto industry, particularly their purchases of American auto parts, if the White House imposed trade sanctions on Japan.

The Clinton Administration has threatened to put punitive tariffs on Japan on Sept. 30 if Tokyo does not agree to open its markets in insurance, government procurement, automobiles and auto parts. The two sides began their final round of negotiations on market-opening this week and currency speculators are already placing their bets as to whether the talks will succeed or fail.

If the negotiations fail, the dollar is expected to weaken even further against the yen; if they succeed, the dollar is likely to strengthen, as speculators conclude that the Administration will not want to use currency to put pressure on Tokyo.

There was some positive news on trade matters for the Administration today, though. The Japanese Finance Ministry informed Washington that the Government in Tokyo intended to put off imposing a consumption tax for three years instead of the two-year delay originally planned. A longer delay in the tax should help stimulate the Japanese economy and the purchase of American goods by Japanese consumers.

There was also some good trade news for the Administration from Capitol Hill, where members of the House Ways and Means Committee and the Senate Finance Committee agreed on legislation that would approve and put in force the global trade accord known as the General Agreement on Tariffs and Trade.

Mickey Kantor, the United States trade representative, said the White House would like to see the legislation be introduced on Monday. Under the fast-track rules governing trade agreements, the House and Senate would then have 90 working days to vote on the measure, with no amendments allowed. President Clinton told reporters today, "I hope it can

Continued on Page D2, Column 5

INSIDE

Police Department Shake-Up

New York City's Police Department has begun the most sweeping management shake-up in a generation to weed out weak supervisors. Page B6.

New York's Tax Burden

New York's state and local tax payments are the second highest in the country, exceeded only by Alaska's, according to a new report. Page B1.

Jury Rules Against Haft

A Federal jury ruled that Herbert H. Haft, the 74-year-old head of one of America's richest families, wrongfully dismissed his son. Page D1.

No Cameras In U.S. Courts

The Judicial Conference voted to deny TV cameras access to Federal civil trials and appeals. Page A18.

Fast Track Turned Bumpy

A Senator's pet project, a new Pennsylvania Station, was a done deal. Then Congress fouled out. Page B1.

Jule Styne, Bountiful Creator Of Song Favorites, Dies at 88

By ELEANOR BLAU

Jule Styne, the versatile, prolific songwriter whose tunes became standards for three generations and the composer of such classic Broadway musicals as "Gypsy," "Gentlemen Prefer Blondes" and "Funny Girl," died yesterday at Mount Sinai Hospital in Manhattan. He was 88 and lived in Manhattan.

The cause was heart failure, said Shirley Herz, his press representative. He had undergone open-heart surgery six weeks ago.

Mr. Styne's enduring songs are legion, among them the Oscar-winning "Three Coins in the Fountain," as well as "I Don't Want to Walk Without You," "Diamonds Are a Girl's Best Friend," "Everything's Coming Up Roses." But his name was always less familiar than his music.

This was probably because of his very flexibility. "You write as well as who you write with," he said, and he usually let a musical's lyricist and star set the tone for the score.

"If you can't be a collaborator," he said, "you don't belong in the theater." Of himself, he once said, "I am the greatest collaborator there is."

In 1987, Mr. Styne estimated that he had written 2,000 songs, had published 1,500 and had 200 hits. "I'm talking about hit hits," he said. "The others were popular, but there were 200 hit hits." Also among them were "It's Been a Long, Long Time," "It's Magic," "Let It Snow! Let It Snow! Let It Snow!," "Time After Time" and "Five Minutes More."

In Hollywood, he teamed up with Sammy Cahn on such romantic fare as "I've Heard That Song Before,"

Continued on Page D19, Column 1

Jule Styne

NEWS SUMMARY A2

Despite Role as Negotiator, Carter Feels Unappreciated

By MAUREEN DOWD

ATLANTA, Sept. 20 — Even now that he is helping make United States foreign policy, even now that he is stopping war on the wing, Jimmy Carter still gets that jilted feeling from the Clinton Administration.

And the worst of it is, he signals that he feels he is being treated shabbily by someone he brought into the State Department, Warren Christopher, a man he once called "the finest public servant I ever have known."

"Rosalynn and I have discussed this a lot, it means a lot to us," he said today, sitting in his office at the Carter Center with one worn loafer up on the glass coffee table, next to a walrus tusk, a cribbage board and a glass dove.

"We haven't come up with a solution to it," said Mr. Carter, 69 years old, in a rambling interview that touched on his role in negotiating a settlement last weekend with Haiti's military rulers, his poetry about the folly of war and his secret efforts to stop the Persian Gulf war.

He circled around but rarely used the name of Mr. Christopher. It was probably inevitable that there would be tension between the former President, who is running around the globe acting like a Secretary of State, and the Secretary of State, who is back in Washington acting frustrated.

It was a telling sign on Saturday afternoon in Washington, when Mr. Christopher and his deputy, Strobe Talbott, showed up in a limousine to take a break at a late-afternoon showing of the Robert Redford movie, "Quiz Show," while Jimmy Carter was in Port-au-Prince struggling to negotiate a last-minute deal that would stop the planned invasion of Haiti.

Jimmy Carter should be basking in his moment of glory. (A CNN poll showed Mr. Carter getting 70 percent of the credit for the peaceful resolution, and President Clinton only 15 percent.) But the former President, as one friend puts it, is a man with "a Mission, capital M, and Moral force, capital M." And with a will of steel, he has forced a reluctant Clinton Administration to accept his help as a global facilitator and peacemaker.

Close friends of Mr. Carter say that he feels he is overdue for a Nobel Peace Prize after he failed to win one for his role in the Camp

Continued on Page A17, Column 1

New York City Hospitals Chief to Lay Off 3,000

By MELINDA HENNEBERGER

The president of New York City's Health and Hospitals Corporation said yesterday that he plans to lay off about 3,000 workers and eliminate hundreds of hospital beds to close a budget gap and make the hospitals more competitive in a shrinking industry.

The president, Dr. Bruce Siegel, who oversees the city's 11 public hospitals and several dozen clinics, said the cuts would be made before the end of the fiscal year next June and would be scattered throughout the system.

Dr. Siegel said that one hospital likely to be hit with "potentially hundreds" of layoffs was Harlem Hospital Center, many of whose 746 beds have been empty on any given day in recent months.

Beds will be taken out of service at other hospitals as well, he said. Though he does not need formal approval to proceed, he said he would give more details of his plan to the agency's board tomorrow.

Union officials said they were flabbergasted by what they knew of the Health and Hospitals Corporation's plan and said that two discussions with the agency earlier this week about the possibilities of such cuts had been extremely contentious.

"They said it translates into 3,000 workers, but they won't give us any details," said Stanley Hill, executive director of District Council 37 of the American Federation of State, County and Municipal Employees. "It's a disaster."

"At Harlem Hospital, they want to eliminate beds and people, but their attitude is not to cooperate and work with us," Mr. Hill said. "You're talking about people's livelihoods and about community services."

Dr. Siegel said the cuts were needed to close a $356 million gap in the agency's $3.6 billion budget and to lower costs to attract referrals from managed-care companies. The Health and Hospitals Corporation has about 8,000 acute-care beds and employs 48,000 workers.

An official involved in meetings about the proposed cuts, who spoke on condition of anonymity, said some treatment programs would be merged, laboratory operations would be consolidated and two surgery units at the Bronx Municipal Hospital Center would be combined. The corporation's difficulties are

Continued on Page B6, Column 3

Figure 3.1 Cover page of the *New York Times*, September 21, 1994. Courtesy of PARS International. This image has been altered from its original form.

then, that the concluding chapter of *Mortevivum* begins in Haiti, where sentiment ends.

The article accompanying the photograph did much to consider the feelings of the American soldiers, men and women who, having newly arrived and eager to be of some use, were feeling "helpless," "frustrated," and "disgusted" at their inability to step in and control the escalating violence amid President Aristide's exile and attempted overthrow. About the nameless Haitian man sprawled on the cover of the international newspaper, though, there is no such consideration. *Times* writer John Kifner wrote of the vendor, "He was a thin man, his arms thrown out to the side, wearing worn tan pants and a white shirt."[3] And there it is: poverty as poetic imagery, murder as state-sanctioned spectacle, and the world of the visible and invisible converge for the imagistic consumption of the *Times* subject.

What is the work of enclosure that proximity engenders? How have viewers been trained to see, in the sliver of space between one person and another, contemporary photographic elision and mortality's hyperpresence? "They, we, inhabit knowledge that the Black body is a sign of immi/a/nent death," Christina Sharpe writes in *In the Wake: On Blackness and Being*, and with this immediacy comes a violent repetition, a fluid temporality, and a discursive trajectory of movement and stasis.[4] For what audience are these images constructed? What progress do they refuse? In this book, I have moved between temporal elongation and quotidian fragility to understand how global obsolescence is articulated through photographic and black embodiment. How might contemporary photographic practices refuse this?

We know that discarding through ocular dismissal happens with the click of the shutter. Because the violence has already been done by external entities, (riot, famine, disaster, war), viewers can participate in multiple and repetitive acts of bodily unprotection. To observe and not interfere. This raises the question, What if observing *is* interfering? What if it inflicts violence through its guise of innocent witnessing, of passive participation? This is what it means to exist on the periphery of photography, on the margins of citizenship and belonging. Revisiting past grievous harm is also what it means to dwell on the cusp of a new century.

I have thus far argued that the proliferation of photographic imagery works to solidify antiblackness through a multitiered apparatus of the visual. Because this apparatus includes photography, there are particular questions the genre requires us to ask, just as there are ways of seeing and being seen that transcend the photographic (even within the realm of photography). If these documentary "scenes of subjection" exist devoid of the attendant historical mechanisms of imperial violence, they can appear to illustrate black obsolescence as destiny. Saidiya Hartman writes, "The emphasis on the joining of race, subjection, and spectacle is intended to denaturalize race and underline its givenness—that is, the strategies through which it is made to appear as if it has always existed, thereby denying the coerced and cultivated production of race."[5] Mortevivum is a scene of subjection that heightens the role of spectacle in the undermining of blackness. A photographic phenomenon that reframes sight.

DOCUMENTARY IMPULSES AND THE ARCHIVE

Newspapers participate in the production of the *everyday*, and the tactile materiality of a newspaper is terminal as soon as it touches your hands. The ease of disintegration, the potential rips and tears, are part of the narrative of communicative obsolescence that produces its own othering. What is solidified through an apparatus of information gathering that ends up in the trash the day after it is considered brand-new? Photographic images. These images are their own genre of legibility. Over time and through thematic repetitions, viewers are trained to align the expectation of death with photographed black subjects—a discarding of a different kind. This is where the work of the contemporary begins.

Sentiment regarding Haiti cements itself during and after the Haitian Revolution (1791–1804). Something about the possibility of black self-governance could scarcely be produced visually without the undertone of dread. Black labor as a conduit to freedom made manifest the false biblical justification for transatlantic slavery. But black subjectivity is not the goal, and this is how we must reckon with the contemporary iterations of "framing" that can contain sight.[6]

When Haiti turned the empire inside out with its revolution, it coupled modernity with black freedom. We are still grappling with the visual meaning of the event. In *The Disciplinary Frame*, John Tagg explicates the utility of the photographic image. "The Camera is, then," Tagg contends, "a place to isolate and discipline light."[7] If we extend this disciplining, then light is both literal and figurative. And photographs are one tool among many to extend imagined subjectivities, and to contain and corrupt those that resist temporal location.[8] "Archives assemble," Michel-Rolph Trouillot writes, and "their assembly work is not limited to a more or less passive act of collecting. Rather, it is an active act of production that prepares facts for historical intelligibility."[9] Contemporary viewers of photography assume, on a fundamental level, that they know Haiti, and that they have known the country for quite a while. What we must interrogate is the temporal layering that creates an air of expectation in opposition to the concept of black sovereignty. The assembled archives open out onto the visual field of ocular refusal—antiblackness as a participatory photographic endeavor.

Multiple external interventions, the overthrow of an imperialist regime, and the (financial/political) repercussions of these actions are enveloped in the visual iconography of Haiti. Underneath this iconography is the external pursuit of black failure and the repetition of the imagined permanence of this failure. Of each of this book's geographical locations, by far the vast majority of images of suffering, death, and loss are from Haiti. This, itself, is telling. Nearly one million Rwandans were murdered during the genocide in 1994, and yet the media images from the nation were scarce and not evenly dispersed. What is it about the small Caribbean nation of Haiti that fractured white supremacist visions of empire? How did the promise of slavery's totalizing capacities engender such imperial refusal that Haiti's revolution was France's melancholy—and America's great fear? To understand a late contemporary global white gaze set against the first black republic to emerge from a history of transatlantic enslavement, we must work our way backward, before the invention of photography but after the invention of blackness.

ANALOG VULNERABILITIES

With the tactile fragility of film, we can explore photography's linear motion (shutter, negative, exposures) alongside its atemporal arc (landscape, location, form). Haiti's revolution, which occupies a hierarchy in the visual register of restricted decipherability, becomes something of a photographic panopticon. It is a place/event through which the Western world surveils black resistance beyond the boundary marker of Haiti, but with the revolution as a triggering afterimage. Relegating the nation to a circular framework of failure is the "archive that assembles," and a doubling mechanism that finds its footing in the presumptive articulation of meaning that the invention of photography, from daguerreotypes to its swift mechanical improvement, would not be impossible without the industrial revolution. Photography, then, was invented in Haiti by way of France, through black laboring bodies.[10] What might it mean to think of photography's invention as a precise by-product of a slave regime so mired in the violence of capitalist pursuit that revolutionary overthrow escaped the depths of consideration? Like a gelatin silver print without a negative trace.

The trace, though, is there. It is prephotographic and postvisual. It is a coercion of imagistic intention that must be negotiated atemporally, lest the potency of the moment shift out of focus, unable to be retrieved. Sentiment organizes the structure of political meaning as a photographic loop of imperialist failure, wrapped in the violence of racial indifference. What a white, class hierarchical visual engagement precipitates is the imagistic deterioration of black subjects, facilitated by an external world order that wants this desperately. Haiti is the visual field upon which melancholy mediates blackness through modernity's extended hands. The emotive labor of violated black embodiment is in the visceral retrieval of its figurative capacities. Viewers can imagine black people both within and beyond the body's utility. To see what is not there and imagine flesh continually removed from its corpus. An emphasis on the extended performance of the body places Haiti beyond the boundary marker of sovereignty, anxiously waiting for permission to enter its place in history. Newspaper imagery reinforces the desire of its intended readership: white subjects. In the context of slavery and corporeality, Saidiya Hartman writes, "If the black body is the vehicle of the other's power, pleasure, and profit, then it is no less true that it is the white or near-white body that makes the captive's suffering visible and discernable."[11] As with the intervention, American soldiers, many of them white, produce the political vision of the moment. This is a moment filled with shadows, dark undertones, and subterfuge.

SHADOWED PEOPLE

Shadows are an important photographic currency. Projections of shapes and figures there and also not there, they are abstractions of form, embodiments with distance, and ghostly matters with the inference of past trauma. They necessitate a certain proximity to conform to the mandates of visuality—a certain mathematical trajectory of both figure and symbolic referent. Critical race theorists have wrestled with the permanent shadow cast upon black subjectivities—a shadow that implies a form of doubling death. In *Raising the Dead*, Sharon Holland navigates this particular terrain "for those beyond the periphery, beyond even a language of the margin, for those literally

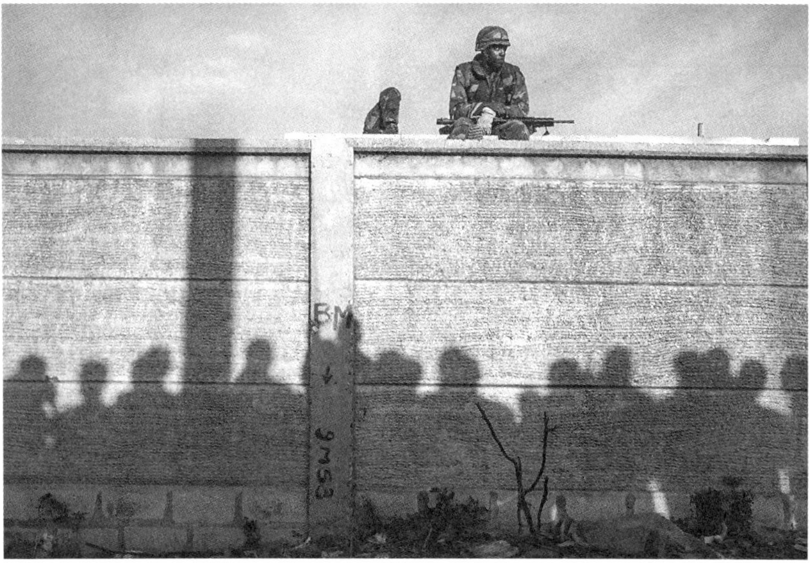

Figure 3.2 Shadowed people.
AP Photo / John McConnico.

'outdoors' and therefore dead to others."[12] In the repetition of shadowed figures against a wall in Port-au-Prince, we see the juxtaposition of "we" and "they," as the only figure visible is the armed American soldier seemingly providing the barrier between sovereign neglect and imperial protection. Although *observing and not interfering*, journalist Rick Bragg imagines the presence of the US Army as one of all-encompassing salvation. "The American show of force was intended as a clear message to the de facto dictatorship of Gen. Raoul Cèdras: No more brutality." [13] *No more brutality . . .*

This "show of force" is one that plays chess with history, marking the United States as the arbiter of global order within the continued primal chaos of the darker world. Frank Wilderson demarcates the space between racialized enslavement and the prison industrial complex, a distance that is not as wide as it may seem. "From the incoherence of Black death," he writes, "America generates the coherence of white life."[14]

These are images that seem to say: *As they come apart (fragment), so shall we coalesce (come together)*. In the temporal elongation that reconfigures the terms of unbelonging, a still photograph intimates movement, even if that movement is a dead walking. This modulation does not neatly correspond to Ariella Azoulay's rendering of the photographic force of the concept. So when Azoulay contends, for instance, that "photography, at times, is the only civic refuge at the disposal of those robbed of citizenship," I want to trouble the waters of this when it is not the case.[15] For the people whose lives are constantly coded via a discourse of unrest, who, starved or slaughtered, offer something unique and necessary to the viewing subject, there may be another contract at play, one that fails to lend itself to a process that is inclusive of blackness without violation.

IN OTHER NEWS

Days after the aircraft carrying the Rwandan president and the president of Burundi was shot down in Kigali in early April 1994, the *New York Times* mentioned the evolving genocide on the front page of the newspaper. Under the headline "Terror Convulses Rwandan Capital as Tribes Battle," there is a universe, one that is constructed as an enclosure, a black-on-black crime spree resembling a "tribal battle." In this construction, there is the palpable absence of empire, the obfuscation of Rwanda as a former German protectorate, the invisible tentacles of the Belgian regime, and the muted presence of the United States as a world leader tasked with responding to human rights violations. Instead, the sliver of space occupied by reporting on the genocide focuses on messages from French officials on the ground and offers very little in the way of understanding what is taking place in the small east-central African country.

Legible mostly as gruesome aftermath corpses, living survivors were disappeared within media coverage that was a situational failure. Privileging dead bodies over living survivors, newspapers and magazines marked the country as a "heart of

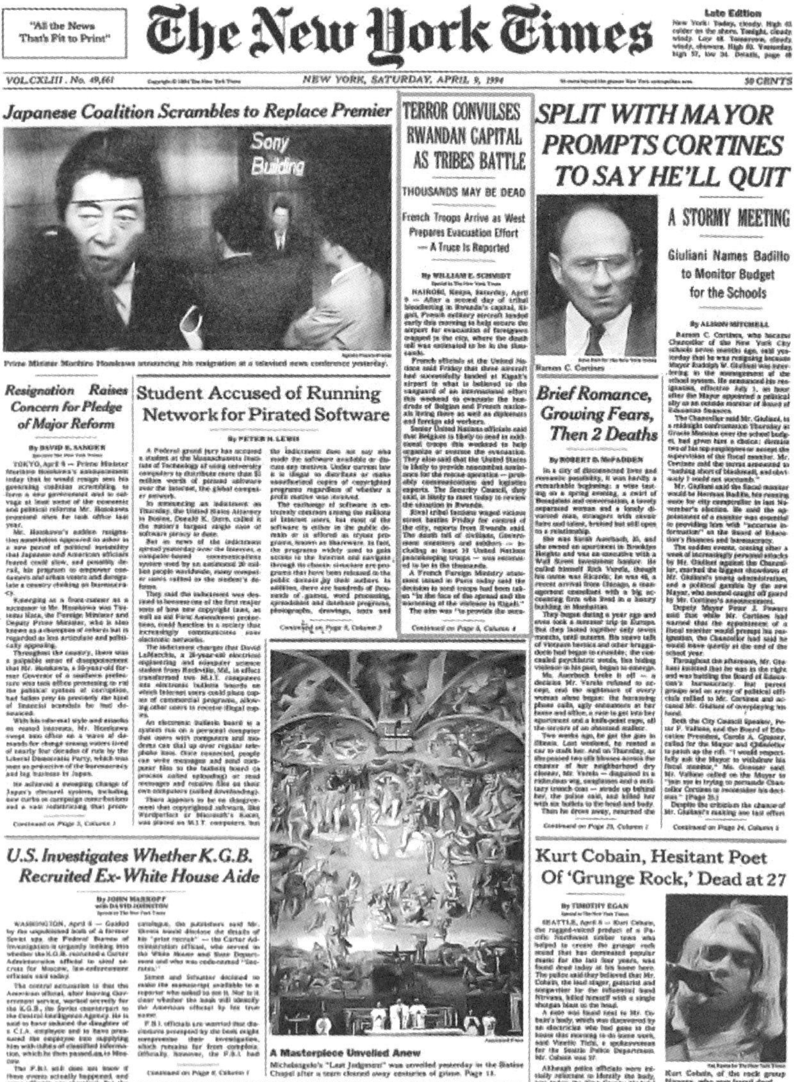

"All the News That's Fit to Print"

The New York Times

Late Edition

VOL. CXLIII . No. 49,661 — NEW YORK, SATURDAY, APRIL 9, 1994 — 50 CENTS

Japanese Coalition Scrambles to Replace Premier

TERROR CONVULSES RWANDAN CAPITAL AS TRIBES BATTLE

THOUSANDS MAY BE DEAD

French Troops Arrive as West Prepares Evacuation Effort — A Truce Is Reported

SPLIT WITH MAYOR PROMPTS CORTINES TO SAY HE'LL QUIT

A STORMY MEETING

Giuliani Names Badillo to Monitor Budget for the Schools

Resignation Raises Concern for Pledge of Major Reform

Student Accused of Running Network for Pirated Software

Brief Romance, Growing Fears, Then 2 Deaths

U.S. Investigates Whether K.G.B. Recruited Ex-White House Aide

Kurt Cobain, Hesitant Poet Of 'Grunge Rock,' Dead at 27

A Masterpiece Unveiled Anew

INSIDE

Figure 3.3 Cover page of the *New York Times*, April 9, 1994. Courtesy of PARS International.

darkness" from which there is no return. Judith Butler writes, "The body implies mortality, vulnerability, agency: the skin and the flesh expose us to the gaze of others, but also to touch, and to violence, and bodies put us at risk of becoming the agency and instrument of all these as well."[16] Are we attuned to this mortality, vulnerability, and agency only when it is untethered from blackness? Can we see it in the dark?

THE INTERIM

Days of protest, marching, and violence mark the removal of Haitian president Jean-Bertrand Aristide. The *New York Times* coverage of the intervention illustrates this in graphic detail. On the last day of September 1994, the newspaper's front page had, as its central image, a photograph of a crowd of Haitians at a rally in Port-au-Prince. Three dead bodies can be seen in the center of the image, surrounded by witnesses—friends and relatives of the deceased—who gather around the horrifying sight. On the far right a man faces the direction of the camera, his mouth agape, his face filled with anguish, and his hands gesturing toward one of the bodies, which is that of a young man. "A Haitian man screamed in mourning over the body of a friend minutes after an explosion in Port-au-Prince," the image description reads. *Screamed in mourning.*

It is difficult to quantify how often facial expressions and bodily gestures made by black people are then misread and/or ignored by white viewers. A cultural rift, maybe, but one that has been rehearsed as a refusal of regard—an eagerness of denial writ visual. A racial apparatus of the eye. "Screamed in mourning" is one way to mute the presence of rage, to siphon anger in the quest for visual obliteration, and to create the thread of destiny out of a national crisis. As with numerous other documentary images published in the *Times*, this one has no photographer attribution. However, there are photographers present in the image. Their telephoto lenses and press passes tell us something about the history of imperialism and conquest that their photographs work to reinforce. "Screamed

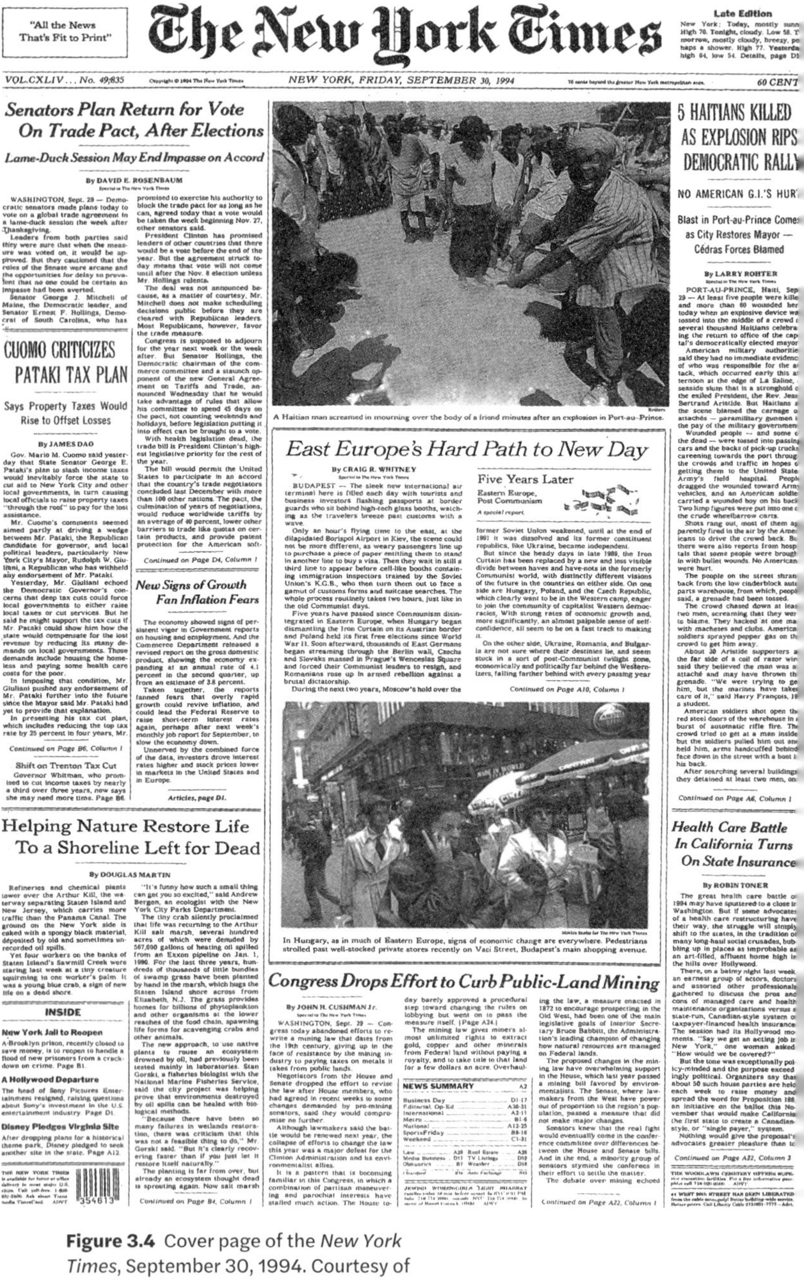

"All the News That's Fit to Print"

The New York Times

Late Edition

New York: Today, mostly sunn High 70. Tonight, cloudy. Low 58. T morrow, mostly cloudy, breezy, po haps a shower. High 77. Yesterda high 64, low 54. Details, page D1

VOL.CXLIV . . . No. 49,835 Copyright © 1994 The New York Times NEW YORK, FRIDAY, SEPTEMBER 30, 1994 76 cents beyond the greater New York metropolitan area. 60 CENT

Senators Plan Return for Vote On Trade Pact, After Elections

Lame-Duck Session May End Impasse on Accord

By DAVID E. ROSENBAUM
Special to The New York Times

WASHINGTON, Sept. 29 — Democratic senators made plans today to vote on a global trade agreement in a lame-duck session the week after Thanksgiving.

Leaders from both parties said they were sure that when the measure was voted on, it would be approved. But they cautioned that the rules of the Senate were arcane and the opportunities for delay so prevalent that no one could be certain an impasse had been averted.

Senator George J. Mitchell of Maine, the Democratic leader, and Senator Ernest F. Hollings, Democrat of South Carolina, who has promised to exercise his authority to block the trade pact for as long as he can, agreed today that a vote would be taken the week beginning Nov. 27, other senators said.

President Clinton has promised leaders of other countries that there would be a vote before the end of the year. But the agreement struck today means that vote will not come until after the Nov. 8 election unless Mr. Hollings relents.

The deal was not announced because, as a matter of courtesy, Mr. Mitchell does not make scheduling decisions public before they are cleared with Republican leaders. Most Republicans, however, favor the trade measure.

Congress is supposed to adjourn for the year next week or the week after. But Senator Hollings, the Democratic chairman of the commerce committee and a staunch opponent of the new General Agreement on Tariffs and Trade, announced Wednesday that he would take advantage of rules that allow his committee to spend 45 days on the pact, not counting weekends and holidays, before legislation putting it into effect can be brought to a vote.

With health legislation dead, the trade bill is President Clinton's highest legislative priority for the rest of the year.

The bill would permit the United States to participate in an accord that the country's trade negotiators concluded last December with more than 100 other nations. The pact, the culmination of years of negotiations, would reduce worldwide tariffs by an average of 40 percent, lower other barriers to trade like quotas on certain products, and provide patent protection for the American soft-

Continued on Page D4, Column 1

CUOMO CRITICIZES PATAKI TAX PLAN

Says Property Taxes Would Rise to Offset Losses

By JAMES DAO

Gov. Mario M. Cuomo said yesterday that State Senator George E. Pataki's plan to slash income taxes would inevitably force the state to cut aid to New York City and other local governments, in turn causing local officials to raise property taxes "through the roof" to pay for the lost assistance.

Mr. Cuomo's comments seemed aimed partly at driving a wedge between Mr. Pataki, the Republican candidate for governor, and local political leaders, particularly New York City's Mayor, Rudolph W. Giuliani, a Republican who has withheld any endorsement of Mr. Pataki.

Yesterday, Mr. Giuliani echoed the Democratic Governor's concerns that deep tax cuts could force local governments to either raise local taxes or cut services. But he said he might support the tax cuts if Mr. Pataki could show him how the state would compensate for the lost revenue by reducing its many demands on local governments. Those demands include housing the homeless and paying some health care costs for the poor.

In imposing that condition, Mr. Giuliani pushed any endorsement of Mr. Pataki further into the future since the Mayor said Mr. Pataki had yet to provide that explanation.

In presenting his tax cut plan, which includes reducing the top tax rate by 25 percent in four years, Mr.

Continued on Page B6, Column 1

Shift on Trenton Tax Cut

Governor Whitman, who promised to cut income taxes by nearly a third over three years, now says she may need more time. Page B6.

New Signs of Growth Fan Inflation Fears

The economy showed signs of persistent vigor in Government reports on housing and employment. And the Commerce Department released a revised report on the gross domestic product, showing the economy expanding at an annual rate of 4.1 percent in the second quarter, up from an estimate of 3.8 percent.

Taken together, the reports fanned fears that overly rapid growth could revive inflation, and could lead the Federal Reserve to raise short-term interest rates again, perhaps after next week's monthly job report for September, to slow the economy down.

Unnerved by the combined force of the data, investors drove interest rates higher and stock prices lower in markets in the United States and in Europe.

Articles, page D1.

Reuters

A Haitian man screamed in mourning over the body of a friend minutes after an explosion in Port-au-Prince.

East Europe's Hard Path to New Day

By CRAIG R. WHITNEY
Special to The New York Times

Five Years Later
Eastern Europe, Post Communism
A special report.

BUDAPEST — The sleek new international air terminal here is filled each day with tourists and business investors flashing passports at border guards who sit behind high-tech glass booths, watching as the travelers breeze past customs with a wave.

Only an hour's flying time to the east, at the dilapidated Borispol Airport in Kiev, the scene could not be more different, as weary passengers line up to purchase a piece of paper entitling them to stand in another line to buy a visa. Then they wait in still a third line to appear before cell-like booths containing immigration inspectors trained by the Soviet Union's K.G.B., who then turn them out to face a gamut of customs forms and suitcase searches. The whole process routinely takes two hours, just like in the old Communist days.

Five years have passed since Communism disintegrated in Eastern Europe, when Hungary began dismantling the Iron Curtain on its Austrian border and Poland held its first free elections since World War II. Soon afterward, thousands of East Germans began streaming through the Berlin wall, Czechs and Slovaks massed in Prague's Wenceslas Square and forced their Communist leaders to resign, and Romanians rose up in armed rebellion against a brutal dictatorship.

During the next two years, Moscow's hold over the former Soviet Union weakened, until at the end of 1991 it was dissolved and its former constituent republics, like Ukraine, became independent.

But since the heady days in late 1989, the Iron Curtain has been replaced by a new and less visible divide between haves and have-nots in the formerly Communist world, with distinctly different visions of the future in the countries on either side. On one side are Hungary, Poland, and the Czech Republic, which clearly want to be in the Western camp, eager to join the community of capitalist Western democracies, With strong rates of economic growth and, more significantly, an almost palpable sense of self-confidence, all seem to be on a fast track to making it.

On the other side, Ukraine, Romania, and Bulgaria are not sure where their destinies lie, and seem stuck in a sort of post-Communist twilight zone, economically and politically far behind the Westernizers, falling farther behind with every passing year

Continued on Page A10, Column 1

Miklos Szabo for The New York Times

In Hungary, as in much of Eastern Europe, signs of economic change are everywhere. Pedestrians strolled past well-stocked private stores recently on Vaci Street, Budapest's main shopping avenue.

5 HAITIANS KILLED AS EXPLOSION RIPS DEMOCRATIC RALLY

NO AMERICAN G.I.'S HUR

Blast in Port-au-Prince Come as City Restores Mayor — Cédras Forces Blamed

By LARRY ROHTER
Special to The New York Times

PORT-AU-PRINCE, Haiti, Sep 29 — At least five people were kille and more than 60 wounded her today when an explosive device wa tossed into the middle of a crowd several thousand Haitians celebra ing the return to office of the cap tal's democratically elected mayor

American military authoritie said they had no immediate evidenc of who was responsible for the a tack, which occurred early this a ternoon at the edge of La Saline, seaside slum that is a stronghold c the exiled President, the Rev. Jean Bertrand Aristide. But Haitians a the scene blamed the carnage o attachés — paramilitary gunmen i the pay of the military governmen

Wounded people — and some o the dead — were tossed into passing cars and the backs of pick-up trucks careening towards the port throug the crowds and traffic in hopes o getting them to the United State Army's field hospital. People dragged the wounded toward Army vehicles, and an American soldie carried a wounded boy on his back Two limp figures were put into one o the crude wheelbarrow carts.

Shots rang out, most of them ap parently fired in the air by the Amer icans to drive the crowd back. Bu there were also reports from hosp tals that some people were brough in with bullet wounds. No American were hurt.

The people on the street shran back from the low cinderblock aut parts warehouse, from which, peopl said, a grenade had been tossed.

The crowd chased down at leas two men, screaming that they wer to blame. They hacked at one ma with machetes and clubs. America soldiers sprayed pepper gas on th crowd to get him away.

About 30 Aristide supporters a the far side of a coil of razor wir said they believed the man was a attaché and may have thrown th grenade. "We were trying to ge him, but the marines have take care of it," said Harry François, 19 a student.

American soldiers shot open th red steel doors of the warehouse in burst of automatic rifle fire. Th crowd tried to get at a man inside but the soldiers pulled him out an held him, arms handcuffed behind face down in the street with a boot his back.

After searching several buildings they detained at least two men, on

Continued on Page A6, Column 1

Health Care Battle In California Turns On State Insurance

By ROBIN TONER

The great health care battle o 1994 may have sputtered to a close i Washington. But if some advocate of a health care restructuring have their way, the struggle will simply shift to the states, in the tradition o many long-haul social crusades, bub bling up in places as improbable a an art-filled, affluent home high i the hills over Hollywood.

There, on a balmy night last week an earnest group of actors, doctor and assorted other professional gathered to discuss the pros an cons of managed care and health maintenance organizations versus state-run, Canadian-style system o taxpayer-financed health insurance The session had its Hollywood mo ments. "Say we get an acting job i New York," one woman asked "How would we be covered?"

But the tone was exceptionally pol icy-minded and the purpose exceed ingly political. Organizers say tha about 50 such house parties are hel each week to raise money an spread the word for Proposition 18 an initiative on the ballot this No vember that would make California the first state to create a Canadian style, or "single payer," system.

Nothing would give the proposal' advocates greater pleasure than t

Continued on Page A22, Column 3

Helping Nature Restore Life To a Shoreline Left for Dead

By DOUGLAS MARTIN

Refineries and chemical plants tower over the Arthur Kill, the waterway separating Staten Island and New Jersey, which carries more traffic than the Panama Canal. The ground on the New York side is caked with a spongy black material, deposited by old and sometimes unrecorded oil spills.

Yet four workers on the banks of Staten Island's Sawmill Creek were staring last week at a tiny creature squirming in one worker's palm. It was a young blue crab, a sign of new life on a dead shore.

"It's funny how such a small thing can get you so excited," said Andrew Bergen, an ecologist with the New York City Parks Department.

The tiny crab silently proclaimed that life was returning to the Arthur Kill salt marsh, several hundred acres of which were denuded by 567,000 gallons of heating oil spilled from an Exxon pipeline on Jan. 1, 1990. For the last three years, hundreds of thousands of little bundles of swamp grass have been planted by hand in the marsh, which hugs the Staten Island shore across from Elizabeth, N.J. The grass provides homes for billions of phytoplankton and other organisms at the lower reaches of the food chain, spawning life forms for scavenging crabs and other animals.

The new approach, to use native plants to rouse an ecosystem drowned by oil, had previously been tested mainly in laboratories. Stan Gorski, a fisheries biologist with the National Marine Fisheries Service, said the city project was helping prove that environments destroyed by oil spills can be healed with biological methods.

"Because there have been so many failures in wetlands restoration, there was criticism that this was not a feasible thing to do," Mr. Gorski said. "But it's clearly recovering faster than if you just let it restore itself naturally."

The planting is far from over, but already an ecosystem thought dead is sprouting again. Now salt marsh

Continued on Page B4, Column 1

INSIDE

New York Jail to Reopen

A Brooklyn prison, recently closed to save money, is to reopen to handle a flood of new prisoners from a crackdown on crime. Page B1.

A Hollywood Departure

The head of Sony Pictures Entertainment resigned, raising questions about Sony's investment in the U.S. entertainment industry. Page D1.

Disney Pledges Virginia Site

After dropping plans for a historical theme park, Disney pledged to seek another site in the state. Page A12.

Congress Drops Effort to Curb Public-Land Mining

By JOHN H. CUSHMAN Jr.
Special to The New York Times

WASHINGTON, Sept. 29 — Congress today abandoned efforts to rewrite a mining law that dates from the 19th century, giving up in the face of resistance by the mining industry to paying taxes on metals it takes from public lands.

Negotiators from the House and Senate dropped the effort to revise the law after House members, who had agreed in recent weeks to some changes demanded by pro-mining senators, said they would compromise no further.

Although lawmakers said the battle would be renewed next year, the collapse of efforts to change the law this year was a major defeat for the Clinton Administration and its environmentalist allies.

It is a pattern that is becoming familiar in this Congress, in which a combination of partisan maneuvering and parochial interests have stalled much action. The House today barely approved a procedural step toward changing the rules on lobbying but went on to pass the measure itself. [Page A24.]

The mining law gives miners almost unlimited rights to extract gold, copper and other minerals from Federal land without paying a royalty, and to take title to that land for a few dollars an acre. Overhauling the law, a measure enacted in 1872 to encourage prospecting in the Old West, had been one of the main legislative goals of Interior Secretary Bruce Babbitt, the Administration's leading champion of changing how natural resources are managed on Federal lands.

The proposed changes in the mining law have overwhelming support in the House, which last year passed a mining bill favored by environmentalists. The Senate, where lawmakers from the West have power out of proportion to the region's population, passed a measure that did not make major changes.

Senators knew that the real fight would eventually come in the conference committee over differences between the House and Senate bills. And in the end, a minority group of senators stymied the conferees in their effort to settle the matter.

The debate over mining echoed

Continued on Page A22, Column 1

NEWS SUMMARY A2

Business Day	D1-17
Editorial, Op-Ed	A30-31
International	A2-11
Metro	B1-6
National	A12-25
SportsFriday	B8-16
Weekend	C1-31

Law	A20	Real Estate	A26
Media Business	D17	TV Listings	D19
Obituaries	B7	Weather	D16

Figure 3.4 Cover page of the *New York Times*, September 30, 1994. Courtesy of PARS International. This image has been altered from its original form.

in mourning" is an abstraction of sight that ignores the indexicality (hands pointing) of the man's gesture. This witness is the only reason the photograph is on the cover of the *Times*. This man's anguish is what propels the framing of the photograph and the document's utility as an addendum to the article.

Five days earlier, on September 25, a dark image shows US marines "subduing two Haitians" after a skirmish in which the marines killed eight people. "Details were sketchy," Eric Schmitt's article reports. The photograph provided by the Associated Press is sketchy as well. Two (maybe three?) soldiers are in the process of "subduing" men who are on the ground. Everything is black. The image is difficult to see clearly. This, of course, is part of the point. Chaos lives in the interstices of the dark, or so we are constantly told. People, places, cultures, and nations—all are utilized to demarcate the sense of "not there" and "not us" that dominates extrajuridical US policy.

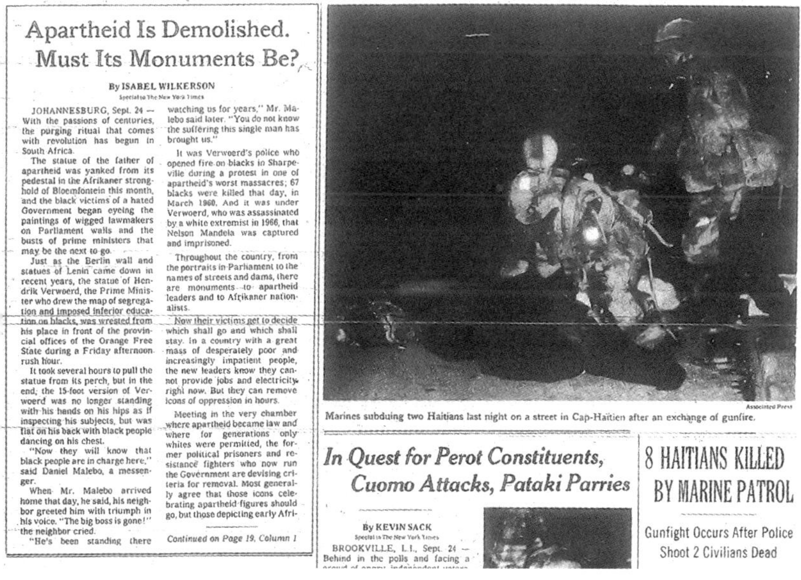
Apartheid Is Demolished. Must Its Monuments Be?

By ISABEL WILKERSON
Special to The New York Times

JOHANNESBURG, Sept. 24 — With the passions of centuries, the purging ritual that comes with revolution has begun in South Africa.

The statue of the father of apartheid was yanked from its pedestal in the Afrikaner stronghold of Bloemfontein this month, and the black victims of a hated Government began eyeing the paintings of wigged lawmakers on Parliament walls and the busts of prime ministers that may be the next to go.

Just as the Berlin wall and statues of Lenin came down in recent years, the statue of Hendrik Verwoerd, the Prime Minister who drew the map of segregation and imposed inferior education on blacks, was wrested from his place in front of the provincial offices of the Orange Free State during a Friday afternoon rush hour.

It took several hours to pull the statue from its perch, but in the end, the 15-foot version of Verwoerd was no longer standing with his hands on his hips as if inspecting his subjects, but was flat on his back with black people dancing on his chest.

"Now they will know that black people are in charge here," said Daniel Malebo, a messenger.

When Mr. Malebo arrived home that day, he said, his neighbor greeted him with triumph in his voice. "The big boss is gone!" the neighbor cried.

"He's been standing there watching us for years," Mr. Malebo said later. "You do not know the suffering this single man has brought us."

It was Verwoerd's police who opened fire on blacks in Sharpeville during a protest in one of apartheid's worst massacres; 67 blacks were killed that day, in March 1960. And it was under Verwoerd, who was assassinated by a white extremist in 1966, that Nelson Mandela was captured and imprisoned.

Throughout the country, from the portraits in Parliament to the names of streets and dams, there are monuments to apartheid leaders and to Afrikaner nationalists.

Now their victims get to decide which shall go and which shall stay. In a country with a great mass of desperately poor and increasingly impatient people, the new leaders know they cannot provide jobs and electricity right now. But they can remove icons of oppression in hours.

Meeting in the very chamber where apartheid became law and where for generations only whites were permitted, the former political prisoners and resistance fighters who now run the Government are devising criteria for removal. Most generally agree that those icons celebrating apartheid figures should go, but those depicting early Afri-

Continued on Page 19, Column 1

Associated Press

Marines subduing two Haitians last night on a street in Cap-Haïtien after an exchange of gunfire.

In Quest for Perot Constituents, Cuomo Attacks, Pataki Parries

By KEVIN SACK
Special to The New York Times

BROOKVILLE, L.I., Sept. 24 — Behind in the polls and facing a

8 HAITIANS KILLED BY MARINE PATROL

Gunfight Occurs After Police Shoot 2 Civilians Dead

Figure 3.5 Marines subduing two Haitians in Cap-Haitien. Courtesy of PARS International. This image has been altered from its original form.

"All the News That's Fit to Print"

The New York Times

VOL.CXLIV . No. 49,830 Copyright © 1994 The New York Times NEW YORK, SUNDAY, SEPTEMBER 25, 1994 $2.60 beyond the greater New York metropolitan area

Apartheid Is Demolished. Must Its Monuments Be?

By ISABEL WILKERSON

Special to The New York Times

JOHANNESBURG, Sept. 24 — With the passions of centuries, the purging ritual that comes with revolution has begun in South Africa.

The statue of the father of apartheid was yanked from its pedestal in the Afrikaner stronghold of Bloemfontein this month, and the black victims of a hated Government began eyeing the paintings of wigged lawmakers on Parliament walls and the busts of prime ministers that may be the next to go.

Just as the Berlin wall and statues of Lenin came down in recent years, the statue of Hendrik Verwoerd, the Prime Minister who drew the map of segregation and imposed inferior education on blacks, was wrested from his place in front of the provincial offices of the Orange Free State during a Friday afternoon rush hour.

It took several hours to pull the statue from its perch, but in the end, the 15-foot version of Verwoerd was no longer standing with his hands on his hips as if inspecting his subjects, but was flat on his back with black people dancing on his chest.

"Now they will know that black people are in charge here," said Daniel Malebo, a messenger.

When Mr. Malebo arrived home that day, he said, his neighbor greeted him with triumph in his voice. "The big boss is gone!" the neighbor cried.

"He's been standing there watching us for years," Mr. Malebo said later. "You do not know the suffering this single man has brought us."

It was Verwoerd's police who opened fire on blacks in Sharpeville during a protest in one of apartheid's worst massacres; 67 blacks were killed that day, in March 1960. And it was under Verwoerd, who was assassinated by a white extremist in 1966, that Nelson Mandela was captured and imprisoned.

Throughout the country, from the portraits in Parliament to the names of streets and dams, there are monuments to apartheid leaders and to Afrikaner nationalists.

Now their victims get to decide which shall go and which shall stay. In a country with a great mass of desperately poor and increasingly impatient people, the new leaders know they cannot provide jobs and electricity right now. But they can remove icons of oppression in hours.

Meeting in the very chamber where apartheid became law and where for generations only whites were permitted, the former political prisoners and resistance fighters who now run the Government are devising criteria for removal. Most generally agree that those icons celebrating apartheid figures should go, but those depicting early Afri-

Continued on Page 19, Column 1

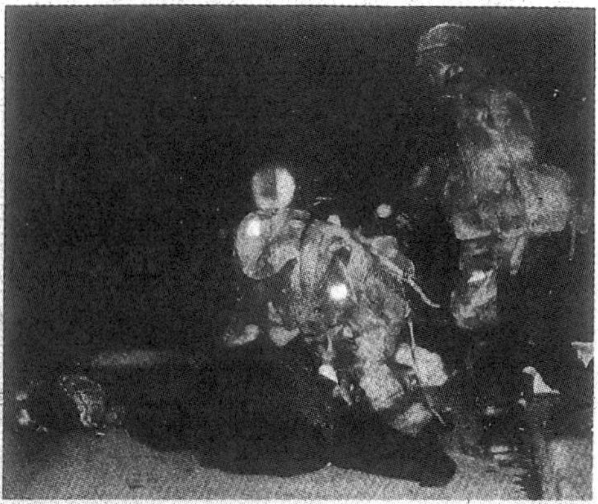

Associated Press

Marines subduing two Haitians last night on a street in Cap-Haïtien after an exchange of gunfire.

Local Governments Lose Millions In Complex and Risky Securities

By LESLIE WAYNE

In 1990, Virgil Swartzlander, the treasurer of Sandusky County, Ohio, for more than 30 years, began investing in a new type of highly speculative security cooked up by Wall Street. So did his friend, Maurice Kline, treasurer of nearby Portage County. Now, after $10 million in losses of taxpayer money, they say they did not fully understand what they were buying.

These men, along with dozens of other officials of towns, colleges and at least one Indian tribe across the country, thought they could get higher returns from new and risky investments called mortgage derivatives. But as interest rates have risen, these investments have dropped sharply in value, and taxpayers now face multimillion-dollar losses.

In Ohio alone, municipalities lost at least $13 million. In Texas, Odessa Junior College has $22 million in investments that cannot be sold. The City Colleges of Chicago have $96 million in highly questionable investments. And the Shoshone Indian tribe in Wyoming has lost about $5 million — leaving it without money to buy clothes and food for needy children or provide financial assistance to adults.

Now that these investments have gone awry, many local officials say they were pushed into unsuitable choices by aggressive brokers. But others say there was greed on both sides — the brokers seeking large commissions and the local officials gambling for big returns that would make them look good, rather than placing public money into conservative investments like certificates of deposit that offered modest returns but virtually no risk.

"The profits to brokers for selling these derivatives have been fat and a lot of local officials wanted to

In Quest for Perot Constituents, Cuomo Attacks, Pataki Parries

By KEVIN SACK

Special to The New York Times

BROOKVILLE, L.I., Sept. 24 — Behind in the polls and facing a crowd of angry, independent voters, Gov. Mario M. Cuomo let loose a blistering attack today on Senator George E. Pataki, accusing him of raising taxes as Mayor of Peekskill, achieving nothing in the Legislature and unseating the only Republican woman in the Senate.

For his part, Mr. Pataki, appearing before the same crowd about a half hour after Mr. Cuomo left, seemed content to play the serene front-runner, and his treatment of the Governor was far more gentle than Mr. Cuomo had received from some disaffected constituents.

Mr. Cuomo was heckled relentlessly as he spoke to a small crowd at a candidate's fair on the C. W. Post Campus of Long Island University that was sponsored by United We Stand, America, Ross Perot's political organization. But the Governor gave as good as he got. And when the heckling continued after his speech, he traded insults in a face-to-face confrontation with a pair of men who cursed him in both English and Italian.

Although the candidates never crossed paths, their exchange was about as close as they have come to a debate so far in the 1994 campaign. And the event showed the impor-

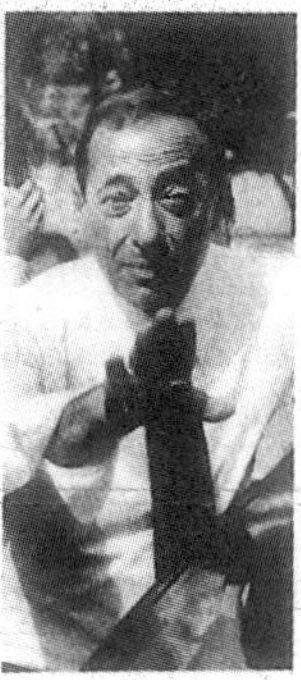

Gov. Mario M. Cuomo was heckled at a fair sponsored by Ross Perot's political organization.

8 HAITIANS KILLED BY MARINE PATROL

Gunfight Occurs After Police Shoot 2 Civilians Dead

By ERIC SCHMITT

Special to The New York Times

CAP-HAÏTIEN, Haiti, Sunday, Sept. 25 — At least 10 Haitians were killed here Saturday night in two clashes involving American marines, the Haitian police and civilians, marine officials said.

Details were sketchy, but shooting reportedly started when Haitian police officers fired on a crowd of several hundred supporters of the exiled President, the Rev. Jean-Bertrand Aristide, when the crowd advanced on a police station in this northern port city.

Marine armored patrols responded to the shooting and returned fire when they were shot at, apparently by Haitian security forces, marine officials said. The marines killed eight Haitians, including at least one senior police officer, they said. One American, a sailor working with the marines as an interpreter, was injured.

Two Haitians were reported killed in the initial clash between civilians and security forces at the police station.

The gunfight was the first between United States and Haitian forces

Figure 3.6 Cover page of the *New York Times*, September 25, 1994. Courtesy of PARS International.

That we have no photograph of the Haitians killed by marines splayed across the front page of the *Times* is one indication that mortevivum necessitates an absent index. There is no single person to point to in order to say, "this is the person who committed the act." No death dealer among all this death. So instead we have spontaneous slaughter that reifies the law of the corporeal as if an act of nature swept people off the earth. From "screamed in mourning," we now have "nothing to see here."

This leaves on-site witnesses with the impossible task of seeking and deciphering the occupation of space that public acts of violence engender. And because these are public acts, they cull the register of engagement forcefully, leaving gaping holes of understanding to hover unencumbered. The daytime photo of people surrounding dead bodies and reacting, in real time, to the horror of the emergent scene is replaced by the visual of a (covert?) military action that produces multiple deaths that occur (we are to assume) outside of the frame of the photograph. Death in the dark or death in the light—the images illustrate how little this matters for black subjects. The matter, according to the reiterated set of images, *is* black death. Of the dozens of image choices editors of daily papers have, how is it possible that the more inhumane the photograph of a black person, the quicker the rush to display it? Antiblackness frames this photographic interface, its arc and reverberations, across temporal, national, and discursive fields. Like "screams in mourning" when the mourners are perpetually black.[17]

THE OTHER SIDE OF THE (WHITE) VISUAL WORLD

On what was the 904th day of the siege of Sarajevo, the *New York Times* featured a photograph of a hospital worker at a Kosovo Hospital calmly folding sheets for use at the facility. The image description reveals that the hospital has lost its electricity during the Bosnian War (1992–1995), necessitating the manual labor of workers like this one to sustain its operation. There is something organized and peaceful about the photograph. The framing functions as an enclosure, with several Bosnian subjects existing within the protective (albeit cloth) boundary, seemingly removed from the onslaught of the violence taking place outside. The man in the forefront of the image is not looking at the photographer, but the man standing to his immediate left is doing just that. He looks in the direction of the photographer or just beyond them. Perhaps his eye is focused on someone or something outside the frame. It is not easy to tell. There is at least one more person who is present in the photograph. A forearm in motion.

The image accompanying the *Times* article is detached from the article's headline ("Sarajevo's Unending Travail"), but not completely. Roger Cohen's piece emphasizes how much (or how little) progress has been made by the Bosnian government in the war against the Serbs. Cohen asks, "Is such a long war—undermining Europe, destabilizing the Balkans and straining transatlantic relations—acceptable to the United States?" The political investment in what is "acceptable to the United States" frames the image that accompanies the piece in contrast to the dozens of images of dead bodies connected to Haiti's political upheaval.[18] The difference between newspaper coverage of Bosnia and coverage of Haiti functions to effectively differentiate the space between black fungibility and white value. What Gloria Wekker refers to as *white innocence* pervades the visual offerings that occupy media imagery.[19] By the end of the twentieth century, viewers are fully entrenched in the visual training they have received.

Days into the newspaper coverage of the intervention in Haiti, the *New York Times* international section is marked with reporting that concerns the siege in Sarajevo and the consequent political interests represented by the United States. Cohen writes, "The end result could be a dirty little war in Bosnia, with America quietly supplying arms to the Bosnian Muslims, Russia quietly supplying materials to the Serbs through Serbia, and the border secured against any wider conflagration."[20] There is something worthy and retrievable

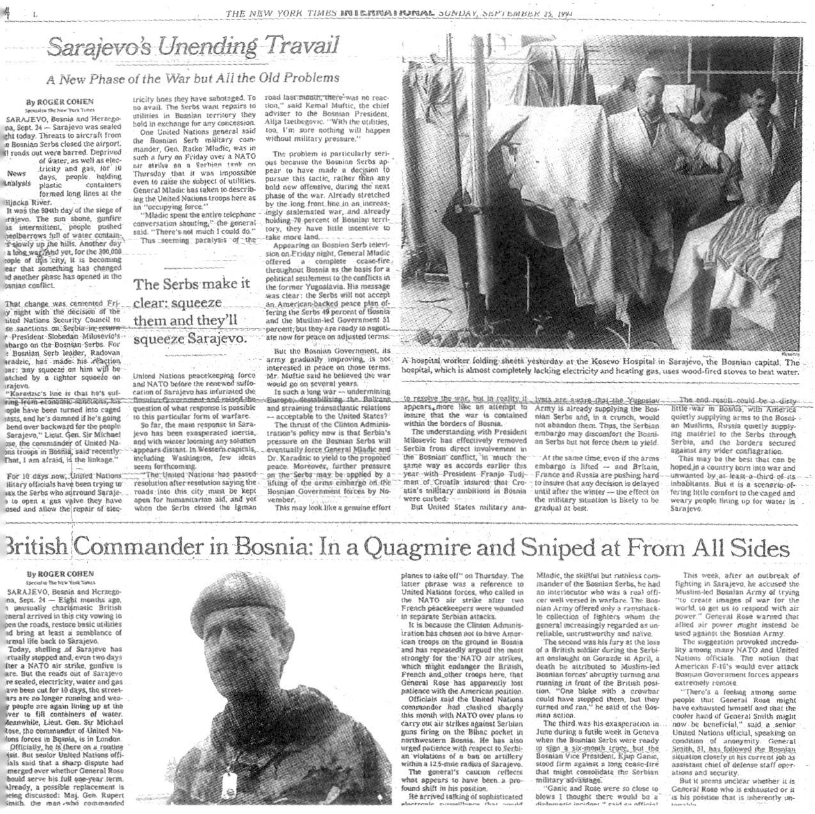

4 L THE NEW YORK TIMES INTERNATIONAL SUNDAY, SEPTEMBER 25, 1994

Sarajevo's Unending Travail

A New Phase of the War but All the Old Problems

By ROGER COHEN
Special to The New York Times

SARAJEVO, Bosnia and Herzegona, Sept. 24 — Sarajevo was sealed ght today. Threats to aircraft from e Bosnian Serbs closed the airport. ll roads out were barred. Deprived of water, as well as electricity and gas, for 10 days, people holding plastic containers formed long lines at the iljacka River.

News Analysis

It was the 904th day of the siege of ajevo. The sun shone, gunfire as intermittent, people pushed heelbarrows full of water contains slowly up the hills. Another day a long war. And yet, for the 300,000 ople of this city, it is becoming ear that something has changed d another phase has opened in the snian conflict.

That change was cemented Fri y night with the decision of the ited Nations Security Council to se sanctions on Serbia in return President Slobodan Milosevic's bargo on the Bosnian Serbs. For Bosnian Serb leader, Radovan radzic, has made his reaction ar: any squeeze on him will be atched by a tighter squeeze on rajevo.

"Karadzic's line is that he's suf ing from economic sanctions, his ople have been turned into caged asts, and he's damned if he's going bend over backward for the people Sarajevo," Lieut. Gen. Sir Michael se, the commander of United Nans troops in Bosnia, said recently. That, I am afraid, is the linkage."

For 10 days now, United Nations ilitary officials have been trying to ax the Serbs who surround Saraje to open a gas valve they have osed and allow the repair of electricity lines they have sabotaged. To no avail. The Serbs want repairs to utilities in Bosnian territory they hold in exchange for any concession.

One United Nations general said the Bosnian Serb military commander, Gen. Ratko Mladic, was in such a fury on Friday over a NATO air strike on a Serbian tank on Thursday that it was impossible even to raise the subject of utilities. General Mladic has taken to describing the United Nations troops here as an "occupying force."

"Mladic spent the entire telephone conversation shouting," the general said. "There's not much I could do."

This seeming paralysis of the

The Serbs make it clear: squeeze them and they'll squeeze Sarajevo.

United Nations peacekeeping force and NATO before the renewed suffocation of Sarajevo has infuriated the [illegible] and raised the question of what response is possible to this particular form of warfare.

So far, the main response in Sarajevo has been exasperated inertia, and with winter looming any solution appears distant. In Western capitals, including Washington, few ideas seem forthcoming.

"The United Nations has passed resolution after resolution saying the roads into this city must be kept open for humanitarian aid, and yet when the Serbs closed the Igman road last month, there was no reaction," said Kemal Muftic, the chief adviser to the Bosnian President, Alija Izetbegovic. "With the utilities, too, I'm sure nothing will happen without military pressure."

The problem is particularly serious because the Bosnian Serbs appear to have made a decision to pursue this tactic, rather than any bold new offensive, during the next phase of the war. Already stretched by the long front line in an increasingly stalemated war, and already holding 70 percent of Bosnian territory, they have little incentive to take more land.

Appearing on Bosnian Serb television on Friday night, General Mladic offered a complete cease-fire throughout Bosnia as the basis for a political settlement to the conflicts in the former Yugoslavia. His message was clear: the Serbs will not accept an American-backed peace plan offering the Serbs 49 percent of Bosnia and the Muslim-led Government 51 percent, but they are ready to negotiate now for peace on adjusted terms.

But the Bosnian Government, its army gradually improving, is not interested in peace on those terms. Mr. Muftic said he believed the war would go on several years.

Is such a long war — undermining Europe, destabilizing the Balkans and straining transatlantic relations — acceptable to the United States?

The thrust of the Clinton Administration's policy now is that Serbia's pressure on the Bosnian Serbs will eventually force General Mladic and Dr. Karadzic to yield to the proposed peace. Moreover, further pressure on the Serbs may be applied by a lifting of the arms embargo on the Bosnian Government forces by November.

This may look like a genuine effort to resolve the war, but in reality it appears more like an attempt to insure that the war is contained within the borders of Bosnia.

The understanding with President Milosevic has effectively removed Serbia from direct involvement in the Bosnian conflict, in much the same way as accords earlier this year with President Franjo Tudjman of Croatia insured that Croatia's military ambitions in Bosnia were curbed.

But United States military analysts are aware that the Yugoslav Army is already supplying the Bosnian Serbs and, in a crunch, would not abandon them. Thus, the Serbian embargo may discomfort the Bosnian Serbs but not force them to yield.

At the same time, even if the arms embargo is lifted — and Britain, France and Russia are pushing hard to insure that any decision is delayed until after the winter — the effect on the military situation is likely to be gradual at best.

The end result could be a dirty little war in Bosnia, with America quietly supplying arms to the Bosnian Muslims, Russia quietly supplying matériel to the Serbs through Serbia, and the borders secured against any wider conflagration.

This may be the best that can be hoped in a country born into war and unwanted by at least a third of its inhabitants. But it is a scenario offering little comfort to the caged and weary people lining up for water in Sarajevo.

Reuters

A hospital worker folding sheets yesterday at the Kosevo Hospital in Sarajevo, the Bosnian capital. The hospital, which is almost completely lacking electricity and heating gas, uses wood-fired stoves to heat water.

British Commander in Bosnia: In a Quagmire and Sniped at From All Sides

By ROGER COHEN
Special to The New York Times

SARAJEVO, Bosnia and Herzegona, Sept. 24 — Eight months ago, n unusually charismatic British eneral arrived in this city vowing to pen the roads, restore basic utilities d bring at least a semblance of rmal life back to Sarajevo.

Today, shelling of Sarajevo has rtually stopped and, even two days fter a NATO air strike, gunfire is are. But the roads out of Sarajevo re sealed, electricity, water and gas ave been cut for 10 days, the streetars are no longer running and weay people are again lining up at the ver to fill containers of water. Meanwhile, Lieut. Gen. Sir Michael Rose, the commander of United Naions forces in Bosnia, is in London.

Officially, he is there on a routine isit. But senior United Nations offiials said that a sharp dispute had merged over whether General Rose hould serve his full one-year term. Already, a possible replacement is eing discussed: Maj. Gen. Rupert Smith, the man who commanded

planes to take off" on Thursday. The latter phrase was a reference to United Nations forces, who called in the NATO air strike after two French peacekeepers were wounded in separate Serbian attacks.

It is because the Clinton Administration has chosen not to have American troops on the ground in Bosnia and has repeatedly argued the most strongly for the NATO air strikes, which might endanger the British, French and other troops here, that General Rose has apparently lost patience with the American position.

Officials said the United Nations commander had clashed sharply this month with NATO over plans to carry out air strikes against Serbian guns firing on the Bihac pocket in northwestern Bosnia. He has also urged patience with respect to Serbian violations of a ban on artillery within a 12.5-mile radius of Sarajevo.

The general's caution reflects what appears to have been a profound shift in his position.

He arrived talking of sophisticated

Mladic, the skillful but ruthless commander of the Bosnian Serbs, he had an interlocutor who was a real officer well versed in warfare. The Bosnian Army offered only a ramshackle collection of fighters whom the general increasingly regarded as unreliable, untrustworthy and naïve.

The second was his fury at the loss of a British soldier during the Serbian onslaught on Gorazde in April, a death he attributed to Muslim-led Bosnian forces' abruptly turning and running in front of the British position. "One bloke with a crowbar could have stopped them, but they turned and ran," he said of the Bosnian action.

The third was his exasperation in June during a futile week in Geneva when the Bosnian Serbs were ready to sign a six-month truce, but the Bosnian Vice President, Ejup Ganic, stood firm against a long cease-fire that might consolidate the Serbian military advantage.

"Ganic and Rose were so close to blows I thought there would be a

This week, after an outbreak of fighting in Sarajevo, he accused the Muslim-led Bosnian Army of trying "to create images of war for the world, to get us to respond with air power." General Rose warned that allied air power might instead be used against the Bosnian Army.

The suggestion provoked incredulity among many NATO and United Nations officials. The notion that American F-16's would ever attack Bosnian Government forces appears extremely remote.

"There's a feeling among some people that General Rose might have exhausted himself and that the cooler hand of General Smith might now be beneficial," said a senior United Nations official, speaking on condition of anonymity. General Smith, 51, has followed the Bosnian situation closely in his current job as assistant chief of defense staff operations and security.

But it seems unclear whether it is General Rose who is exhausted or it is his position that is inherently un-

Figure 3.7 Interior page of *The New York Times*, September 25, 1994. Courtesy of PARS International.

here, something able to be made legible and it doesn't have to announce itself to register. "The invisibility of whiteness as a racial position," Richard Dyer laments, "is of a piece with its ubiquity."[21] Ubiquity functions here in its visual disavowal, the empty space between object and subject that viewers navigate, aided or not. Dyer continues:

> Death may in some traditions be a vivid experience, but within much of the white tradition it is a blank that may be immateriality (pure spirit) or else just nothing at all. This is within the logics of whiteness even if it is not at the forefront of white identity. White people have a colour, but it is a colour that also signifies the absence of colour, itself a characteristic of life and presence. In the transparent representation of the culture of light, the white face has to be read in the blanks on the paper or screen. To be positioned as an overseeing subject without properties may lead one to wonder if one is a subject at all.[22]

To leave whiteness on this mortal coil is to engender a vulnerability that whiteness refuses to occupy. It is to lay bare the contradictions born of binary modes of seeing, and it is a difficult endeavor. As a result, documentary images, particularly as they exist in the *New York Times* and other periodicals, reinforces the idea that whiteness and death are intermingled, but also projections of cultural refusal. So much so that white vulnerability is rendered precious and black fungibility mundane. *What is the proof that white people die?* This is an archival question still yet unanswered.

September 1994 was a difficult month to be black within the pages of the *New York Times*. Over the course of that tumultuous month, the newspaper featured numerous corpses in various states of decay, nearly all featuring a body marked by its vicarious distance from the eager eyes of the viewer. The removal of the *Times* subject from the violation on display does a tremendous amount of cultural work. For the suburban American subject, gifted with the relative and physical distance of belonging, the images can sadden and disturb, enlighten and enrage. Given the range of possibility, it is little wonder that the temporal multiplicity of *blackness as woundedness* exists so fully as to be commonplace. What we can gather from the pioneering scholarship in existence for the last hundred years on lynching is that this phenomenon of public violence has a tangible linchpin: the keepsake. In a desire to revisit the experience and a communally-inspired quest to share the occasion with others, photographs and postcards became key to this display. The difference now is the keepsake is delivered to our homes daily or viewed privately over the internet or retrieved without the viewer having to leave the comfort of the domestic sphere.

In a September 26, 1994, image from the US intervention, a group of mourning women dressed in white stand over the corpse of a loved one lying in a Port-au-Prince street. They seem only tangentially aware of the multiple photographers clamoring together to capture the moment of unearthed anguish. The shadowed people are the ones with the power. Their lenses repeat a story of conquest and articulated self-destruction, as the sun's position casts their silhouettes on the ground close to the dead man's body.

Two hundred years after the invention of photography, it is still absence and hyperpresence that naturalizes and delineates. Dead black bodies normalized through the absence of dead white bodies; "that has been" replaced by a lulling "this should be." Given photography's conflicted relationship with representing the other, it is no wonder that its earliest resonance coincides with an intractable difference—negative to positive—an optical opposition. "Being a spectator of calamities taking place in another country is a quintessential modern experience," Susan Sontag tells us.[23] "In fact, there are many uses of the innumerable opportunities a modern life supplies for regarding at a distance, through the medium of photography—other people's pain."[24] How might we attempt to address the trauma black people experience while they grapple with humanity so fraught that its very visibility is a problem? "Acts of remembrance," Edwidge Danticat writes,

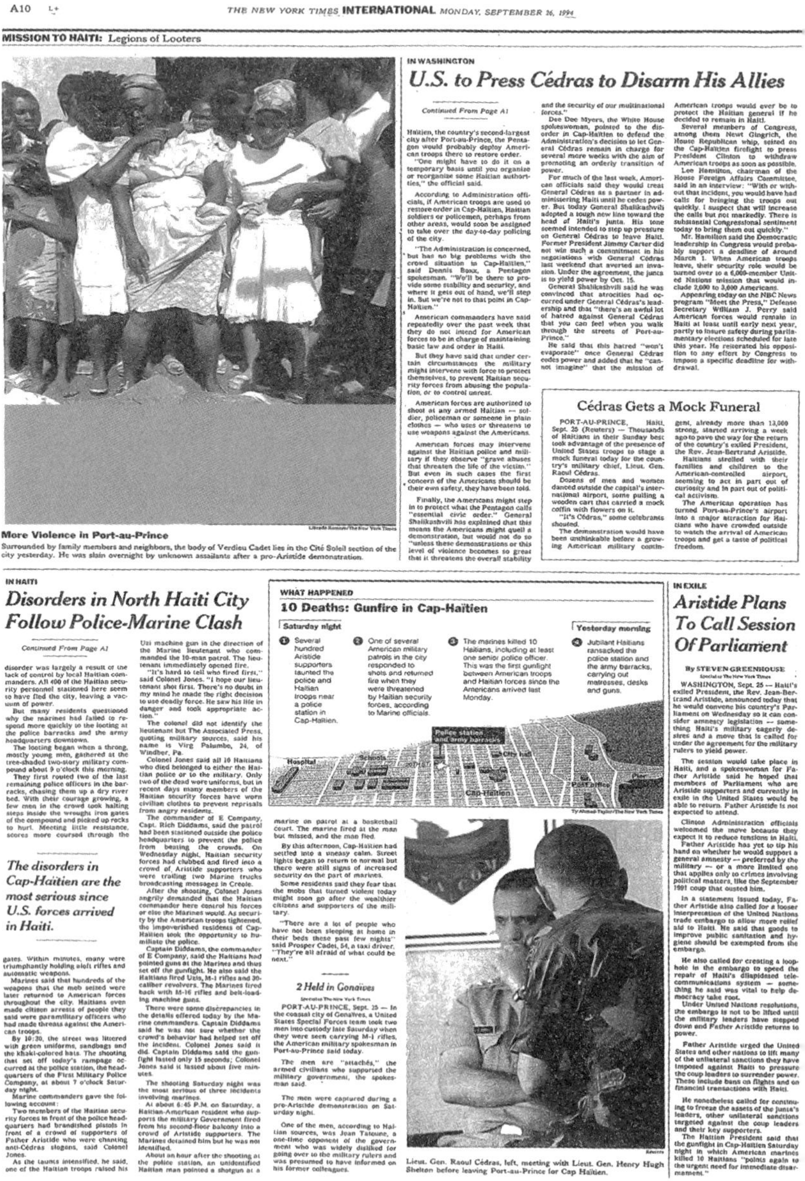

A10 L+ THE NEW YORK TIMES INTERNATIONAL MONDAY, SEPTEMBER 26, 1994

MISSION TO HAITI: Legions of Looters

IN WASHINGTON

U.S. to Press Cédras to Disarm His Allies

Continued From Page A1

Haïtien, the country's second-largest city after Port-au-Prince, the Pentagon would probably deploy American troops there to restore order.

"One might have to do it on a temporary basis until you organize or reorganize some Haitian authorities," the official said.

According to Administration officials, if American troops are used to restore order in Cap-Haïtien, Haitian soldiers or policemen, perhaps from other areas, would soon be assigned to take over the day-to-day policing of the city.

"The Administration is concerned, but has no big problems with the crowd situation in Cap-Haïtien," said Dennis Boxx, a Pentagon spokesman. "We'll be there to provide some stability and security, and where it gets out of hand, we'll step in. But we're not to that point in Cap-Haïtien."

American commanders have said repeatedly over the past week that they do not intend for American forces to be in charge of maintaining basic law and order in Haiti.

But they have said that under certain circumstances the military might intervene with force to protect themselves, to prevent Haitian security forces from abusing the population, or to control unrest.

American forces are authorized to shoot at any armed Haitian — soldier, policeman or someone in plain clothes — who uses or threatens to use weapons against the Americans.

American forces may intervene against the Haitian police and military if they observe "grave abuses that threaten the life of the victim." But even in such cases the first concern of the Americans should be their own safety, they have been told.

Finally, the Americans might step in to protect what the Pentagon calls "essential civic order." General Shalikashvili has explained that this means the Americans might quell a demonstration, but would not do so "unless these demonstrations or this level of violence becomes so great that it threatens the overall stability and the security of our multinational forces."

Dee Dee Myers, the White House spokeswoman, pointed to the disorder in Cap-Haïtien to defend the Administration's decision to let General Cédras remain in charge for several more weeks with the aim of promoting an orderly transition of power.

For much of the last week, American officials said they would treat General Cédras as a partner in administering Haiti until he cedes power. But today General Shalikashvili adopted a tough new line toward the head of Haiti's junta. His tone seemed intended to step up pressure on General Cédras to leave Haiti. Former President Jimmy Carter did not win such a commitment in his negotiations with General Cédras last weekend that averted an invasion. Under the agreement, the junta is to yield power by Oct. 15.

General Shalikashvili said he was convinced that atrocities had occurred under General Cédras's leadership and that "there's an awful lot of hatred against General Cédras that you can feel when you walk through the streets of Port-au-Prince."

He said that this hatred "won't evaporate" once General Cédras cedes power and added that he "cannot imagine" that the mission of American troops would ever be to protect the Haitian general if he decided to remain in Haiti.

Several members of Congress, among them Newt Gingrich, the House Republican whip, seized on the Cap-Haïtien firefight to press President Clinton to withdraw American troops as soon as possible.

Lee Hamilton, chairman of the House Foreign Affairs Committee, said in an interview: "With or without that incident, you would have had calls for bringing the troops out quickly. I suspect that will increase the calls but not markedly. There is substantial Congressional sentiment today to bring them out quickly."

Mr. Hamilton said the Democratic leadership in Congress would probably support a deadline of around March 1. When American troops leave, their security role would be turned over to a 6,000-member United Nations mission that would include 2,000 to 3,000 Americans.

Appearing today on the NBC News program "Meet the Press," Defense Secretary William J. Perry said American forces would remain in Haiti at least until early next year, partly to insure safety during parliamentary elections scheduled for late this year. He reiterated his opposition to any effort by Congress to impose a specific deadline for withdrawal.

Cédras Gets a Mock Funeral

PORT-AU-PRINCE, Haiti, Sept. 25 (Reuters) — Thousands of Haitians in their Sunday best took advantage of the presence of United States troops to stage a mock funeral today for the country's military chief, Lieut. Gen. Raoul Cédras.

Dozens of men and women danced outside the capital's international airport, some pulling a wooden cart that carried a mock coffin with flowers on it.

"It's Cédras," some celebrants shouted.

The demonstration would have been unthinkable before a growing American military contingent, already more than 13,000 strong, started arriving a week ago to pave the way for the return of the country's exiled President, the Rev. Jean-Bertrand Aristide.

Haitians strolled with their families and children to the American-controlled airport, seeming to act in part out of curiosity and in part out of political activism.

The American operation has turned Port-au-Prince's airport into a major attraction for Haitians who have crowded outside to watch the arrival of American troops and get a taste of political freedom.

Librado Romero/The New York Times

More Violence in Port-au-Prince

Surrounded by family members and neighbors, the body of Verdieu Cadet lies in the Cité Soleil section of the city yesterday. He was slain overnight by unknown assailants after a pro-Aristide demonstration.

IN HAITI

Disorders in North Haiti City Follow Police-Marine Clash

Continued From Page A1

disorder was largely a result of the lack of control by local Haitian commanders. All 400 of the Haitian security personnel stationed here seem to have fled the city, leaving a vacuum of power.

But many residents questioned why the marines had failed to respond more quickly to the looting at the police barracks and the army headquarters downtown.

The looting began when a throng, mostly young men, gathered at the tree-shaded two-story military compound about 9 o'clock this morning. They first routed two of the last remaining police officers in the barracks, chasing them up a dry river bed. With their courage growing, a few men in the crowd took halting steps inside the wrought iron gates of the compound and picked up rocks to hurl. Meeting little resistance, scores more coursed through the gates. Within minutes, many were triumphantly holding aloft rifles and automatic weapons.

The disorders in Cap-Haïtien are the most serious since U.S. forces arrived in Haiti.

Marines said that hundreds of the weapons that the mob seized were later returned to American forces throughout the city. Haitians even made citizen arrests of people they said were paramilitary officers who had made threats against the American troops.

By 10:30, the street was littered with green uniforms, sandbags and the khaki-colored hats. The shooting that set off today's rampage occurred at the police station, the headquarters of the First Military Police Company, at about 7 o'clock Saturday night.

Marine commanders gave the following account:

Two members of the Haitian security forces in front of the police headquarters had brandished pistols in front of a crowd of supporters of Father Aristide who were chanting anti-Cédras slogans, said Colonel Jones.

As the taunts intensified, he said, one of the Haitian troops raised his Uzi machine gun in the direction of the Marine lieutenant who commanded the 10-man patrol. The lieutenant immediately opened fire.

"It's hard to tell who fired first," said Colonel Jones. "I hope our lieutenant shot first. There's no doubt in my mind he made the right decision to use deadly force. He saw his life in danger and took appropriate action."

The colonel did not identify the lieutenant but The Associated Press, quoting military sources, said his name is Virg Palumbo, 24, of Windber, Pa.

Colonel Jones said all 10 Haitians who died belonged to either the Haitian police or to the military. Only two of the dead wore uniforms, but in recent days many members of the Haitian security forces have worn civilian clothes to prevent reprisals from angry residents.

The commander of E Company, Capt. Rich Diddams, said the patrol had been stationed outside the police headquarters to prevent the police from beating the crowds. On Wednesday night, Haitian security forces had clubbed and fired into a crowd of Aristide supporters who were trailing two Marine trucks broadcasting messages in Creole.

After the shooting, Colonel Jones angrily demanded that the Haitian commander here control his forces or else the Marines would. As scrutiny by the American troops tightened, the impoverished residents of Cap-Haïtien took the opportunity to humiliate the police.

Captain Diddams, the commander of E Company, said the Haitians had pointed guns at the Marines and thus set off the gunfight. He also said the Haitians fired Uzis, M-1 rifles and 30-caliber revolvers. The Marines fired back with M-16 rifles and belt-loading machine guns.

There were some discrepancies in the details offered today by the Marine commanders. Captain Diddams said he was not sure whether the crowd's behavior had helped set off the incident. Colonel Jones said it did. Captain Diddams said the gunfight lasted only 15 seconds; Colonel Jones said it lasted about five minutes.

The shooting Saturday night was the most serious of three incidents involving marines.

At about 6:45 P.M. on Saturday, a Haitian-American resident who supports the military Government fired from his second-floor balcony into a crowd of Aristide supporters. The Marines detained him but he was not identified.

About an hour after the shooting at the police station, an unidentified Haitian man pointed a shotgun at a marine on patrol at a basketball court. The marine fired at the man but missed, and the man fled.

By this afternoon, Cap-Haïtien had settled into a uneasy calm. Street lights began to return to normal but there were still signs of increased security on the part of marines.

Some residents said they fear that the mobs that turned violent today might soon go after the wealthier citizens and supporters of the military.

"There are a lot of people who have not been sleeping at home in their beds these past few nights" said Prosper Cadet, 54, a taxi driver. "They're all afraid of what could be next."

2 Held in Gonaïves

Special to The New York Times

PORT-AU-PRINCE, Sept. 25 — In the coastal city of Gonaïves, a United States Special Forces team took two men into custody late Saturday when they were seen carrying M-1 rifles, the American military spokesman in Port-au-Prince said today.

The men are "attachés," the armed civilians who supported the military government, the spokesman said.

The men were captured during a pro-Aristide demonstration on Saturday night.

One of the men, according to Haitian sources, was Jean Tatoune, a one-time opponent of the government who was widely disliked for going over to the military rulers and was presumed to have informed on his former colleagues.

WHAT HAPPENED

10 Deaths: Gunfire in Cap-Haïtien

Saturday night

1 Several hundred Aristide supporters taunted the police and Haitian troops near a police station in Cap-Haïtien.

2 One of several American military patrols in the city responded to shots and returned fire when they were threatened by Haitian security forces, according to Marine officials.

3 The marines killed 10 Haitians, including at least one senior police officer. This was the first gunfight between American troops and Haitian forces since the Americans arrived last Monday.

Yesterday morning

4 Jubilant Haitians ransacked the police station and the army barracks, carrying out mattresses, desks and guns.

Police station and army barracks
Hospital
Schools
City hall
Cap-Haïtien
Pier
Post office

Ty Ahmad-Taylor/The New York Times

Reuters

Lieut. Gen. Raoul Cédras, left, meeting with Lieut. Gen. Henry Hugh Shelton before leaving Port-au-Prince for Cap Haïtien.

IN EXILE

Aristide Plans To Call Session Of Parliament

By STEVEN GREENHOUSE

Special to The New York Times

WASHINGTON, Sept. 25 — Haiti's exiled President, the Rev. Jean-Bertrand Aristide, announced today that he would convene his country's Parliament on Wednesday so it can consider amnesty legislation — something Haiti's military eagerly desires and a move that is called for under the agreement for the military rulers to yield power.

The session would take place in Haiti, and a spokeswoman for Father Aristide said he hoped that members of Parliament who are Aristide supporters and currently in exile in the United States would be able to return. Father Aristide is not expected to attend.

Clinton Administration officials welcomed the move because they expect it to reduce tensions in Haiti.

Father Aristide has yet to tip his hand on whether he would support a general amnesty — preferred by the military — or a more limited one that applies only to crimes involving political matters, like the September 1991 coup that ousted him.

In a statement issued today, Father Aristide also called for a looser interpretation of the United Nations trade embargo to allow more relief aid to Haiti. He said that goods to improve public sanitation and hygiene should be exempted from the embargo.

He also called for creating a loophole in the embargo to speed the repair of Haiti's dilapidated telecommunications system — something he said was vital to help democracy take root.

Under United Nations resolutions, the embargo is not to be lifted until the military leaders have stepped down and Father Aristide returns to power.

Father Aristide urged the United States and other nations to lift many of the unilateral sanctions they have imposed against Haiti to pressure the coup leaders to surrender power. These include bans on flights and on financial transactions with Haiti.

He nonetheless called for continuing to freeze the assets of the junta's leaders, other unilateral sanctions targeted against the coup leaders and their key supporters.

The Haitian President said that the gunfight in Cap-Haïtien Saturday night in which American marines killed 10 Haitians "points again to the urgent need for immediate disarmament."

Figure 3.8 Interior page of the *New York Times*, September 26, 1994. Courtesy of PARS International. This image has been altered from its original form.

"like pieces of art, can also surface out of daily rituals, even interrupted ones. A place setting left unused at a dinner table. An oversize shoe into which we slip a foot. A tearstained journal in which we scribble a few words about unclaimed bones."[25] But what of a visual politics of remembrance that insists upon the destruction of black subjects? How can this mandate be undone?

For the short period in which US soldiers were stationed in Port-au-Prince, the cover images of the *New York Times* engendered the idea of *Haiti as death knell*. In a chaotic barrage of violent images, the narrative of impossible black governance takes on new meaning at the end of the year, particularly as South Africa is months into its new nationhood. From the earliest black republic in the western hemisphere to the most recent nation to renew itself after decades of white supremacist juridical rule, Haiti is a nation of contrasts, reconfigurations, and renewals.

The body of the soldier is shadowed to a silhouette, but his automatic rifle is not. The weapon is clearly displayed, leaning diagonally across the soldier's knee, in close proximity to a small child sitting against a walled barrier. Her arms are crossed and resting on her knees. There is a straw sun hat on her head that is slanted to her right. In an extended reading of this image, the viewer, it must be presumed, is encouraged to imagine the future of Haiti (as represented by the child) as one that is always under the gun, a history that collapses two hundred years of independence into a single referendum on the nation's fraught sovereignty. That this intervention, the second major occupation of Haiti by the United States, is barely noted in the newspaper should strike one as odd, and yet documentary photographs endeavor to normalize military interference. It is as if Haiti is ever the small child, set against a barrier, waiting for an external paternalistic rescue. So both inexperience and imminent death stalk the photograph as it appears to the viewer. As with the majority of these swiftly taken shots, there is no name attributed to the photographed

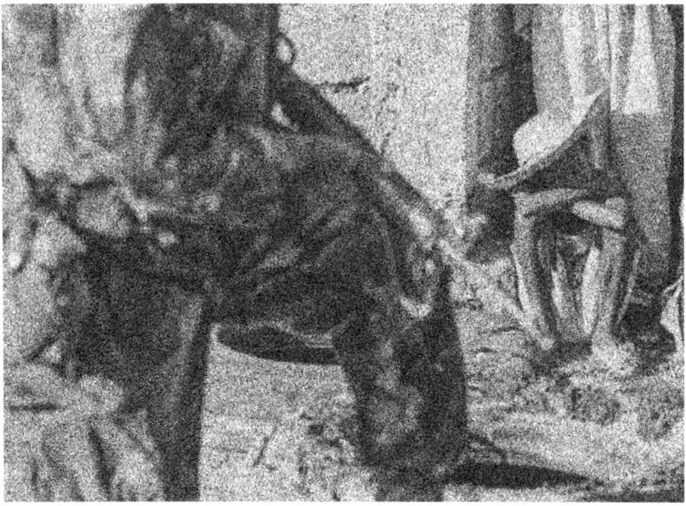

Figure 3.9 AP Photo / John McConnico, September 22, 1994.

subject and no further information provided. A trace of photographic training (a Barthesian *studium noir*) operates at an angle, a slant that diverges away from black subjectivity. This slant facilitates a diagonal slope of care moving from invisible and omnipresent whiteness to ubiquitous but discardable blackness. That so many children are figured centrally in these images denotes the racial parameters of ocular investment assumed by *Times* readers and viewers. If, as Pooja Rangan asserts, "the prehistory of participatory documentary offers us one possible model for recouping the dialectical potential of the figure of the child," then what does it tell us about the visual expectation of what Rangan refers to as "feral innocence" that operates "as fetish"?[26] Are viewers to be trusted with the bodies of others when there is so much at stake?

The child's right eye can barely be seen in the photograph. The left eye is completely obscured by shadow. The one eye stares out from the darkness and into the perception of light. Scholars of black and white photography have purposely tussled with binaries of light and dark, "good" and "bad," and this is the inflection the image offers. What is the "bad" on view here? Is it conditional (the intervention), national (Haiti as a "bad" sovereign), generational (and the children suffer), or racial (blackness as imminent death)? Here, shadow (shade) demarcates the photographic space between object and subject as the rifle at the center of the image (the object) indexes the child at the far right of the photograph (the subject). Little room is left to say what is present outside the imagery of force and failure. Fragments of space are available to occupy the eye beyond the structure of this binary: Force that is necessary due to the elongation of national (read: racial) failure. Failure that has been destined since the founding of Haiti after the revolution. Force and failure bracket the imagistic engagement Haiti has with the media as this is the only narrative that has been allowed to prosper. External force and internal failure. The idea of revolution, of freedom, is repeatedly undermined.

SAINT DOMINGUE GIVES BIRTH TO HAITI

Haiti enters the visual field of the Atlantic world narrative under its former name, Saint Domingue. As contemporary historians have noted, part of Haiti's deployment in the political imaginary is measured through the multiple crops the colony yielded for the empire of France. According to Laurent Dubois, "The livelihood of as many as a million of the 25 million inhabitants of France depended directly on the colonial trade."[27] This trade was then as brutal and corporeally divisive as the contemporary entrapments of "good intentions," intoned by a visual relationship intimately encoded to show a nation in a constant state of upheaval. Before it was a modern site of imperialist deflection, it was the most profitable colony possession in the West—the bright light of early material and corporeal capitalism.[28]

In the way Haiti entered the global imaginary, it resembles the modern flashpoints of repeated engagement: a place and a people to fear, an infected and infecting populous (revolution, insubordination, disease, vodou, trauma), and the site of death on death. The specificity of the circumstantial is a large part of my interest here. Essentially, my aim in this book has been to use photography as a focal point of national and civic engagement postulating the viewer (Western, white) as the arbiter of inclusive humanity.

In the introduction to *Scenes of Subjection*, Saidiya Hartman speaks of those mainstays of racial violence in literature that "immure us to pain by virtue of their familiarity," noting that "they reinforce the spectacular character of black suffering." Of the pained body of the enslaved, she writes: "Are we witnesses who confirm the truth of what happened in the face of the world-destroying capacities of pain, the distortions of torture, the sheer unrepresentability of terror, and the repression of dominant accounts? Or are we voyeurs fascinated with and repelled by exhibitions of terror and sufferance? What does the exposure of the violated body yield? At issue here is the precariousness of empathy and the uncertain line between witness and spectator."[29] It is in this narrow space between witness and spectator that our imagistic sensibilities take form, cultivating the photographic rupture between the living and the dead, the subject and the subjected. W. E. B. Du Bois's famous query—"How does it feel to be a problem?"—has, by the end of the twentieth century, evolved. The question is now, "How do we solve the problem of black people?" And the answer is: visually. In other words, on the cusp of the twenty-first century, there remains a desire to see black people in a constant state of impending death. And photography delivers, aided by white supremacy. Christina Sharpe writes, "For if we are lucky, we live in the knowledge that the wake has positioned us as no-citizen," and from this position something new may be deciphered. Something new can emerge.[30]

In the days forward, scenes from the intervention inflect the flashpoint of engagement from a very specific emotive register. An absence of interest in the health, safety, and well-being of Haitians presents itself as a *cartography of the ocular*. This cartography narrows the field of vision for the *Times* subject, as blackness is easily consolidated into mortevivum—a proximity to death repeatedly rendered photographically. In the production of this default subjectivity, photographs mediate the space between citizenship and sentiment, and traverse this ground by following a road previously paved for white comfort and black suffering. No matter the geography, the comfort of the viewer, assumed to be white, is what foregrounds these images. This comfort creates silos of safety that are framed by the reinforced citizenship of global whiteness. Haiti is the figurative focal point that opens out onto modernity—the temporal aperture allowing light to enter but never self-illuminate. Illumination, as it has been articulated in a white supremacist production, is the province of the white West, and nowhere/no one else. *As they fall apart (disintegrate), so shall we coalesce (come together).* It all begins with Haiti.

In the days that follow, the *New York Times* will feature rhetorical replays of the tale of a white Bronco and a black defendant, news magazine covers with corrupted and manipulated photographs will be crafted to further darken the lack of distinction between race and extreme acts of violence. This will all happen in the span of the same month of registered visuality and display.

The months of inquiry into what will be eventually called the "trial of the century" occupy prime real estate in the *Times*. For the future trial in criminal court, *People v. O. J. Simpson*, race, class, fame, and violence seem to coalesce into a veritable circus of rage and entertainment. During the start-up to the trial that would dominate news media outlets for most of 1994 and 1995, in which Simpson would be acquitted of double murder, much was made of the circumstances surrounding the case, its famous defendant, and the racial discord engendered by the allegations. During the year, multiple pages were devoted to reporting on the murders and analyzing the evidence to be presented at the trial while synthesizing concurrent discussions about race in America. Simultaneous and astounding, the timing of the articles coincides with the intervention in Haiti, so

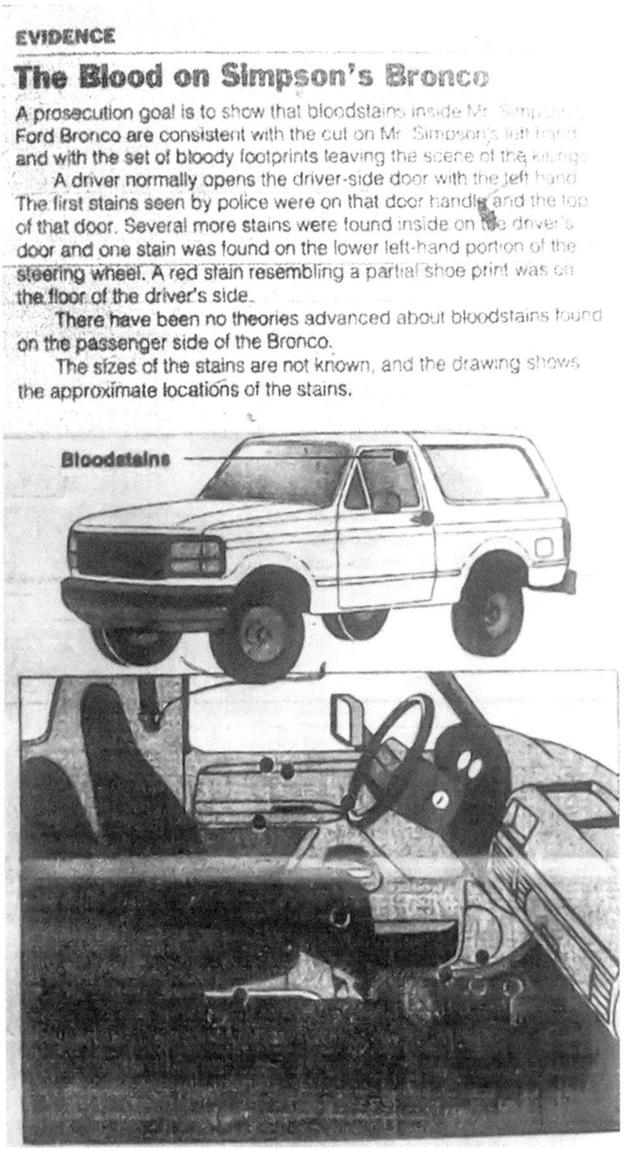

EVIDENCE

The Blood on Simpson's Bronco

A prosecution goal is to show that bloodstains inside Mr. Simpson's Ford Bronco are consistent with the cut on Mr. Simpson's left hand and with the set of bloody footprints leaving the scene of the killings.

A driver normally opens the driver-side door with the left hand. The first stains seen by police were on that door handle and the top of that door. Several more stains were found inside on the driver's door and one stain was found on the lower left-hand portion of the steering wheel. A red stain resembling a partial shoe print was on the floor of the driver's side.

There have been no theories advanced about bloodstains found on the passenger side of the Bronco.

The sizes of the stains are not known, and the drawing shows the approximate locations of the stains.

Figure 3.10 O. J. Simpson's Ford Bronco is entered into evidence. Courtesy of Los Angeles Police Department.

much so that there seems to be a cleanly distributed overlap between the island nation's destiny and Simpson's.

A visual stitching of documentary alignment becomes useful in its aggregate form. Images of mourning, like those appearing in the *New York Times*, highlight the temporal infrequency employed by viewers when those imbued with sympathy are visually set against those who are to engender no such thing. "These journalistic photographs," Barthes contends, "are received (all at once), perceived. I glance through them, I don't recall them; no detail (in some corner) ever interrupts my reading: I am interested in them," he continues. "I do not love them."[31] He does not have to "love them," but what is striking is that Barthes finds these photographs only of momentary interest, and never more than an aberration of investment. It is here, in the space of emotive extensions of care, that blackness is reified as a glance and a glance away. Regard and disregard. But the art of black study, the effort to find and reinforce a ritual of looking that produces the very intentional practice it uses to sustain itself, this must be the way forward.

Days of mourning follow the public display of dead bodies photographed and printed on the cover of the *New York Times*. The dead appear to be subjects worthy of investigation, but in truth they are objects of discourse, of dispossession. Sporadic information is provided about the dead and occasional notifications of funerals given. Family members are photographed in black, coming from or going to funeral processions. Amid a string of chaotic images connoting the spontaneity of national violence occurring in Haiti, there are interspersed scenes of gathered mourning practices presented for the viewer. Between the clarity of images of the dead and the photographic subterfuge of US military practices abroad, news media outlets curate this cartography of the ocular, which is centered around deserving deaths and invisible lives. Documentary photographs invest the viewer in a myriad of emotive mechanisms designed to bring an event into perspective. It matters that this perspective is a practiced loophole into which antiblackness slips. A space for nonblack pontification and black resistance, most of which happens as viewers sit with the quotidian task of news gathering. In the documentary apparatus of photography, eyes invested in the particularities of truth-making settle on a theme. The result is a transcription of antiblackness rendered visual.

"NO GRAPHIC WARNING"

One month after the massive earthquake that took place in Haiti on January 12, 2010, news media outlets refused to show images that might further upset the viewing public. Interestingly, these images were of the accident that killed a Winter Olympics luge athlete from the nation of Georgia, and not of the hundreds of thousands of Haitians killed by the earthquake. Viewers who watched the luge video were outraged by the sight and wrote in to various media outlets so that the video would be removed. The earthquake in Haiti, seen by tens of millions of Americans in an eerie loop of repeating imagery—corpses lining city streets, maimed, wounded, and semiconscious Haitian citizens recovering from severe trauma—did not elicit the same outrage. And if it did, it failed to move the media to the same ethical consideration of the dead.

For days and weeks after the accident at the Winter Olympics in Vancouver, viewers questioned the ethics of looking as it pertained to Nodar Kumaritashvili's luge crash. Viewers left responses to a question posed by Newsvine: Should the luge video have been aired on TV? A full 50 percent of survey participants said the video should not have been shown. With comments ranging from "A horrific video for loved ones & friends to have seen" to "if it were my family member (or even me) I wouldn't have wanted the world to see it," people were disturbed that the video was shown at all, never mind multiple times.[32] On the question of the earthquake in Haiti, there is no such dilemma. No "loved ones" or "friends" to consider. No family members to grieve for the dead, survive them, or mourn in private. There is no viewer backlash once documentary images proliferate in the media. It's worth examining why death and blackness are aligned via information-gathering sites that purport to bring news to the masses.

Contemporary videos of black people shot to death by police, wrestled to the ground and suffocated, or tased to death are ubiquitous in the United States and beyond its borders. Incredibly, even when the friends and family members of the victims of these public deaths request that photos and video footage of their dead bodies remain out of the public domain via social media, these requests are aggressively ignored.[33] Is antiblackness an ill that documentary impulses expose without the possibility of resolution? Can geography provide the template of meaning-making where black subjectivity can live and breathe without the threat of obliteration?

For Ariella Azoulay, what she terms the *civil contract of photography* "is a way to delineate part of the newly constructed space of civil relations that has been opened—and even necessitated—by photography."[34] For Haiti, this "newly constructed space of civil relations" is actually centuries old, but the advent of photographic practices extends the vibrancy of this familiar paradigm of destabilizing epistemology. Simply put, empires (France, Britain, Spain, the United States) participated in processes of mortevivum: rigidly discarding and objectifying based on a prescribed manipulation of ocular intimacies. They did so before the advent of photography, and therefore may have produced a *predetermined* negotiated proximity that provided the racialized gaze a viable (*violate*able) silver gelatin scapegoat. A corporeal *catastrophe*, as Azoulay might term it, that unfurls and repeats in a cadence of failed black self-governance.

And so it might be said that Haiti registers photographically to replace slave success (and revolutionary overthrow of the empire) with modernity's revenge: a visual culture determined to illustrate, with devastating immediacy, how little that has meant to the world. Although two hundred years of black independence has bored a hole into the hegemonic currency of the West, it is a hole filled with photographs of *nationhood as failure*. As an imagistic site of perpetual ruin, Haiti's relationship to the larger world falls under the thumb of what Ann Laura Stoler terms *imperial formations*. These formations are not tethered to a single, recognizable empire; rather, they are "*states of deferral* that mete out promissory notes that are not exceptions to their operation but constitutive of them: imperial guardianship, trusteeships, delayed autonomy, temporary intervention, conditional tutelage, military takeover in the name of human rights and security measures in the name of peace."[35] Haiti's status as a nation of the formerly enslaved and nonwhite eliminates its very capacity to be seen as a sovereign power. Because Haiti's emergence as a sovereign nation coincides with US imperialist missions (also involving enslaved peoples) that were easily threatened by the frightening concept of black revolution within or without the empire, a popular and enduring refrain emerges: that catastrophe follows all efforts to resist paternalistic protection.

Imperial dispossession is a photographic practice, an existing archive of destruction, enslavement, and scopic control. Its afterimage is a series of textual offerings that foreshadow the punitive return facilitated by the start of the Haitian Revolution. We are entering the third century of misaligned aggression: financial, political, social, historical. *Archives assemble.* Let us also consider the visual narrative of revolution that, curated and maintained for over two hundred years, resists consistent attempts at reinterpretation. As news media outlets merge temporalities, as they pertain to black agency and resistance, the productive deployment of sovereign failure is an antiblack photographic refrain. The viewer's projected investment extends the proliferation of the maimed (or contained) black world subject, offering the viewer the ability to slaughter with the eye those who have been foisted out of time. This is what it means to live perpetually in the psychic photographic space of black peoples' demise. A history of violence that repeats itself. A living thing, a dead offering.

CONCLUSION: WE, STILL

Two figures appear in a diptych, both highlighting the space between what was and what could have been. Photographer Dawoud Bey's *Birmingham Project* features an African American adult and a child side by side in a photograph. The child represents the age of one of the four girls murdered in the bombing of the Sixteenth Street Baptist Church in Birmingham, Alabama, in 1963. The adult represents the age the murdered girl would be had she survived. There is much imagistic control exhibited in the series. Each subject sits calmly, facing the viewer and marking the space of complicity—national, racial—that haunts the memory of the event. Four girls, aged eleven to fourteen, dead on a warm September morning. A series of black-and-white photographs, intimate in their construction, meditative in their presentation, and unyielding in their mission. On this subject, bell hooks writes, "Spaces of agency exist for black people, wherein we can both interrogate the gaze of the Other but also look back, and at one another, naming what we see."[1] Noting the importance of the returned gaze, hooks is determined to locate the spaces of resistant looking that animate black subjectivities. What she calls an *oppositional gaze* allows those caught in a vortex of violent imagery a place of redress and response.

"The four girls are a kind of mystic and abstract presence," Bey states in an interview. "I knew that I wanted to make work that gave them a more tangible, palpable presence." [2] This "more tangible palpable presence" allows for viewers to envelop a spatial realm without restricting the delicate work of healing from racial violence. The photographs offer a sliver of space, represented by the white line separating the two images in the diptych, where it is possible to bring black childhood and adulthood together without harm. But the nation, like the rest of the world, does not seem to be ready to imagine blackness outside of violence. Bey seeks to engender a visual enclosure that allows for recognition and indictment to coexist. The space between the two subjects is the burden of history and memory that should have been able to hold Addie Mae Collins, Cynthia Wesley, Carole Robertson, and Carol Denise McNair within it. Instead, viewers are asked to grapple with their absence and the nation's resistance to address domestic terrorism when the terror is white supremacist in nature.

As a student in high school, Jacquie Jones came across the lynching photograph from Indiana discussed in chapter 1. "I remember how long, how intently I looked at that photograph," she writes. The image was, according to Jones, "reproduced carelessly . . . added as an afterthought to whatever the text was, no doubt . . . something about it was so matter of fact."[3] The choice to show black subjects in various states of injury and death is done both carelessly and with the full force of intention. Little is thought of what this exposure does to black viewers, who are not assumed to be embodied in the term *viewer*.[4] Courtney R. Baker writes, "Considering the black body as a seeing body rather than a body to be seen is itself a significant move."[5] Jones is asked to process both the "seeing body" and the "body to be seen" in one visual exchange.

How do you evade capture when the containing apparatus is a photograph? Michael S. Harper tussles with this question in a series of poetic offerings I refer to as his *darkroom poems*. The suite of poems was first published in his 1972 collection *Song: I Want a Witness*. Beginning with "The Negatives," Harper engenders a black enclosure that he likens to a womb—a dark space of creation imbued with its own logic of protection where black lives can be imagined as matter.[6] In his attempt to mute the violence of photography's repetitive relationship to antiblackness, Harper's poems emphasize the violence inherent in any interaction with the external world, where white supremacy orients the way people are able to be seen. To hold blackness in its precise measure and to enclose it with care guarantees little. It is the effort, then, to render black subjectivity in all of its varied complexity that makes the gestural endeavor worthy of the pursuit. And yet, there is always the possibility that this will not ever be enough.

Although not exclusively its domain, the United States has a stranglehold on media images disseminated across the world. In this way, the United States structures the temperament of investment far beyond its borders. And because the nation's history is intertwined with black enslavement, indigenous slaughter and removal, theft and unacknowledged violence, the land is haunted and so are its people. Images manage the visuality of order where before only chaos thrived. Photographs reinforce a national "we" that never was and never will be. Out of this chaos, black photographers and image makers worked to offer the viewer evidence of range of visual possibilities embodied by members of the black diaspora.

The movement from displaying graphic death on photographic film to current video presentations has been facilitated by the advent of digital imaging technologies and social media. It is the next stage of the violent evolutionary tactics meted out against black subjects. Now, instead of a still image contained and held within a frame, we have moving images, films that provide corporeal presence and then cause viewers to witness their deaths. Snuff films, though they are rarely called by that name. And it is the long history of imagistic disregard that gives these death videos their point of origin. The desire to see black people on the precipice of death is something we should name and unpack. At its center is the understanding, created over time and with violent precision, that black life is so devoid of value that it need not be held with any regard. But regard is held; and so is the murderous application of a look. A practice of racial sociopathy where the understanding, implicit in the display of dying black subjects, is that this is the arena of belonging to which we are relegated. From Laquan McDonald and Eric Garner to Philando Castille and George Floyd, there is a ready audience eager to watch us die.

This very evening, as I write this conclusion, Memphis police will release bodycam footage of Tyre Nichols, a twenty-nine-year-old black man beaten to death by five black police officers. White supremacy, as we know, has no race. "Blacks know something about black cops," James Baldwin writes in *The Devil Finds Work*. "They know how much the black cop has to prove, and how limited are his means of proving it."[7] Having seen the video, Nichols's family released their own images to represent their loved one. In a mixture of still images and video clips, we see Nichols doing what he loves—skateboarding—gliding on and off railings and ledges, his body lanky and long. His moves are joyful and effortless. The release of the officers' bodycam footage, a snuff film with a 6:00 p.m. EST scheduling time, was then discussed heavily on social media, with the understanding that black people would yet again be traumatized without recourse.

Elizabeth Alexander's vital question about the visuality of suffering black folks have to navigate is instrumental. "Can you be black and look at this?" is an insular question posed to the people most affected by repeated viewings of anti-black violence. "Black bodies in pain for public consumption,"

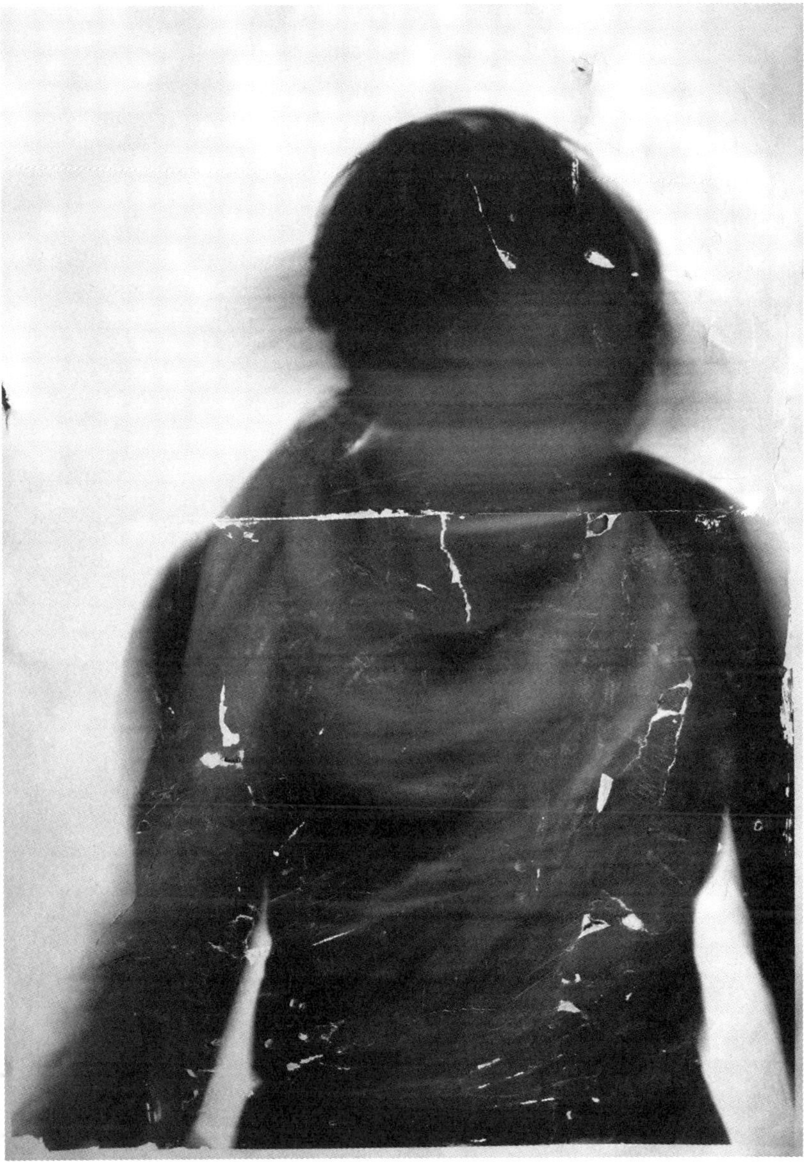

Figure 4.1 Sandra Brewster, Blur *1, 2/3*, 2016-17. Courtesy of the artist.

Alexander writes, "have been an American national spectacle for centuries."[8] Not just national, but global—a global spectacle that takes black pain and black death as its point of departure. The "paranoid color wheel" that James Baldwin articulates is the gleaming void of meaning that encircles black being.[9] Navigating this requires vigilance, patience, fortitude, and mercy. Because, like most antiblack structures of order, this too must be seen through the spectacle of race. Black subjects gather within an externally imposed visual forfeiture of worth rendered photographically. Instead of acquiescing to the dispossession on offer, alternate sites of retrieval are deployed by the collective, with the understanding that even this might not work.

Sandra Brewster's 2017 series *It's All a Blur* (or *Blur*) features photographic portraits in motion, parsing out the space between stillness and movement. Taken over a series of years, Brewster's photographs give the viewer a way to temper the harm of a one-sided gaze. Her subjects are photographed while in motion, moving their heads from side to side. The result is a print blurred with painterly figuration *within* abstraction. The subject's face is faded out, thickening the texture of the image. This is a present haunting—figures there and also not there. Blackness bathed in the protective submersion of anonymity. Harper continues:

She shades the prints bathed
in what iron water there is,
artesian iron spring water;
pictures of wintergreen
blur in darkness,
the second hand stops.[10]

The "second hand stops" in a swirl of recognition that the image is beyond the fixations of time.

On a saturated blue archival print Carrie Mae Weems offers the viewer one way to *blur in darkness* and evade the fixed delineation of photographic antiblackness. Part of her 2016

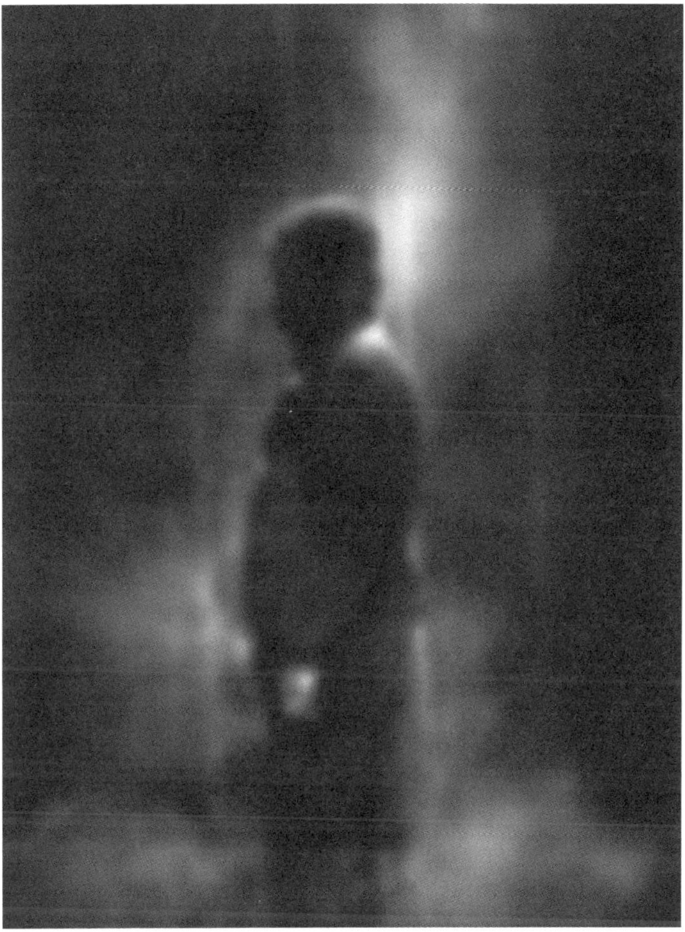

Figure 4.2 Carrie Mae Weems, *All the Boys (Profile 1)*, 2016. Courtesy of the artist.

series *The Usual Suspects*, Weems casts a shadowed figure / a figure as shadow into the visual field. Accompanied by quantitative death data that enters the public sphere through the media, Weems focuses instead on black life—individual, collective—that undergirds the violences experienced. Weems aims to hold fast to the humanity of black subjects killed violently and often publicly, thus not afforded such measure. Each archival print serves as a reminder—that there is someone in the image—*somebody* in the frame. That they are remembered. Regarded. Loved.

Temporality is a fixation that blackness cannot abide. Photography aids and abets, but this is not the whole story. We *blur in darkness* where legibility is the command. But our existence, such that it is, is a phenomenon that seeps through the frame of the photograph to reveal the world beyond it. A world of patient looking that envelops the subject with the determined patience of the beloved who would recognize your body from a silhouette presented to them in low light. A look that reminds you that you "will not die here." *We will not die here,* in the two-dimensional space of disregard that is deployed under the moniker of *evidence*. We will continue to exceed the frame of the photograph so that it will not be the only way to define us. We will have beauty without terror and without violence. And we will have justice, "for the living and the dead," as Toni Morrison assures us.[11] Everything else is detritus.

US

It was the first time I got choked up during a presentation, and the last time I have shown graphic images of black death while giving a talk. While I had quietly agreed to manage the psychic toll of this project for myself, I had not thought enough about the book's presence as a traumatizing force that other black people would have to guard themselves against. To evade, like a series of triggers with no warnings or a public showing of *Gone with the Wind* that nobody told you would be playing at your favorite theater. I was a visiting Martin Luther King fellow at

We will continue to exceed the frame of the photograph so that it will not be the only way to define us. We will have beauty without terror and without violence.

the Massachusetts Institute of Technology for the 2017–2018 academic year, and this was my project presentation talk. These talks are public and are often attended by faculty and staff at the institution. This talk was the first time I was presenting work on photography and antiblackness to an audience that was more than 50 percent black. And there I was, being asked a question that was so devastating in its perplexing simplicity that I was instantly overcome with emotion. "Why do they hate us so much?" was the woman's question. I can only remember responding, "I don't know." And I still don't. What I do know is that pleasure is derived for some just by having a proximity to viewing black people in pain. And photographs of black suffering proliferate so that this can be done with little recourse for the victims of such violence.

In her poem "photograph," Lucille Clifton lingers lovingly over an image of her grandsons "spinning in their joy" while the poet, their grandmother, registers a prayer that is also a lamentation:

universe
keep them turning
turning
black blurs against the window
of the world
for they are beautiful
and there is trouble coming
round and round and round[12]

The speaker speaks of not only an inner vision deepened by racial intuition, but "trouble coming" that she can hear or touch, and an understanding of the world shaped by the meaning making of blackness as fungibility. Yet in her mind's eye, there is the photograph: grandsons who are safe and free, children at play, "black blurs" that she wants to hold to that moment, that freedom, in the hopes that this image is normalized over the proliferation of photographs marked as documentary but aggressively participating in aestheticizing black death. We have many examples of the devastating immediacy that attends black engagements with public space. This poem provides the possibility of containing this engagement, this effort to use dark space in a more meaningful way.

I think about that day at MIT a lot. I think about the way my tunnel vision exposed me to the fallacies embedded in the project. I think of the woman who posed a question within a wail. I think of my inability to give her an answer that made any sense. "For from our original expectations of increased intimacy and broader knowledge," Toni Morrison writes, "media presentations deploy images and language that narrow our view of what humans look like (or ought to look like) and what in fact we are like."[13] This is still the case, particularly when photography deepens a two-dimensional relationship with the aftermath of slavery and Western imperialist violences framed within. And black subjects fight for the kind of photographic redemption song worthy of our complex humanity, our complex history. Harper writes,

She shakes the developing tank
as a uterus
mixing developer
to the negatives
where no light appears . . .
a simple enlarger,
a bulb with a shade,
images born through her lens
packed on the contact sheet;
fatted negatives under thick
condenser glass,
prints from her uterus,
cramps from her developing tank.[14]

We live in the exposure to light that corrupts our relationship to the external world. We live with the knowledge of our imagistic dispossession.

And yet, this is not the end of our story. We are not remanded to the strictures of a singular photographic display. Exceeding the frame of capture is one way we navigate the world of the visual when that world is eager to violently include us. In this way, we alter the temporalities of containment that disallow our complex humanity. Our complex vision. We are so much more than the way we are imagined by others. My hope is that we continue to gravitate toward representations that reflect our interior lives while leaving room for the exigencies of movement, stillness, and time.

We are so much more than the way we are imagined by others.

ACKNOWLEDGMENTS

This book has lived with me like a second self I took everywhere I went. From writing *Mortevivum*, I have learned patience and purpose, fury, and profound sorrow. I have been fortunate to come through the other side of its creation a better human, and this is in no small part due to the support I have had around me. I want to begin with Victoria Hindley at the MIT Press, who held an admirable certainty about this book when I did not. I thank you for your code of ethics, your insight and vision, the way that you listen, and all you are able to see. Gabriela Bueno Gibbs, Mary Reilly, Kathleen Caruso, Melinda Rankin, Allison Levy, and the whole Brown University Digital Publications team have my profound thanks for the work that has gone into shaping this project into its current form. To the anonymous reviewers of the book manuscript, I am grateful for the time and effort you put into your suggestions and comments.

The first seed of *Mortevivum* was presented at the Feeling Photography conference in Toronto, ON, in 2009. I thank the organizers, Thy Phy, Elspeth Brown, and the members of the Toronto Photography Seminar for the opportunity to be part of that important conversation. My essay, "Regarding the Pain of the Other: Photography, Famine, and the Transference of Affect," was later published in the edited collection *Feeling Photography* (2014). I have presented parts of this project in one form or another to audiences at Emory University, the Massachusetts Institute of Technology, the University of Pennsylvania, Simmons University, The University of Toronto, Brown University, Tufts University, CUNY Graduate Center, Harvard University, and OCAD University, Toronto. I want to thank series editors Gabrielle Moser and Adrienne Huard, SAGE Publications, and the *Journal of Visual Culture* for the opportunity to reprint a portion of my essay "You and Eye in the Afterlives of Images" in *Mortevivum*.

This project was supported by a Martin Luther King Jr. Visiting Fellowship at the Massachusetts Institute of Technology. My enduring appreciation goes to Sandy Alexandre, Helen Elaine Lee, Mary C. Fuller, Wyn Kelly, Joaquin Terrones, Ed Bertschinger, and Sophia Hasenfus for making my time there so incredibly productive. I completed the book manuscript in my first semester as the Richard D. Cohen Fellow at Harvard University's W. E. B. Du Bois Research Institute at the Hutchins Center. To Henry Louis Gates Jr., Abby Wolf, Krishna Lewis, and the rest of the Hutchins Center community, I want you to know that my time there was a gift of black studies centrality, and it came at the exact moment it was needed. To my *fellow-fellows*: your effortless brilliance does not surprise me, but your remarkable cross-disciplinary engagement and care will stay with me for a long time.

The years I spent at Mount Holyoke College have given me great colleagues and greater friends. Iyko Day made the Five Colleges area a refuge for scholars of color seeking communion. I aim to create community with such elegance and precision. David Hernández, aside from being my left-handed comrade, is a sonically attuned master of musical selections.

Each of his suggestions have made their way into my sound lists. Wesley Yu marks this world with a seemingly effortless calm disposition and genuine interest in others. He makes me want to read medieval literature *for fun*. Ellen Alvord is what joy in a museum looks like. I will always take the opportunity to visit an exhibition space with her. Suparna Roychoudhury mixes wit with wicked humor and blends this with intellectual energy. I thank Vanessa Rosa, Sarah Stefana Smith, Meredith Coleman-Tobias, and Ren-yo Hwang for good food, good humor, and great joy. My first chairs at Mount Holyoke, Amy E. Martin (English) and Preston Smith II (Africana Studies) made my introduction to the college pleasant and comfortable. I thank Dorothy Mosby, Elizabeth Young, Nigel Alderman, Lucas Wilson, Andrea Lawlor, Chris Benfey, and Kate Singer for the time we have spent in conversation.

Eunsong Kim is that friend that most do not deserve, me included. I am so grateful that we crossed paths (thanks, Lisa!). Sandy Alexandre is the epitome of *deep, soul kin*. My goal is to keep earning the friendship she gives. Jyoti Puri is a perfect example of a purpose-driven life. Chiwen Bao helps me to remember what is most important as I move through my days. Helen Elaine Lee *goes hard* and loves harder. Sarika Chandra puts good humor to good use while also using her scholarly integrity to benefit others. Caroline Light continues to inspire me with her moral code and her jovial nature. To DJ Lynnée Denise, I thank you for your eye, and your pristine ear.

At Dartmouth College I have had the great fortune to be in good company. Donald Pease is as generous with his time and expertise as he is kind. Trica Keaton, Alexander Chee, Peter Orner, Colleen Boggs, Vievee Francis, Patricia Stuelke, Michael A. Chaney, Eng-Beng Lim, Jed Dobson, Matthew Olzmann, Naaborko Sackeyfio-Lenoch, Desirée J. Garcia, Laura Edmonson, Joshua Bennett, Jeff Sharlet, Mary Coffey, Tommy O'Malley, Monika Otter, Iyabo Kwayana, Andrew McCann, Ayo Coly, Mingwei Huang, Matthew Delmont, Melanie Benson Taylor, Alisa Swindell, and Katherine Gibbel—thank you for welcoming me with such care. Charlotte Bacon is a source of genuine motivation and my work is better because of this. Michaela S. Benton was my research assistant for the 2021–2022 academic year, and her mix of enthusiasm and vigilance helped the book reach this point.

I will be endlessly in debt to Lisa Lowe, for all the reasons she knows and some she may not. I thank her for her continued mentorship, for her infectious laughter, and for our friendship. Roderick Ferguson is a model of humanity and scholarly grace I wish to emulate. My appreciation goes out to Paul Gilroy for his continued support and helpful advice. I thank Michael Boyce Gillespie, Jennifer L. Morgan, Lisa Uddin, Karin Vélez, Kymberly Newberry, Sa Whitley, Trica Keaton, Elizabeth Maddock Dillon, Jovonna Jones, Iyko Day, and Vievee Francis for good humor and laughter. Katherine O'Callaghan and Malcom Sen graciously allowed me to be a small part of their life when I lived in South Hadley. For this I am thankful.

Former students and now current academic colleagues Jenna Sciuto, Tesla Cariani, Asimina Nikolopoulou, Anni Pullagura, Laura Hartmann-Villalta, Kiara Hill, Liz Polcha, and Victoria Papa remind me of the importance of the connections you make along the way.

I could not have completed this work if not for the conversations I have had and continue to have with my cohort of black women who *do-not-suffer-fools*. To say that our work is the fuel that propels us is to say a thing. So thank you: Nicole N. Ivy, Patricia A. Lott, Kaysha Corinealdi, Martine Jean, Helen Elaine Lee, Moya Bailey, Nikki A. Greene, Christina Sharpe, Dell Marie Hamilton, Trimiko Melancon, Faith Lois Smith, Julie Crooks, Sandy Alexandre, Sarah Haley, Marcia Chatelain, Shana Redmond, Zakiyyah Iman Jackson, Toby Sisson, Vanessa Monique Liles (my plus-one, my road traveler), Kia Melchor Quick Hall, Misty De Berry, Amanda Russhell Wallace, Aneeka A. Henderson, Trimiko Melancon, and Nadine Adjoa Smith (and of course, Ayo).

I was wrestling with the contours of this project when I decided to create a scholarly working group on race and visual culture. The Dark Room: Race and Visual Culture Studies Seminar began in 2012 and has been the most sustaining force in my scholarly world. What started as a way to think through the axes of engagement between black feminism, black studies, and visual culture studies is now so much more than that. We are every part the collective I imagined we would be. To Nikki A. Greene, Nicole Morris Johnson, Patricia A. Lott, Rachel Afi Quinn, Jasmine Elizabeth Johnson, Kelli Moore, Autumn Marie Womack, Patrica A. Banks, Samantha A. Noël, Kellie Carter Jackson, Zoé Samudzi, Sarah J. Jackson, Anique Jordan, Bakirathi Mani, Irene Mata, Alexandrina Agloro, K. Melchor Quick Hall, Brittnay Proctor-Habil, Brandy Monk-Payton, LaRose Davis, Rachel Mordecai, Sonya Donaldson, Stéphanie Larrieux, and Alicia Ellis, thank you for reminding me of the power of community.

I have Shirley Carrie Hartman to thank for any clarity that exists in this book. While I have secretly been calling her an "alliteration killer" and a "hater of fragments," the truth is she has shaped *Mortevivum* in ways I could not. Sometimes fragments are a cry for help.

My siblings are remarkable people. They have always managed to give me the space to be myself in their presence. I will forever be grateful for that.

My father, Harold "Sylvester" Brown remains my constant compass, having shown me what it means to put good out in the world and to do so with intention. After a contentious divorce and the loss of his visitation with us, my father, a bus driver, chose his bus route to move through our neighborhood so that he could occasionally set his eyes on his children and make sure we were okay. He gave me my first camera at sixteen, and a word processer when I was eighteen. Most importantly, he has given me my temperament and my commitment to grace.

This book is dedicated to him.

NOTES

INTRODUCTION

1. Roland Barthes, *Camera Lucida: Reflections on Photography*, trans. Richard Howard (New York: Hill and Wang, 1981), 79.

2 Michael S. Harper, *Images of Kin: New and Selected Poems* (Champaign: University of Illinois Press, 1977), 132.

3. In the "disciplining" sphere of photography, black subjects have had to contend with bifurcated representation: one part interest and one part exploitation. The latter emphasis has dominated a global field of vision that continues to shape the order of investment from healthcare to law, social engagements, and everything in between.

4. John Tagg, *The Disciplinary Frame: Photographic Truths and the Capture of Meaning* (Minneapolis: University of Minnesota Press, 2009).

5. Barthes, *Camera Lucida*, 32.

6. In Walt Whitman's "Song of Myself," Section 51, the speaker declares, "Do I contradict myself? / very well then I contradict myself, / (I am large, I contain multitudes)." Whitman, "Song of Myself," in *Leaves of Grass* (New York: Simon & Schuster, [1855] 2006).

7. Social progressives in the late nineteenth century in the United States were fixated on photography's potential to aid in the documentation of the ills that society seemed determined to produce. "The 1890s had begun with American society in the grip of a long crisis," Alan Trachtenberg writes. "For a dozen years the economy had fallen, creating hardship, especially for farmers and workers. Labor conflicts had grown sharp and frequently violent, as industrial workers increasingly resorted to the strike to defend their interests and win recognition of their unions. As conditions worsened, cities became a major focus of attention." Overlapping with the Great Black Migration from the rural south to cities and to the north, African Americans make up a good number of the human subjects traced during this time in American history. Trachtenberg, *Reading American Photographs: Images as History: Mathew Brady to Walker Evans* (New York: Hill & Wang, 1990), 170.

8. Alexander Gardner, *Gardner's Photographic Sketch Book of the Civil War* (New York: Dover Publications, 1959).

9. Anthony W. Lee and Elizabeth Young examine Gardner's *Sketch Book* for all its symbolic representations of the racial status quo. Lee writes, "Black men and women visibly appear in only six of its one hundred images, and only in their most caricatured antebellum roles—as meek servants, childish entertainers, or brute laborers for their white folk." Lee and Young, *On Alexander Gardner's Photographic Sketch Book of the Civil War* (Berkeley: University of California Press, 2008), 47.

10. Michèle Pearson Clarke, "A Dark Horse in Low Light: Black Visuality and the Aesthetics of Analogue Photography," lecture, Gallery 44, Toronto, ON, November 9, 2017.

11. Clarke, "A Dark Horse in Low Light."

12. Beaumont Newhall, "The Mirror with a Memory," in *The History of Photography from 1839 to the Present Day* (New York: Museum of Modern Art, 1964), 17.

13. Deborah Willis, *A Small Nation of People: W. E. B. Du Bois and African American Portraits of Progress* (Washington, DC: Library of Congress, 2003), 51.

14. Bongani Madondo, "Making Memories: Reshooting Postcards from the Edge of South Africa's Pop Culture History," *Daily Maverick*, July 10, 2021.

15. Lisa Lowe, *The Intimacies of Four Continents* (Durham, NC: Duke University Press, 2015), 60.

16. Martin A. Berger, *Sight Unseen: Whiteness and American Visual Culture* (Berkeley: University of California Press, 2005), 57.

17. Krista A. Thompson, *An Eye for the Tropics: Tourism, Photography, and Framing the Caribbean Picturesque* (Durham, NC: Duke University Press, 2006), 78.

18. Media images traffic in the visual repetition of a *Muslim other*, one who can be folded neatly into an articulation of terrorism that is legible to a mass audience. For more on media representation and Muslim identity, see Evelyn Asultany, *Arabs and Muslims in the Media: Race and Representation after 9/11* (New York: NYU Press, 2012).

19. Deborah E. McDowell, "Viewing the Remains," in *The Familial Gaze*, ed. Marianne Hirsch (Hanover, NH: University Press of New England, 1999), 155.

20. McDowell, "Viewing the Remains," 155.

21. Lucille Clifton, "the photograph: a lynching," in *Blessing the Boats: New and Selected Poems 1988–2000* (New York: BOA Editions, Ltd., 2000), 19.

22. Jacqueline Goldsby, *A Spectacular Secret: Lynching in American Life and Literature* (Chicago: University of Chicago Press, 2006), 229.

23. James Baldwin, *Going to Meet the Man: Stories* (New York: Vintage Books, 1995), 232.

24. Saidiya Hartman, *Scenes of Subjection: Terror, Slavery, and Self-Making in Nineteenth-Century America* (Oxford: Oxford University Press, 1997), 23.

25. In Gwendolyn Brooks's famous poem about Emmett Till's lynching at the hands of white supremacists in Money, Mississippi in 1955, she presents the wife of one of the murderers, Carolyn Bryant, as immersed in the gendered application of racial patriarchy. "It was necessary," Brooks writes of the white woman whose complaint about fourteen-year old Till set the lynching in motion, "To be more beautiful than ever. / The beautiful wife. / For sometimes she fancied he looked at her as though / Measuring her. As if he considered, Had she been worth it? / Had *she* been worth the blood, the cramped cries, the little stuttering bravado, / The gradual dulling of

those Negro eyes, . . . He must never conclude / That she had not been worth It." Brooks, "A Bronzeville Mother Loiters in Mississippi. Meanwhile, a Mississippi Mother Burns Bacon," in *Blacks* (Chicago: Third World Press, 2000), 335–336.

26. Baldwin, *Going to Meet the Man*, 246–247.

27. Sandy Alexandre, *The Properties of Violence: Claims to Ownership in Representations of Lynching* (Jackson: University of Mississippi Press, 2012), 45.

28. Baldwin, *Going to Meet the Man*, 245.

29. Baldwin, *Going to Meet the Man*, 248.

30. Mark Sealy, *Decolonising the Camera: Photography in Racial Time* (London: Lawrence & Wishart, 2019), 113–114.

31. James Baldwin, *The Evidence of Things Not Seen* (New York: Owl Books, 1985), 2.

32. Simone Browne, *Dark Matters: On the Surveillance of Blackness* (Durham, NC: Duke University Press, 2015), 50.

33. Toni Morrison, *The Bluest Eye* (New York: Holt, Rinehart and Winston, 1970), 36.

34. Aimé Césaire, *Discourse on Colonialism*, trans. Joan Pinkham (New York: Monthly Review Press, 2000), 47.

35. In *White Innocence: Paradoxes of Colonialism and Race* (Durham, NC: Duke University Press, 2016), Gloria Wekker examines the structure of racial stratification in a Dutch context that willfully refuses to acknowledge its own racism and xenophobia.

36. John Berger, *About Looking* (New York: Pantheon Books, 1980), 55.

37. Stuart Hall, *Selected Writings on Race and Difference*, ed. Paul Gilroy and Ruth Wilson Gilmore (Durham, NC: Duke University Press, 2021), 102.

38. Pumla Gobodo-Madikizela, *A Human Being Died that Night: A South African Woman Confronts the Legacy of Apartheid* (New York: Mariner Books, 2003), 61.

CHAPTER 1

1. Bill Keller, "The Man for South Africa's Future," *New York Times*, May 1, 1994, 1.

2. Keller, "Man for South Africa's Future," 1.

3. Dionne Brand, *A Map to the Door of No Return: Notes to Belonging* (Toronto: Vintage Canada, 2001), 35.

4. Achille Mbembe, *Critique of Black Reason* (Durham, NC: Duke University Press, 2017), 55.

5. "Voyage through death," Robert Hayden writes. "Voyage whose chartings are unlove." Hayden, "Middle Passage," in *Collected Poems* (New York: Liveright Publishing, 1985), https://www.poetry foundation.org/poems/43076/middle-passage.

6. White life set against default black death functions much in the same way as the rhetoric around freedom is structured through the concept of unfreedom, which black subjects, enslaved or free, occupy.

7. Quoted in "Living Memory: A Meeting with Toni Morrison," in *Small Acts: Thoughts on the Politics of Black Cultures*, Paul Gilroy (London: Serpent's Tail, 1993), 178.

8. *Oxford English Dictionary Online*, s.v. "empire, n.," accessed August 28, 2018, http://www.oed.com.

9. *Oxford English Dictionary Online*, s.v. "empire, n."

10. Peter Magubane, *Soweto Riots, South Africa*, 1976. International Center of Photography.

11. Giorgio Agamben, *Homo Sacer: Sovereign Power and Bare Life* (Palo Alto, CA: Stanford University Press, 1998).

12. Saidiya Hartman, *Scenes of Subjection: Terror, Slavery, and Self-Making in Nineteenth-Century America* (Oxford: Oxford University Press, 1997).

13. Ken Gonzales-Day, *Lynching in the West: 1850–1935* (Durham, NC: Duke University Press, 2006), 88.

14. Tina Campt, *Image Matters: Archive, Photography, and the African Diaspora in Europe* (Durham, NC: Duke University Press, 2012), 127.

15. Natasha Trethewey, *Native Guard: Poems* (Boston: Mariner Books, 2006), 30. "Native Guard" is a suite of ten poems about the military regiment.

16. Library of Congress, Prints & Photographs Division (http://www .loc.gov/pictures/).

17. Susan Sontag, *Regarding the Pain of Others* (New York: Picador, 2003), 70.

18. Toni Morrison, *The Origin of Others* (Cambridge, MA: Harvard University Press, 2017), 59.

19. Tiffany Willoughby-Herard, *Waste of a White Skin: The Carnegie Corporation and the Racial Logic of White Vulnerability* (Oakland: University of California Press, 2015), 95.

20. Martin A. Berger, *Seeing through Race: A Reinterpretation of Civil Rights Photography* (Berkeley: University of California Press, 2011).

21. Peter Magubane, *Magubane's South Africa* (New York: Knopf, 1978), 52.

22. Bénédicte Boisseron, *Afro-Dog: Blackness and the Animal Question* (New York: Columbia University Press, 2018), 39, 51, 76.

23. John Berger, *About Looking* (New York: Pantheon Books, 1980), 57.

24. The subtitle of the exhibition, *Photography and the Bureaucracy of Everyday Life*, gives some context to the day-to-day oppressions the apartheid regime imposed, which were meted out in images meant to reinforce the power of white supremacy on black subjects (see https://www.icp.org/exhibitions/rise-and-fall-of-apartheid).

25. Frantz Fanon, *The Wretched of the Earth* (New York: Grove Press, 1963), 7.

26. Paul Gilroy, *Postcolonial Melancholia* (New York: Columbia University Press, 2004), 105.

27. Hartman discusses the abolitionists' attempt to utilize the discourse of empathy in order to reify their centrality as the figure of investment. "The difficulty and slipperiness of empathy" is that the one who is the intended focus of this empathy gets lost in the gesture. She writes, "Properly speaking, empathy is a projection of oneself into another in order to better understand the other." Further, she asks: "Can the white witness of the spectacle of suffering affirm the materiality of black sentience only by feeling for himself?" Hartman, *Scenes of Subjection*, 18–19.

28. Christina Sharpe, *Monstrous Intimacies: Making Post-Slavery Subjects* (Durham, NC: Duke University Press, 2010), 87.

29. Berger, *About Looking*.

30. Ariella Azoulay, *The Civil Contract of Photography* (New York: Zone Books, 2008), 146.

31. W. J. T. Mitchell, "What Pictures Want," *October* 77 (Summer 1996): 75.

32. Magubane, *Magubane's South Africa*, 11.

33. Trethewey, *Native Guard: Poems*.

34. Jacqueline Goldsby, *A Spectacular Secret: Lynching in American Life and Literature* (Chicago: University of Chicago Press, 2006), 231.

35. Charles Mills, *Blackness Visible: Essays on Philosophy and Race* (Ithaca, NY: Cornell University Press, 1998), 70.

36. Trethewey, *Native Guard: Poems*, 29, 30; emphasis in original.

37. Kirk Savage, *Standing Soldiers, Kneeling Slaves: Race, War, and Monument in Nineteenth-Century America* (Princeton, NJ: Princeton University Press, 1997), 162, 167.

38. Karla F. C. Holloway, *Passed On: African American Mourning Stories* (Durham, NC: Duke University Press, 2002), 6.

39. Claudia Rankine, *Citizen: An American Lyric* (Minneapolis: Graywolf Press, 2014), 69.

40. Achille Mbembe, "Necropolitics," in *Public Culture* 15, no. 1 (Winter 2003): 11–40.

41. Frantz Fanon, *Concerning Violence* (New York: Penguin Books, 2008).

42. Elizabeth Alexander, *The Black Interior: Essays* (Minneapolis: Graywolf Press, 2004).

43. Azoulay, *Civil Contract of Photography*, 146.

44. Trethewey, *Native Guard: Poems*, 28; emphasis in original.

45. Trethewey, *Native Guard: Poems*, 28–29; emphasis in original.

46. Drew Gilpin Faust, *This Republic of Suffering: Death and the American Civil War* (New York: Vintage Press, 2008), 57.

47. Tina Campt, *Listening to Images* (Durham, NC: Duke University Press, 2016), 7.

48. Sontag, *Regarding the Pain of Others*, 85.

49. Yve-Alain Bois, Douglas Crimp, and Rosalind Krauss, "A Conversation with Hans Haacke," *October* 30 (Autumn 1984): 23–48.

50. James Q. Whitman, *Hitler's American Model: The United States and the Making of Nazi Race Law* (Princeton, NJ: Princeton University Press, 2017), 138.

51. Leigh Raiford, *Imprisoned in a Luminous Glare: Photography and the African American Freedom Struggle* (Chapel Hill: University of North Carolina Press, 2011), 62–63.

52. Lisa Lowe, *The Intimacies of Four Continents* (Durham, NC: Duke University Press, 2015), 35.

53. Zahid Chaudhary, *Afterimage of Empire: Photography in Nineteenth-Century India* (Minneapolis: University of Minnesota Press, 2012), 64.

54. Azoulay, *Civil Contract of Photography*, 282–283.

55. Nelson Mandela's inauguration speech, May 10, 1994; see https://www.sanews.gov.za/south-africa/read-nelson-mandelas-inauguration-speech-president-sa.

56. Christina Sharpe, *In the Wake: On Blackness and Being* (Durham, NC: Duke University Press, 2016), 106.

CHAPTER 2

1. "Don't despair too much if you see beautiful things destroyed, if you see them perish. Because the best things are always growing in secret." Ben Okri, *Astonishing the Gods* (London: Orion Publishing Group), 53.

2. Alfredo Jaar interview, accessed May 3, 2023, https://art21.org/read/alfredo-jaar-the-rwanda-project/.

3. Roland Barthes, *Camera Lucida: Reflections on Photography*, trans. Richard Howard (New York: Hill and Wang, 1981).

4. Jae Emerling, *Photography History and Theory* (New York: Routledge, 2012), 107.

5. Mahmood Mamdani, *When Victims Become Killers: Colonialism, Nativism, and the Genocide in Rwanda* (Princeton, NJ: Princeton University Press, 2001), 185.

6. Mamdani, *When Victims Become Killers*, 185.

7. Transmissions from Radio Télévision Libre des Mille Collines (RTLM) contributed to the role ordinary citizens played in the violence occurring during the genocide.

8. Here, Mbembe engages Frantz Fanon's theorizing of the imprint of imperial violence on all that comes after. In the center of what Mbembe calls "the terror of democracy," we can visualize the looping demands of "representation" that fail to offer black subjects the capacity for three-dimensional existence afforded others. Instead, there exists what Fanon calls "a death in life" that repeats. Achille Mbembe, *Necropolitics* (Durham, NC: Duke University Press, 2019), 139.

9. Thy Phu, *Warring Visions: Photography and Vietnam* (Durham, NC: Duke University Press, 2022), 21.

10. See https://www.pulitzer.org/winners/staff-35.

11. Mamdani, *When Victims Become Killers*, 87.

12. Mamdani, 80.

13. Edgar Roskis, "A Genocide without Images: White Film Noirs," in *The Media and the Rwanda Genocide*, ed. Allan Thompson (London: Pluto Press, 2007), 239–240.

14. Filmmaker Kivu Ruhorahoza's recent cinematic offering, *Father's Day* (2022), narrates the contemporary Rwandan social condition with the COVID-19 pandemic and the aftermath of the genocide through a series of recovery movements that tie the lush landscape with its undertone of national violence. In the film a series of women, all recovering in one way or the other from the ripple effects of the genocide, find strength and solace in one another.

15. Ángeles Donoso Macaya, *The Insubordination of Photography: Documentary Practices under Chile's Dictatorship* (Gainesville: University of Florida Press, 2020), 16.

16. Donoso Macaya, *Insubordination of Photography*, 166.

17. Saidiya Hartman, *Scenes of Subjection: Terror, Slavery, and Self-Making in Nineteenth-Century America* (Oxford: Oxford University Press, 1997), 22.

18. Susan Sontag, *On Photography* (London: Noonday Press, 1989), 93.

19. Mamdani, *When Victims Become Killers*, 194.

20. Pieter Hugo and Susan Dominus, "Portraits of Reconciliation," *New York Times Magazine*, April 6, 2014, https://www.nytimes.com/interactive/2014/04/06/magazine/06-pieter-hugo-rwanda-portraits.html.

21. See https://www.nytimes.com/interactive/2014/04/06/magazine/06-pieter-hugo-rwanda-portraits.html.

22. Ulrich Baer, *Spectral Evidence: The Photography of Trauma* (Cambridge, MA: MIT Press, 2002), 69.

23. Michel-Rolph Trouillot, *Silencing the Past: Power and the Production of History* (Boston: Beacon Press, 1995), 48.

24. Christina Sharpe, *In the Wake: On Blackness and Being* (Durham, NC: Duke University Press, 2016), 15.

25. Zakiyyah Iman Jackson, *Becoming Human: Matter and Meaning in an Antiblack World* (New York: New York University Press, 2020), 46.

26. Bakirathi Mani, *Unseeing Empire: Photography, Representation, South Asian America* (Durham, NC: Duke University Press, 2020), 147.

27. Dionne Brand, *A Map to the Door of No Return: Notes to Belonging* (Toronto: Vintage Canada, 2001), 96.

28. Ariella Aïsha Azoulay, *Potential History: Unlearning Imperialism* (New York: Verso Books, 2019), 284.

29. Jacques Ranciere. *The Emancipated Spectator* (New York: Verso, 2008), 96.

30. Trouillot, *Silencing the Past*, 49.

31. Jackson, *Becoming Human*, 166.

32. The King's College UCL photographic exhibition "*Rwanda in Photographs—Death Then, Life Now*, curated by Zoe Norridge and Mark Sealy, aimed to examine the "complexities of life after genocide" through ten contemporary photographers whose work endeavored to move past the horrors the nation was still memorially mired within (see https://www.kcl.ac.uk/cultural/projects/archive/2014/rwanda-in-photographs).

33. Alfredo Jaar, *Let There Be Light: The Rwanda Project 1994–1998* (Barcelona: ACTAR, 1998).

34. Paul Gilroy, *Postcolonial Melancholia* (New York: Columbia University Press, 2004), 89.

35. Gilroy, *Postcolonial Melancholia*.

36. Barbie Zelizer, *About to Die: How News Images Move the Public* (Oxford: Oxford University Press, 2010), 20.

37. Zelizer, *About to Die*, 21.

38. Marita Sturken and Lisa Cartwright, *Practices of Looking: An Introduction to Visual Culture* (Oxford: Oxford University Press, 2001).

39. Sturken and Cartwright, *Practices of Looking*, 21–22.

40. Zelizer, *About to Die*, 124.

41. Mehdi Chebil, "'Pushed Back Because We're Black': Africans Stranded at Ukraine-Poland Border," France 24, February 28, 2022, https://www.france24.com/en/europe/20220228-pushed-back-because-we-re-black-africans-stranded-at-ukraine-poland-border.

CHAPTER 3

1. Mary Renda's book *Taking Haiti: Military Occupation and the Culture of U.S. Imperialism, 1915–1940* (Chapel Hill: University of North Carolina Press, 2001) traces the 1915 intervention in Haiti through the lens of US imperialism and paternalistic impulses. She writes in part, "Formally, the United States was at peace with Haiti. Consistent with the official state of affairs, paternalism conferred on the United States the status of an elder brother, in Haiti on a mission of paternal care and guidance" (135).

2. Barthes is interested in the space between *has been* and *is to be* that photography seems particularly suited to manipulate. In an extended discussion of the promise and the perils of photography, Barthes muses: "Photography transformed subject into object, and even, one might say, into a museum object: in order to take the first portraits (around 1840) the subject had to assume long poses under a glass roof in the bright sunlight; to become an object made one suffer as much as a surgical operation; then a device was invented, a kind of prosthesis invisible to the lens, which supported and maintained the body in its passage to immobility: this headrest was the pedestal of the statue I would become, the corset of my imaginary essence." Roland Barthes, *Camera Lucida: Reflections on Photography*, trans. Richard Howard (New York: Hill and Wang, 1981), 13.

3. John Kifner, "Police Crush Rally as American Troops Watch," *New York Times*, September 21, 1994, 1.

4. Christina Sharpe, *In the Wake: On Blackness and Being* (Durham, NC: Duke University Press, 2016), 71.

5. Saidiya Hartman, *Scenes of Subjection: Terror, Slavery, and Self-Making in Nineteenth-Century America* (Oxford: Oxford University Press, 1997), 57.

6. Haiti is particularly pertinent in this regard, as most of the news information contemporary readers have of the nation situate Haiti in relation to chaos and inconsistent political leadership. Erica Caple James writes in part, "A long tradition of misrepresenting the Haitian nation and its culture, especially on the part of Westerners, complicates many recent as well as older depictions of the country's plight." James, *Democratic Insecurities: Violence, Trauma, and Intervention in Haiti* (Berkeley: University of California Press, 2010), 9.

7. John Tagg, *The Disciplinary Frame: Photographic Truths and the Capture of Meaning* (Minneapolis: University of Minnesota Press, 2009), 1.

8. Tagg, *Disciplinary Frame*, 1.

9. Michel-Rolph Trouillot, *Silencing the Past: Power and the Production of History* (Boston: Beacon Press, 1995), 52.

10. Laboring bodies on the plantations of Saint Domingue brought wealth to France before and even after slavery ended. See Catherine Porter, Constant Méheut, Matt Apuzzo, and Selam Gebrekidan, "The Root of Haiti's Misery: Reparations to Enslavers," *New York Times*, updated November 16, 2022, https://www.nytimes.com/2022/05/20/world/americas/haiti-history-colonized-france.html.

11. Hartman, *Scenes of Subjection*, 20.

12. Sharon Holland, *Raising the Dead: Readings of Death and (Black) Subjectivity* (Durham, NC: Duke University Press, 2000).

13. Rick Bragg, "Mission to Haiti: In Port-au-Prince; Cheers and Signs of Relief as Beatings Subside," *New York Times*, September 23, 1994, A12.

14. Frank Wilderson III, "The Prison Slave as Hegemony's (Silent) Scandal," *Social Justice* 30, no. 2 (2003): 18–27, 23.

15. Ariella Aïsha Azoulay, *The Civil Contract of Photography* (New York: Zone Books, 2012), 121.

16. Butler, *Precarious Life: The Powers of Mourning and Violence* (New York: Verso, 2006), 26.

17. In a *New York Times* editorial, linguist Michel De Graff wrestles with the lessons he was taught to absorb concerning his native tongue, Kreyòl. De Graff writes, "I consider the description of Haiti as the poorest nation of the Western Hemisphere to be a gross misrepresentation; Haiti is, rather, the nation most impoverished by the effects of white supremacy. The emissary of Charles X imposed an insurmountable financial ransom, but the French educational model, a supposed war bounty, was every bit as brutal: a linguistic ransom, a powerful tool for mental colonization. Haiti's French-speaking elites, who have enforced that mandate, have always lived as far away as possible—geographically, socially, culturally, religiously and linguistically—from the majority Kreyòl-speaking population. They have never created a system to adequately teach French to those who did not grow up speaking it. Instead these Haitian elites favor teaching in French—an option that's guaranteed to multiply the privilege they already enjoy and to ensure that most of their fellow citizens cannot share it." Michel De Graff, "As a Child in Haiti, I Was Taught to Despise My Language and Myself," *New York Times*, October 12, 2022.

18. Roger Cohen, "Sarajevo's Unending Travail," *New York Times*, September 25, 1994, 14.

19. Gloria Wekker, *White Innocence: Paradoxes of Colonialism and Race* (Durham, NC: Duke University Press, 2016).

20. Cohen, "Sarajevo's Unending Travail," 14.

21. Richard Dyer, *White: Essays on Race and Culture* (London: Routledge, 1997), 2.

22. Dyer, *White*, 207.

23. Susan Sontag, *Regarding the Pain of Others* (New York: Picador, 2003), 18.

24. Sontag, *Regarding the Pain of Others*, 13.

25. Edwidge Danticat, *The Art of Death: Writing the Final Story* (Minneapolis: Graywolf Press, 2017), 56.

26. Pooja Rangan, *Immediations: The Humanitarian Impulse in Documentary* (Durham, NC: Duke University Press, 2017), 59, 47.

27. Laurent Dubois, *Avengers of the New World: The Story of the Haitian Revolution* (Cambridge, MA: Harvard University Press, 2004), 21.

28. Profits from slavery in Saint Domingue sustained much of the nation of France for most of the eighteenth century and well beyond.

29. Hartman, *Scenes of Subjection*, 3.

30. Sharpe, *In the Wake*, 22.

31. Barthes, *Camera Lucida*, 41.

32. The Newsvine survey is one of the few places where you can ascertain how people are processing, in real time, filmed accidents that involve people dying.

33. After Michael Brown was shot and killed in Ferguson, Missouri, his family asked that images of his dead body lying in the street not be circulated via social media. Their requests were largely ignored.

34. Azoulay, *Civil Contract of Photography*, 89.

35. Ann Laura Stoler, "Imperial Debris: Reflections on Ruins and Ruination," *Cultural Anthropology* 23, no. 2 (May 2008): 191–219, 193.

CONCLUSION

1. See bell hooks, "The Oppositional Gaze: Black Female Spectators," in *The Feminism and Visual Culture Reader*, ed. Amelia Jones (New York: Routledge Press, 2003), 95.

2. "Dawoud Bey on 6 Photos That Pushed his Work Forward," as told to Sasha Bonét, https://www.vulture.com/article/dawoud-bey-photo-whitney-retrospective.html.

3. Jacquie Jones, "How Come Nobody Told Me about the Lynching," in *Picturing Us: African American Identity in Photography*, ed. Deborah Willis (New York: New Press, 1994), 153.

4. Jones, "Nobody Told Me about the Lynching," 153.

5. Courtney R. Baker, *Humane Insight: Looking at Images of African American Suffering and Death* (Champaign: University of Illinois Press, 2015), 51.

6. Michael S. Harper, *Song: I Want a Witness* (Pittsburgh: University of Pittsburgh Press), 1972.

7. James Baldwin, *The Devil Finds Work* (New York: Vintage Books, 1976), 63.

8. Elizabeth Alexander, *The Black Interior* (St. Paul, MN: Graywolf Press, 2004), 177.

9. James Baldwin, *The Evidence of Things Not Seen* (New York: Owl Books, 1985).

10. Harper, *Song*, 50.

11. In Toni Morrison's *Beloved*, Baby Suggs implores those recovering from the horrors of slavery to practice release. "Cry," she tells them, "for the living and the dead. Just cry." Morrison, *Beloved* (New York: Plume, 1987), 88. See also Harper, *Song*.

12. Lucille Clifton, "photograph," in *Quilting: Poems 1987–1990* (New York: BOA Editions, Ltd., 1990), 51.

13. Toni Morrison, *The Origin of Others* (Cambridge, MA: Harvard University Press, 2017), 37.

14. Harper, *Song*, 50.

INDEX

American Civil War
  aftermath of, 5, 24, 43
  black soldiers' visual absence in, 12, 15, 23–26, 29
  and images of black subservience, 10
  and photography, xii, xiv, xviii, 14
Antiblackness, 36, 38, 43, 52, 100
  and citizenship, 76
  and disregard of the dead, 69
  global enforcement of, 58
  in the media, 66, 101
  ubiquity of, 45, 55, 66
  and the viewer, 53
Apartheid. *See* South Africa
Archives of indifference, 22
Aristide, Jean-Bertrand, 83
Baldwin, James, 106, 108
Bey, Dawoud, 103–104
Biko, Steve, 37
Birmingham Project (Bey), 103–104
Black agency, 102
Black civil disobedience, 18
Black Civil War soldiers. *See* American Civil War
Black death
  and American Civil War photography, 12
  and citizenship, 14
  digital proliferation, 24
  hypervisibility of, 59, 67–68, 87
  as impending, xix
  and photograph of Steve Biko, 37

as spectacle, 108
and white life, 37, 60, 80, 127n6
witnessing of, 29
Black diaspora, and visual possibilities of, 105
Black embodiment, 75, 79
Blackness
alignment with death, 4–5, 8, 11
seeing, xiv, 12
and temporality, 22
value of, xx
Black pain, 41, 91, 96, 108
consumption of, 106
indifference to, 22
pleasure in, xxx, 112
Black sovereignty, 16, 39, 77
Black subjectivity, 12, 24–25, 27, 51, 54, 94, 101, 105
Bluest Eye, The (Morrison), xxx
Bosnian War, media coverage of, 87–90
Brewster, Sandra, 107–108

Carnivorous voyeurism, 22
Cartography of the ocular, xx, 9, 96
and black death, 99
Castille, Philando, 106
Césaire, Aimé, xxxii
Citizen: An American Lyric (Rankine), 26–27
Citizenship, 10, 12, 22, 24, 27, 33
Civil rights movement (US), 17, 38
and Soweto uprising, 23
Clifton, Lucille, xxiii–xxiv, 112–113
Corporeal catastrophe, 101
Corporeal destruction, 55

Danticat, Edwidge, 91, 93
Dead bodies, 55, 101
in the media, xxii, xxxi, 83, 88, 99
privileging over survivors, 61, 81
Devil Finds Work, The (Baldwin), 106
Disregard
and black pain, 43
of the dead, 55, 60, 106
photographic, xxiii, 55, 69
and the viewer, 39, 45, 65
Du Bois, W. E. B., 96

Empire, 9, 33, 47, 77
etymology of, 5
global legacy of, 47, 52, 63, 77, 81 95
photography and, 4, 29, 37
racial construction of, 7, 16, 22, 43
and surveillance, 41
Evidence of Things Not Seen (Baldwin), xxix
Evidentiary, the, 53, 69

Floyd, George, 106
Fungibility, xx, 25, 58
as blackness, 51, 69, 90, 112
photographic, 8
and the viewer, 69
and white value, 88

Gadsden, Walter, 16–17, 70–71
Gardner, Alexander, xiv, 124n9
Gardner's Photographic Sketch Book of the Civil War (*see* American Civil War)
Garner, Eric, 106
Going to Meet the Man (Baldwin), xxv–xxx

Haiti
and coverage of Bosnia in 1994, 88
media coverage of intervention, 78, 83, 85–87, 93, 99
portrayal as sovereign failure, xxxiv, 95, 97, 102
and sentiment, 75, 77
US military intervention in 1994, 73, 133n1
Haitian Earthquake (2010), and images of the dead, 100–101
Haitian Revolution, 77–78
and modernity, 79, 101
Harper, Michael S., 105, 108, 113
Hayden, Robert, 4
Hugo, Pieter. *See* Rwandan genocide, "Portraits of Reconciliation"

Imaginary(ies)
American, 12, 24
blackness in, 51
imperial, 52
photographic, 22, 39
Imperial violence, 42
Invisible Man (Ellison), xxx

Jaar, Alfredo, 48–49, 51–52, 66
Jim Crow, 43

King, Rodney, 29

Legibility, xxiii, 27, 76, 110
Let There Be Light: The Rwanda Project 1994–1998 (Jaar), 48–52
Looking, 18, 51, 68, 110
ethics of, 100–101
pleasure of, 14
power of, xxx
resistant, 104
as ritual, 99

Magubane, Peter, 7–8, 17–19, 23–24, 27, 29
Magubane's South Africa (Magubane), 19
Mandela, Nelson, presidential election of, 1–2, 4, 41–42
Media
control of, 58
and dehumanization, 113
ethics of, 60
hypervisibility of black death in, 55, 59
and journalistic truth, 53–54
and temporality, 81, 102
value of black life and death, 36
white death and, 68
"Middle Passage" (Hayden), 4
Modernity
geographies of, 39
and whiteness, 37
Morrison, Toni, 5, 110, 113
Mortevivum, 76
and black subjects, 69
as death's proximity to blackness, 4–5, 15, 97
and empire, 101
as photographic production, xx, xxxi
and vicarious murder, xxv
and white collectivity, 26

Natchwey, James, 53–54
Native Guard (Trethewey), 25
Newspapers. *See New York Times*
New York Times
coverage of Bosnian War, 87–88
coverage of Mandela's election, 1–3, 42, 44

coverage of Rwandan genocide, 47, 51, 81–82, 89
coverage of US military intervention in Haiti, 73–74, 83–85, 92–93
coverage of Zulu protest for sovereignty, 39–40
and documentary photography, 90, 99
photograph of Walter Gadsden, 16–17
and O. J. Simpson trial, 97
Nichols, Tyre, 106

Objectification, violence of, xvii
Okri, Ben, 48

Paris Exposition of 1900, xvii
Parks, Gordon, 6
Photography, 28, 43, 59, 97, 110, 113
analog, xii, xxi
and antiblackness, xii, 33, 58–59, 69, 76, 100, 105
and black suffering, 20, 91, 94, 96, 112
and citizenship, 81
digitization of, xxi
and dispossession, 102
documentary, 53, 58, 63–64
and eugenics, xii, xxxii
as evidence, xvii, xx, 26, 110
history of, 5, 39, 101
and imperialism, 16, 37, 57, 60–61, 78, 101
lynching, xxiv–xxv, 9, 12, 14, 24, 29, 60
and oppositional gaze, 104
portraits in, xvii, 108
Police Dog Attack (Hudson), 17. *See also* Magubane, Peter
Rankine, Claudia, 26
Rwanda, 69
colonial history of, 57, 81
Rwandan genocide, 65
and critique of black governance, 52, 56, 66
humanizing survivors of, 48–49
images of aftermath, 54, 58, 64, 67, 81
media coverage of, 52, 58–59, 70, 77–78
"Portraits of Reconciliation," 61–63
and visual indifference, 53, 68

Sempervivum, xxxi
logic of, 29
and whiteness, 4–5, 15, 60
Sentiment, 97
and *Mortevivum*, 75
public, 68
structure of, 78–79
September 11, 2001, xxi, 27, 55
Shadows
as aesthetic of haunting, 16
and black death, 79
as empire, 43
Sharpeville Massacre. *See* South Africa
Slavery, 4, 10, 22, 78
and corporeality, 79
formation of surveillance in, xxx
legacy of, 12, 14, 18, 113
transatlantic, 5, 77
Social media, images of black death on, 59, 101, 105–106
Song: I Want a Witness (Harper), 105

South Africa, 52, 93
apartheid era, 4, 18, 22–23, 28
Apartheid Museum, 31, 35–36
and black citizenship, xxxiii, 24, 27–28, 33
and empire, 5
history of photography, 4, 16, 37, 41–43
and Mandela's election, 1–2
and Nazism, 38
rebranding of, 39–40
Rise and Fall of Apartheid exhibition, 20–21
Sharpeville massacre, 23, 28
Truth and Reconciliation Commission, 42
and the United States, 7, 9, 15, 17–19, 23, 29, 43
Soweto Riots (Magubane) 7, 16
Surveillance, xxx, 41, 69

Transnational blackness, 27
Trauma
photographs of, 62
racialized, 36
visualized effects of, 53
Trethewey, Natasha, 12, 24–25

Ukraine
and African students, 69
international response, 69–70
Russian invasion of, 69
United States
global reach of media images, 105
history of racial violence, xxiv, 9–10, 17–18, 29, 101
indifference to Rwandan genocide, 67
intervention in Haiti in 1994, 80, 93
and pursuit of whiteness, 15
and racial segregation, 5, 37–38, 43
response to invasion of Ukraine, 69
stereographs of black laborers, 14

Viewer, the, 36, 38–39, 63–64, 68
altering gaze of, 51, 105, 108
and indifference, xiv, 20, 53, 62, 91
racial identity, 96–97
relationship to the subject, 68
and voyeuristic participation, 23, 75–76, 102
as witness, 28
Violence
corporeal, 38
of the gaze, 31, 76
photographic, 23–24, 28, 70
state-sanctioned, 27
and the viewer, 61
visual refusal of, 49
visual reproduction of, 37
Voici Alcan (Haacke). *See* Black death

Weems, Carrie Mae, 108–110
White supremacy, xxxi, 2, 16, 20, 45, 105–106
Confederate preservation of, 14
global legacy of, xxiii, 5, 18, 41–42
and photographic production, 56, 60, 96
and US model for Nazi Germany, 38